# THE
# LEARNING-CENTERED
# UNIVERSITY

# THE
# LEARNING-CENTERED UNIVERSITY

Making College a More Developmental,
Transformational, and Equitable Experience

STEVEN MINTZ

JOHNS HOPKINS UNIVERSITY PRESS | *Baltimore*

© 2024 Johns Hopkins University Press
All rights reserved. Published 2024
Printed in the United States of America on acid-free paper

2  4  6  8  9  7  5  3  1

Johns Hopkins University Press
2715 North Charles Street
Baltimore, MD 21218
www.press.jhu.edu

Library of Congress Cataloging-in-Publication Data

Names: Mintz, Steven, 1953– author.
Title: The learning-centered university : making college a more developmental,
transformational, and equitable experience / Steven Mintz.
Description: Baltimore, Maryland : Johns Hopkins University Press, 2024. |
Includes bibliographical references and index.
Identifiers: LCCN 2023016703 | ISBN 9781421448022 (hardcover) |
ISBN 9781421448039 (ebook)
Subjects: LCSH: Student-centered learning—United States. | Transformative learning—
United States. | Education, Higher—Aims and objectives—United States. |
Educational equalization—United States.
Classification: LCC LB1027.23 .M568 2024 | DDC 378.73—dc23/eng/20230607
LC record available at https://lccn.loc.gov/2023016703

A catalog record for this book is available from the British Library.

Special discounts are available for bulk purchases of this book. For more information,
please contact Special Sales at specialsales@jh.edu.

# CONTENTS

*Preface*  vii

*Acknowledgments*  xv

INTRODUCTION.  Higher Education's Post-pandemic Future  1

1.  Higher Education's Perfect Storm  18

2.  The Challenges Ahead  28

3.  The Shifting Higher Education Landscape  53

4.  Lessons from the History of American Higher Education  83

5.  A Learner- and Learning-Centered Vision for the Future of Higher Education  102

6.  Thinking outside the Box  110

7.  From Teaching to Learning  133

8.  Enhancing Teaching and Learning with Technology  159

9.  Rethinking Assessment  170

10.  Helping Students Become Better Writers  179

11.  Standing Up for Equity  191

12.  Supporting Student Success at Scale  204

13.  Campus Flash Points  217

14.  The Future of the Humanities  247

15. How Innovation Happens    269

EPILOGUE    283

*Appendixes*
*1. Insights from the Science of Learning    299*
*2. The Lexicon of Academic Innovation    304*
*3. Next-Generation Pedagogies    310*
*4. Technology-Enhanced Active Learning Tools    314*
*5. Strategies for Enhancing Equity and Student Success    317*

*Notes    319*
*Index    337*

# PREFACE

As gaps in income, wealth, living standards, and access to quality schools and health care widen, as disparities between so-called superstar cities and decaying industrial towns and rural communities in flyover country swell, and as differences in politics and values along educational, class, ethnic, gender, racial, and political lines intensify, it has become increasingly imperative that we address these gulfs in a systematic way. In US society, higher education represents the most promising solution to the nation's biggest challenges: stagnating incomes and productivity, persistent inequalities of wealth, and political polarization.

If higher education is to meet these challenges, it must adapt. The cost of attendance and educational debt are too high, retention and completion rates are too low, and learning and employment outcomes are too uncertain. Inequalities exist in every facet of higher education. In terms of spending per student on instruction and support, cost after financial aid, and admission to the most selective, well-resourced campuses, American colleges and universities are among the nation's most stratified and status-conscious institutions.

In this book, I offer practical, realistic strategies for addressing higher education's challenges of access, affordability, equity, degree attainment, and postgraduation employment outcomes. As an experienced academic administrator, educational technologist, teaching center director, and director of student success initiatives, I know firsthand the barriers to educational innovation. As a published scholar with expertise in the transition to adulthood, and as a faculty member who has taught over 40,000 students in face-to-face classes (and many more online and via instructional television), I am closely in touch with students' shifting needs and aspirations.

The book begins by delineating the challenges facing American higher education. These include dramatic shifts in the composition of the student body, broken business models, and shaken public confidence in the value of a college education. I first examine higher education's shifting landscape—the new providers, educational models, delivery modalities, instructional staffing models, and credentials that are radically disrupting the educational ecosystem. I then turn to the profound changes taking place in the student body, which increasingly consists of groups whom campuses have historically treated poorly: commuter and part-time students, community college transfer students, working adults, family caregivers, international students, and students with disabilities. I also examine how colleges and universities might best help traditional-aged undergraduates navigate the tangled transition to adulthood.

Next, I place higher education's current challenges in a historical perspective and identify a series of timely, actionable lessons that can be drawn from the history of American higher education and heeded today as institutions strive to implement reforms. I then shift to the heart of the academic enterprise: how we might rethink college curricula and degree requirements, strengthen teaching and learning, reimagine assessment, and improve student supports. My overarching goals are to make degree pathways more coherent and synergistic; pedagogies more engaging, interactive, and outcome focused; and the academic experience itself more learner and learning centered, with the larger goal of cultivating a college education that is less transactional and more developmental, transformative, and intellectually challenging.

My educational vision incorporates a Deweyesque emphasis on authentic, active, collaborative, inquiry-driven, project-based, and experiential learning as well as civic engagement, skills-building, and immersion in the big ethical, cultural, political, social, and scientific issues of the day. This vision seeks to reaffirm higher education's civic and public purpose and better prepare today's extraordinarily diverse student body for the complex array of personal and societal challenges they will face as adults.

I next look at a series of flash points and areas of controversy involving the future of education technology, equity, career preparation, and the professoriate, along with the fate of the humanities. I show how technology can enhance a college education by empowering, not replacing, instructors and making the learning process more active and collaborative. I also examine how to embed career preparation across the undergraduate experience, how the humanities can best adapt to an environment that prioritizes marketable skills and workplace-ready credentials, and how the professoriate ought to change at a time when tenure and academic freedom seem threatened. I conclude the book by offering practical, pragmatic strategies for driving academic innovation and overcoming resistance to essential transformations.

The literature on educational innovation is vast, so why should you read this book? The answer is threefold. First, this book's argument is grounded in authentic firsthand experience. It builds not just on research studies but on hard-won experiences, good and bad. This book, therefore, can speak to those who confront the day-to-day challenges of academic administration. Second, this book recognizes that the basic challenge facing higher education is not a shortage of ideas but a problem with their implementation. We actually know quite a bit about what needs to be done. It's executing these solutions that's our number-one challenge. This book details both solutions and a sensible path forward. Third, and most importantly, this book articulates a vision of undergraduate education that I think most faculty can embrace. It is founded on a recognition that today's undergraduates differ markedly from those of a generation ago, that the economy and workplaces have also changed in far-reaching ways, and that, as a result, what we teach and how we mentor and prepare students as well as how we assess their learning must evolve.

I am advocating an approach to undergraduate education that is developmental and transformational. It's an education with clear objectives that are not simply cognitive but entail educating the whole person. It's also an approach that seeks to ensure that as many undergraduates as possible get the opportunity to take part in the high-impact educational practices that can transform lives. These practices are currently reserved largely for the most privileged students: those who attend highly selective, well-endowed research universities and liberal arts colleges or who are admitted to public universities' honors programs. The transformational experiences include the opportunity to engage in guided research and supervised internships and participate in a learning community with dedicated faculty mentors, professional advisers, and rich cocurricular activities. I show how such experiences can be scaled.

Achieving this vision will not be easy. It will require broad-access institutions, which serve the vast majority of undergraduates, to better serve the students they have, not those they might prefer to have. These undergraduates represent the new majority—students who have received an uneven high school education and must juggle their studies with work and family responsibilities. Coming, as most do, from lower middle-class and working-class families, these students tend to be highly career focused, debt averse, and concerned, for good reasons, that their dream of receiving a college degree won't work out. These undergraduates are especially likely to drop out of school. They require more advising, more supplemental instruction, more constructive feedback, and more time, energy, and personal attention than previous generations of students customarily received.

To bring these students to a bright future, campuses must innovate. Such innovations entail cultivating a sense of belonging and connection to the institution, faculty members, and classmates. These innovations also involve providing more coherent pathways to a degree, more intensive academic and career advising, a greater emphasis on skills-building, and more wraparound supports. And these innovations must be implemented within the context of resource constraints.

The innovations that I propose require changes across every dimension of a college or university. Faculty must re-envision their roles and embrace their responsibilities as mentors, learning architects, and providers of more extensive and substantive constructive feedback. Institutions must redesign degree pathways and make these routes to a degree more coherent, integrated, and synergistic. Pedagogies must place a greater emphasis on active, collaborative, and inquiry- and project-based learning. Course design and delivery must move beyond the standard instructor-centered lecture and the discussion-based seminar and embrace more experiential learning in the form of practicums, clinicals, studio classes, and community— and field-based courses as well as scaled, supervised research and internship opportunities. In addition, colleges and universities need to embed skills development, career preparation, and the acquisition of job-aligned credentials and certificates across the undergraduate experience.

My larger goal is to rescue and resurrect two conceptions of education that have faded over time: *cura personalis*, the idea of educating the whole person, and *Bildung*, the notion of education as part of a larger process of self-discovery and personal maturation. In my view, institutions must accept a much greater responsibility for educating and assisting the whole student, not just by helping to meet their basic needs for housing, food, transportation, and physical and mental well-being but also by facilitating their emotional and social development and metacognitive (self-reflective) skills.

In addition to promoting students' cognitive growth, colleges and universities must do more to drive maturation across other vectors of development. Institutions need to help students grow morally, socially, and interpersonally. Undergraduates must learn how to function in diverse, multicultural environments and handle interpersonal relationships—whether they involve classmates, friends, or romantic or sexual partners—judiciously, empathetically, and respectfully. Colleges and universities also need to nurture students' intrapersonal development: their capacity to plan, assess their own strengths and weaknesses, manage emotions, delay gratification, overcome distractions and obstacles, and adjust their strategies as needed.

Educational innovation is imperative. I fully recognize that the kinds of innovation I propose will be difficult to institute at the necessary scale. Militating against change are inertia, tradition, institutional rankings, resource constraints, and misguided incentives that downplay the importance of teaching and mentoring. Still, innovation must come. Equity and opportunity require no less.

Some, no doubt, will view the book's prescriptions as out of reach. But dreams can inspire and motivate, and dreams have a funny way of eventually becoming reality. Predicting the future is easy. Anyone can do it. Getting the predictions right, however, is hard. As a historian, I know full well that "unpredictability" is among history's watchwords. Forecasts tend to be futile yet fundamental. In times of uncertainty, the best we can do is speculate, spin scenarios, and prepare accordingly.

A video produced by Microsoft Office Labs in 2009 offered a vision of technology a decade in the future. It included simultaneous translations between languages, touch screens, gesture controls, e-paper, wall-sized smart displays, voice-activated digital assistants, and pocket projectors. All have their counterparts today, but notice what's missing. There are no team-based, mobile collaboration tools, like Slack or Google Docs, and nothing about predictive analytics, apps, machine learning, or cloud storage. The video doesn't envision 3D printing or the omnipresence of GPS (Global Positioning System), let alone the generative artificial intelligence that can write whole articles or create illustrations almost instantly on demand.

Speculating about the future is a fool's game. Forecasts are often wrong for several reasons: they convey a false sense of certainty, extrapolate current trends, and fail to anticipate contingencies—those "unknown unknowns" that include unforeseen events and shifting circumstances. Still, we need to anticipate the challenges that lie ahead.

What will the higher education landscape look like fifteen years from now? Some changes strike me as likely. Many very small colleges—typically those with fewer than a thousand students—and campuses in areas with shrinking populations, I predict, will have closed or merged, forged partnerships and alliances, or adopted shared services. At the same time, alternatives to an education at a traditional brick-and-mortar college will have expanded, posing a serious competitive threat to struggling institutions. An increasingly larger share of the undergraduate population will consist of nontraditional and historically underrepresented students. Costs—driven by the need to expand student services, enhance technology, and invest in new programs in emerging fields of study—will have risen at a rate equal to or faster than inflation.

Other changes strike me as plausible. Institutions will be held more accountable for meeting their diversity, equity, and inclusion benchmarks. Elite institutions will come under increasing attack over their refusal to grow and admit a more representative student body. Virtual internships will become more common. Schools will increase their online offerings and expand online professional master's programs and nondegree programs, even though the market already seems glutted. More community colleges will offer applied bachelor's degrees. And opportunities for students to acquire college credits in high school will expand.

Apart from these predictions, my crystal ball is cloudy. Nevertheless, it's obvious that higher education stands at a crossroads as it struggles with a series of disruptive developments, including shifting student demographics, mounting student debt, rising costs, emerging competition from fully online institutions and alternative providers, and public questioning of higher education's value proposition. Colleges and universities need to contain costs and provide an undergraduate education more efficiently and effectively, without compromising quality or rigor. Institutions also need to figure out how to raise graduation rates dramatically for students who are already in college, a statistic that has barely budged from around 60 percent in six years. So too must this country ensure that many more adults—as many as fifty million who never went to college or dropped out—acquire the credentials they need to obtain the secure, well-paying jobs that the economy requires.

No one knows what the future holds. The future is, it's quite rightly said, a blank page. It's up to us to create that future. The pages that follow offer my prescription for what we need to do if higher education is to fulfill its democratic promise: to open doors, expand horizons, and transform lives.

# ACKNOWLEDGMENTS

The world of academic innovation is largely populated by two discrete groups of people: thought leaders, generally academics with a large social media following but limited practical implementation experience, and experienced administrators, often from continuing education programs or educational technology or publishing companies. I have been fortunate to work alongside innovators with feet firmly planted in both camps, including Marni Baker Stein, who served as the chief innovation officer at the University of Texas's Institute for Transformational Learning before becoming provost at Western Governors University and later the chief content officer at Coursera; Joann Kozyrev, the Institute for Transformational Learning's director of competency-based program design and now Western Governors University's vice president of design and development; and Michael Steiper, who has served as associate provost for student success at the City College of New York's Hunter College. Their dedication to student success knows no bounds.

I owe special thanks to Michael Rutter, my partner-in-arms for Inside Higher Ed's *Higher Ed Gamma* blog and a senior adviser in MIT's Office of the Vice Provost, whose insights into the state and fate of higher education are extraordinary, and to Alexandra Logue, the former executive vice chancellor for academic affairs at the City University of New York, a true warrior for academic equity, whose willingness to share her expertise is legendary.

Academic innovation is a team sport, and I have been enormously fortunate to work alongside a cast of all-stars. These include Hunter College's data gurus Joan Lamb, James Llana, and Arad Namin; its academic and preprofessional advisers extraordinaire Brian Buckwald,

Nikole Feliciano, Elise Harris, Kemile Jackson, Elise Jaffe, Brian Maasjo, Kevin Nesbitt, and Peggy Segal; and its learning center directors, including Christina Medina Ramirez. I also benefited enormously from conversations with Chris Buonocore, who has done more to streamline credit transfer across the CUNY system than anyone I've ever encountered; Stephen Sheets, CUNY's senior research analyst and a leading expert on postgraduation student outcomes; George Mehaffy, who recently retired as vice president of academic leadership and change at the American Association of State Colleges and Universities; and Martin Kurzweil of Ithaka S+R, whose expertise on higher education research has no equal.

My debts to those who have supported my innovation efforts at the University of Texas System and Columbia University can never be repaid. I was especially fortunate to work with Jan E. Allen, now associate dean for academic and student affairs at Cornell University, who took me under her wing and showed me what a student-centered focus is all about, and to Janet Metcalfe, whose knowledge about the learning sciences is something to behold. I will always be grateful to Chancellors Francisco Cigarroa and William McRaven, Executive Vice Chancellors Steven Leslie and Pedro Reyes, and Regents Alex Cranberg, Wallace L. Hall Jr., and Gene Powell, who provided the UT System's Institute for Transformational Learning with unrivaled support. At the University of Texas at Austin, David Laude and Jamie Pennebaker have been ongoing sources of inspiration. I owe special thanks to those who invested in my initiatives: the Bill and Melinda Gates Foundation, especially Art Seavey; the Howard Hughes Medical Institute and its assistant director, Sarah Simmons; the National Endowment for the Humanities; and the Teagle Foundation and its program director, Loni M. Bordoloi Pazich.

To these colleagues and friends, I owe debts that I can never adequately repay. I thank them from the bottom of my heart.

# THE
# LEARNING-CENTERED
# UNIVERSITY

# Higher Education's Post-pandemic Future

THE PANDEMIC THAT SURFACED in early 2020 hit higher education with all the force and fury of an earthquake. In the span of a few mid-semester weeks, colleges and universities closed their campuses, and their faculty and students migrated to remote learning. Even as the pandemic's initial shocks dissipated, it became clear that the higher education landscape had shifted in fundamental ways. The worst was behind us, but the disruptions were not.

Challenges—demographic, financial, and political—that predated the health crisis deepened. Conversations about access, admissions, affordability, equity, and testing intensified. At the same time, changes in the composition of the student body that were already underway accelerated. Now, new concerns—notably, a heightened sensitivity toward equity, worries about higher education's return on investment, and a student mental health crisis—have added to the challenges ahead.

Higher education remains our society's best hope for addressing the most profound issues of our time: stagnating incomes, worsening economic inequalities, productivity slowdowns, persistent racial disparities, and deepening political partisanship. But if our colleges and universities are to continue to fulfill their educational, research, and social and emotional development functions and serve as an engine of economic mobility and local and regional dynamism, these institutions must become more affordable, sustainable, resilient, and successful in bringing all students to graduation.

It's possible that the federal government will step in, eliminating student debt and providing sufficient funds to allow these institutions to proceed as they did before the pandemic. But rather than await a miracle, it is better to develop a forward-looking strategy that is learner and learning centered.

Meeting today's challenges would be difficult under the best of circumstances, but current conditions are anything but optimal. Many institutions never fully recovered financially from the Great Recession that began in late 2007. The stratification of higher education has worsened, with the gaps between institutional resources and student need growing wider. Meanwhile, the pandemic—and the resulting furloughs, layoffs, and cuts in retirement contributions—exacerbated tensions among faculty, staff, and administrators. Institutions are also facing a new age of student activism and protest, which arose in response to police brutality against people of color, symbols of bigotry (including statues and building names), federal actions against undocumented and international students, and tuition and fees charged by colleges not offering in-person instruction or the traditional college experience. One need not be a seer to recognize that campus controversies and conflicts involving admissions, affirmative action, diversity, equity, financial aid, and inclusion will persist and likely intensify.

In the wake of the health crisis, the economic crisis, and the long-overdue reckoning over race, higher education will, and indeed must, change. The crisis will force society to rethink how best to pay for higher education and impel colleges and universities to radically reimagine how best to educate students. Although these crises have created havoc, every crisis also offers opportunities: a chance to rethink, reprioritize, and reinvent. Many institutions of higher education made huge investments in and built a business around a model of mass education that now seems increasingly problematic—a model that included large dormitories and dining halls, enormous lecture halls, massive stadiums, and large-capacity performance venues. In addition, many institutions adopted an enrollment and budgetary strategy that depended on admitting substantial numbers of international, out-of-state, and affluent students willing to pay full tuition—a strategy that no longer seems sustainable or equitable.

Colleges and universities that hope to thrive in the years ahead must contain costs in ways that do not compromise quality, leverage technology to better serve students more efficiently and cost-effectively, and pursue growth markets. These institutions also need to redesign their curricula and reinvent the student experience. Faculty, in turn, must reimagine their roles, priorities, pedagogy, and the courses they teach.

Some view the ongoing crisis as an opportunity for radical disruption. These disruptors propose upending higher education as we have known it. Among the ideas they have advanced are these: substituting short-term certificates and certifications for traditional degrees; replacing standard terms and courses with self-paced, competency-based approaches that award credit for demonstrated learning outcomes rather than seat time; replacing a comprehensive program and course offerings with a much narrower, career-oriented curriculum; swapping tenurable faculty for lower-cost coaches, course mentors, and graders; "unbundling" the college experience by eliminating expensive facilities, laboratories, physical libraries, athletics, and theaters; and developing cheaper, faster alternatives, like boot camps and skills academies, as substitutes for traditional campuses.

I do not fall into the radical camp. I greatly value the defining characteristics of a traditional college education: a physical campus, a curriculum rooted in the liberal arts, and faculty who are active researchers and scholars as well as teachers. Indeed, I believe that accrediting agencies need to subject online institutions, nonprofit as well as for-profit, to far greater scrutiny and make it clear that a college education requires regular, substantive interaction with and feedback from *bona fide* professors. I also believe, however, that we have a great deal to learn from the disruptors and even from the for-profit online universities and their nonprofit successors.

No doubt you've heard the advice: you can't go forward looking in the rearview mirror. But those words of wisdom are actually wrong. Only by looking backward can we move forward. We need to look backward to learn from our mistakes and free ourselves from the ruts we find ourselves in. Looking backward helps us understand trends that are fast approaching. So, let's look back at the recent past and see what we can learn about how we got to where we are today.

If we look rearward, we see that a series of utterly unpredictable developments in the last decade and a half left an indelible imprint on higher education today. The first was the Great Recession, the financial crisis that began in December 2007. It was the Great Recession that brought to a head the mounting concerns over rising tuition and student loans, state cutbacks in higher education spending, college graduates' uneven employment outcomes, and institutions' unproven return on investment. The financial crisis also made the academy inescapably aware of a basic fact: that most students had to work while they earned their degrees. In addition, the financial crisis made it obvious that colleges needed to establish stronger ties to employers and careers. Equally important, the Great Recession triggered a campus version of the Occupy Wall Street movement, as growing numbers of graduate students and even undergraduates unionized and campus activism intensified, evident in campaigns to divest from fossil fuels, in unrest among student athletes, and in fury over campus sexual assaults.

One by-product of the Great Recession was accelerating a shift away from traditional humanities fields to seemingly more lucrative fields in business, engineering, health care, and science. Another outgrowth of the recession was the proliferation of alternatives to college as usual. MOOCs, or massive open online courses, from Stanford, MIT, Harvard, and other major universities that attracted one hundred thousand or more students, were one offshoot of the Great Recession. As tuition mounted and student loan debt soared, the institutions with the greatest resources were under pressure to share their wealth and give back. But because these privileged institutions had no interest in awarding degrees to MOOC takers, disaggregating content, or seriously adapting courses to assist those students with the greatest learning needs, and because the MOOC providers were supposed to be financially self-sustaining, MOOCs inevitably failed to live up to their promise.

Other recession-fueled alternatives to college included boot camps, skills academies, nondegree certificate programs, apprenticeships, and other faster, cheaper paths into the workforce. Yet none of these other paths has succeeded in demonstrating its value as a viable alternative to a traditional college degree. By far the most successful recession-era development was the spectacular growth of nonprofit online universities, including Arizona State Online, Southern New Hampshire University, and Western Governors University, which rapidly supplanted their for-profit counterparts. By targeting the underserved market of working adults and family caregivers and offering a more flexible, convenient education at a somewhat lower price point than brick-and-mortar campuses—along with multiple start dates and, typically, shorter terms—these institutions attracted hundreds of thousands of students. It appears, however, that their enrollment growth largely reflected the decline of such major for-profits as the University of Phoenix.

Yet another consequence of the Great Recession was a demographic shift that continues to carry vast repercussions for higher education today. Birth rates fell sharply, especially among the middle class, which will dramatically decrease the size of the traditional college-aged population in the later 2020s. The youthful population grew much more diverse ethnically and racially, and it increasingly came from lower-income backgrounds, which means that colleges and universities must not only increase financial aid but also figure out how to bring populations they have poorly served in the past to academic and postgraduation success.

Another landmark development was the 2010 publication of *Academically Adrift*, a book that called into question the knowledge and skills students acquired in college. Disputes over the book's methodology and findings proved irrelevant. The book convinced many policy makers and opinion shapers that academic rigor was in free fall and that a substantial share of students showed no improvements in critical thinking, analytical reasoning, or written communication during their college years. As influential in its own way as *Silent Spring*, *The Feminine Mystique*, and *Unsafe at Any Speed*, *Academically Adrift* contributed substantially to the growing doubts among large segments of the population over the value of higher education, even as a college degree was becoming a prerequisite for a stable, secure, and well-paying middle-class job.

One consequence of *Academically Adrift* was to fuel the development of campus teaching and learning centers and to advance scholarship on the science of learning. The learning sciences, including cognitive and developmental psychology and neuroscience, have taught us a great deal about how students learn and how to make studying more efficient and effective and teaching more impactful. The science of learning, in other words, holds out the prospect of using evidence-based techniques to improve instructional design, pedagogy, and assessments; build students' knowledge and skills; and create learning experiences that engage students and stay with them.

A data analytics revolution, too, would leave a lasting imprint on higher education. For the first time, it was possible to analyze a student's academic journey, from recruitment through graduation. Enrollment management specialists and student-success czars could determine with extraordinary accuracy which students were most likely to enroll and how much financial aid would be required to maximize tuition revenue. It was also possible to predict which undergraduates would persevere, sustain their academic momentum, shift majors, transfer, drop out, or graduate as well as how much they'd earn after graduation. Consequently, campuses could now target academic advising and proactively intervene when students were lost or went off track.

Alongside the analytics revolution came a series of other innovations. At great expense, campuses implemented a new digital infrastructure to support enrollment management, budgeting, human resources management, student information systems, and course management. Institutions also turned to various for-profit and nonprofit intermediaries to provide a host of services. These included third-party vendors that provided success coaching, arranged internships, enrolled international students, ran study abroad programs, recruited and enrolled college dropouts, and worked with corporations to make higher education an employee benefit. Without a doubt, the most significant and controversial partnerships were with online program managers who promised to help colleges market their online programs leading to degrees and certificates, typically in exchange for long-term contracts that required institutions to give the online program managers 50 to 70 percent of the revenue that the programs generated. Other collaborations were with firms that offered boot camps, managed and tracked certificates and other alternative credentials, and hosted student portfolios.

Edtech companies and publishers also held out the promise of making higher education more effective and cost efficient by offering personalized and adaptive educational software, interactive courseware, and digital textbooks with rich multimedia, animations and simulations, tutorials, and embedded assessments. In most cases, these highly touted innovations failed to live up to the hype. Much more successful were less ambitious technology tools that made it easier for students to annotate texts collaboratively, manage citations, mine texts, visualize and analyze data, or create blogs, infographics, podcasts, and digital stories. These tools made the academic experience more active, immersive, interactive, and participatory. Looming on the horizon today are tools that leverage artificial intelligence and machine learning as a substitute for scarce advisers and teaching assistants. Examples include essay autograders, chatbots, and automated degree planners and trackers.

Yet another development with far-reaching implications for higher education was the 2016 presidential election, which was at once a product of deepening political polarization and a key contributor to partisan division, inflaming campus protests over diversity, immigration, sexual assault, and student loan repayment and resulting in bitter battles over free speech and academic freedom.

Then came the pandemic. Whatever its other effects, COVID-19 brought with it a growing acceptance of online learning and prompted campuses to make student support services available online. The pandemic also revealed and intensified a campus mental health crisis. With much casual socializing suspended in lockdown and many social rituals and rites of passage curtailed, students' social skills eroded, as did their ability to sustain focus and, in some instances, to interact in a civil manner. Rates of depression and anxiety soared. Accompanying the pandemic were protests over George Floyd's murder at the hands of police officers. Student protesters demanded equity and launched concerted attacks on symbols of inequality and past discrimination. They placed intense pressure on colleges and universities to diversify the professoriate and strengthen diversity, inclusion, and anti-racism initiatives.

The pandemic accelerated and intensified a series of disruptions in higher education. There was the demographic disruption, as many institutions, community colleges above all, experienced an enrollment crunch at the same time that student bodies were growing more diverse, not only in terms of class, ethnicity, and race but in many other respects as well. A majority of students are now nontraditional in some way: they commute to campus; attend part-time; work; parent; have a physical, learning, or psychological disability; or come from a home where English is not the primary language.

There was also the digital disruption that occurred when faculty were forced to move courses online in record time and as many students, initially resistant to online learning, came to discover that digital classes helped them juggle the competing demands on their time. Although a growing acceptance of online education as equivalent to face-to-face education is more common in graduate and professional education than in undergraduate education, a hybrid approach combining online and in-person classes is taking hold, in part reflecting improvements in online instruction that allow for more student engagement.

Then there was the business model disruption. Although temporary federal stimulus funding through the CARES Act (Coronavirus Aid, Relief, and Economic Security Act) mitigated the pandemic's immediate financial impact, underlying cost challenges involving facilities maintenance, infrastructure, overhead, and services remained, while international enrollment, a key revenue generator, declined. Facing deeply entrenched constraints on their ability to increase tuition and fees, the tuition-dependent institutions that make up the vast majority of US colleges and universities found themselves caught in a trap. The cost of higher education is becoming prohibitively expensive for many families, even as the cost of providing a college education rises faster than inflation. Such trends are unsustainable. Without increased government support—directly, through grants and contracts or indirectly, through student debt relief and an increase in the size of Pell Grants—campuses risk pricing out their students.

Disruptive competition has become worrisome as well. Higher education is now more competitive domestically and internationally as universities in Australia, Canada, and the United Kingdom as well as China, Hong Kong, and Singapore vie aggressively for international students and rise steadily in worldwide rankings, thereby putting American preeminence in higher education at risk. Countries such as France and Germany now offer degree programs in English. Within the United States, alternatives to brick-and-mortar universities are attracting more and more students, including a growing number of traditional-aged undergraduates. At the same time, the online market has grown increasingly saturated, closing off that lucrative source of revenue. Not only is competition intensifying, but the higher education market is becoming more stratified and differentiated, divided between wealthy institutions and those that face chronic economic stresses and enrollment challenges, with few new revenue sources available.

Some disruptions have come largely from within: long-overdue demands for greater diversity and equity, improved services and return on investment, and new fields of study, such as artificial intelligence and machine learning, biomedical engineering, biostatistics, cybersecurity, data science, financial technology, and environmental sustainability. These disruptions should prompt campuses to ask some tough questions. Who will our students be in the next five to ten years? Is our curriculum relevant to the changing needs of the economy and preparing students for the future? Are our technology, infrastructure, and services prepared to support the future of education on our campus?

All of which brings us to today. It's important to recognize what hasn't happened. As unemployment rates fell and student loan repayment went into abeyance, interest in alternative paths into the workforce dampened. Recent high school graduates have not flocked in large numbers to fully online universities or boot camps or skills academies or apprenticeships. It seems clear that the overwhelming majority of prospective students want something that resembles, more or less, a traditional college education. Even though online learning achieved a degree of legitimacy inconceivable a dozen years earlier, it's now apparent that most undergraduates want a mixture of online and in-person classes, plus access to online support 24/7. Fully online programs appeal primarily to working adults and graduate students.

That said, students and parents came to care intensely about a college education's return on investment. The popularity of majors that lead directly to well-paying jobs, whether in business, engineering, health care, or information technology, shows no signs of slackening. Despite the movement by some companies and some states to eliminate college degree requirements for certain jobs, most employers still prefer bachelor's degree holders. Additionally, companies favor applicants with certain skills—quantitative ability; facility with relevant software, project management, and marketing or sales; and soft skills such as the ability to communicate clearly, along with on-the-job experience. It is up to colleges and universities to ensure that students acquire the skills and experience that employers demand.

American higher education's recent history has clarified the challenges that today's colleges and universities face. Campuses must control and contain costs, raise completion rates, and improve and verify learning outcomes. These institutions must also offer an education that impresses students as relevant and experiential. Equity, too, is imperative. Institutions must enroll a more diverse student body, including more community college transfer students and those from low-income backgrounds; ensure equal access to high-demand majors; and bring considerably more students to graduation and postgraduation success.

In the chapters to come, I explain how institutions of higher education can institute these imperative changes. Colleges and universities need not reinvent the wheel. Many of the innovations that higher education needs already exist and are practiced at some institutions around the country. Our challenge, in short, is not a shortage of ideas. Rather, it is—as George Mehaffy, former vice president for academic leadership and change at the American Association of State Colleges and Universities, has observed—an implementation problem.

I favor what the educational technologist Michael Feldstein calls a "radically conservative" vision of higher education that conserves "the best parts of an American-style liberal arts education by reimagining it but not rejecting it."[1] I call this vision the learner- and learning-centered university. This is an institution that values scholarship, the liberal arts, a physical campus, and the teacher-scholar. It doesn't offer a narrowly vocational education, but it is career conscious. It's a mission-driven university, and that mission is, above all, to give a diverse student body educational experiences that are second to none in addition to the feedback and mentoring that students need and deserve to prepare them for postgraduation success as adults and professionals.

If we were honest with ourselves, we'd acknowledge that most American colleges and universities have embraced an educational model that doesn't work very well. Only about 60 percent of undergraduates at four-year institutions earn a bachelor's degree, while fewer than 40 percent of community college students ever get a degree or certificate. Even among those who do receive a bachelor's, about 40 percent find themselves underemployed in a field unrelated to their college major. If the nation's K–12 schools had such awful outcomes, politicians and the public would cry foul.

The broad-access institutions that serve the bulk of undergraduates need a new educational model. That's not the model proposed by the self-styled disruptors and innovators who call for cheaper, faster paths into the job market. Some of those disruptors believe that the path forward lies in a fully online, career-focused education; others advocate for a self-directed, self-paced model. Still others think the answer lies in unbundling traditional college by replacing teacher-scholars with course mentors, coaches, and graders; eliminating buildings, fixed-length terms, and extracurricular activities; and substituting stackable, short-term credentials for conventional degrees. Then there are those who want to eliminate tenure and reduce expectations for faculty research.

Even as I reject the disruptors' vision, I recognize that their diagnosis of the weaknesses in today's system of higher education is not wholly wrong. We do need more meaningful accountability and oversight from government and accrediting agencies for quality and outcomes. Of course, those assessments need to be made in a nuanced and mindful way, attentive to an institution's particular mission and the composition of its student body. Yet without greater accountability, complacency is inevitable. Also, our society needs alternative tracks into the workforce for those whose lives make an in-person, full-time college education impossible. But let's not claim that those alternative paths are equivalent to a traditional college education. In addition, institutions as a whole as well as their individual departments need to become more attentive to their graduates' employment prospects. I consider it a moral responsibility to embed career identification and preparation within degree programs and better align courses with the kinds of jobs that graduates will enter.

My vision of a learner- and learning-centered university affirms the value of a physical campus and a professoriate that combines research, teaching, and mentoring while embracing the value of a liberal arts education. This model differs from existing practice in its emphasis on explicit learning and skills outcomes, more coherent and integrated curricular pathways, and the well-rounded development of the whole student—socially, emotionally, ethically, and cognitively. I also endorse introducing alternatives to traditional lecture and seminar courses that involve more active, immersive, participatory, experiential, and inquiry- and project-based learning; a curriculum that cultivates graduates with knowledge and skills in quantitative analysis, social science thinking, and the scientific method along with fluency in the arts, literature, history, philosophy, and the humanities' interpretive techniques; and more explicit preparation for the job market.

Implementing a learner- and learning-centered approach will require far-reaching changes in curricula, pedagogy, assessment, faculty roles, and student support structures. This won't be easy, but it is essential if campuses are to bring many more students to a bright future. The changes I spell out are imperative, first of all, because the student body has changed. The new student majority—which consists of commuting students, part-time students, working students, international students, and students with disabilities, many of whom received an uneven education in high school—needs approaches to teaching and learning that differ from those of the past.

Second, the education our institutions offer needs to adapt to changes in students' life challenges as well as their expectations and aspirations. To paraphrase Donald Rumsfeld, colleges and universities must serve the students they have, not the students they might want. At most broad-access institutions, these are often students who attend part-time, commute, work twenty-five hours a week or more, have transferred, or have family responsibilities. Many are among the first in their families to attend college and therefore need more advising and mentoring than those who are already familiar with college terminology, offices, practices and procedures, requirements, and academic expectations. In addition, many require help with basic needs like food, housing, health care, childcare, transportation, and the unpredictable problems that all too frequently interrupt their educations.

We must also adapt to the fact that today's students, unlike their counterparts of a half century ago, are primarily interested in a glide path to a rewarding career. That means colleges and universities must furnish entering students with a clearly delineated road map to a degree; offer an education students regard as engaging and relevant; provide wraparound academic and nonacademic supports, including intensive, personalized academic, financial, and career advising and ready access to supplemental instruction while eliminating obstacles to timely completion, such as outdated or irrelevant graduation requirements and barriers to transfer.

A learner- and learning-centered institution would strive to maximize students' return on investment and prepare undergraduates not just for their fifth job but for their first. This will require that faculty make sure their teaching is, first and foremost, about advancing their students' welfare. Instructors need to create educational experiences that are intentionally designed to engage and motivate students, tie in with their postgraduation aspirations, offer a sufficient amount of flexibility and options, and help students persevere. We know what to do. Let's look at the steps we need to take to get there.

In terms of policies and practices, we need to incentivize full-time enrollment. We need to offer a robust new-student orientation to introduce students to campus services and provide each one with a degree plan and a personal point of contact. We need to create block schedules that allow students to make more productive use of their time on campus, whether in the morning, afternoon, or evening on specific weekdays or on weekends. We must replace remedial courses with credit-bearing classes that provide corequisite support and supplemental instruction. In addition, we must guarantee the availability of essential gateway courses and make the transfer process seamless by fully articulating degree requirements between four-year and two-year feeder institutions and expediting transfer credit evaluation.

Our curricula need to be rethought and redesigned. We need to create structured, integrated degree pathways into high-demand fields, with courses designed to reinforce one another. We should consider aligning math requirements with students' program of study and associated careers. We should rethink general education by offering for-credit courses that promote personal development, build academic success skills, involve civic engagement and service learning, and address pressing and timely social problems. These courses should broadly introduce students to social science and historical thinking, the frontiers of science, and the art of looking, listening, and reading from multidisciplinary perspectives. We should also supplement lecture courses and seminars with other experiences that feature active and experiential learning.

As institutions reimagine their curricula, they should also reenvision the courses they offer, if students are to acquire a range of knowledge and competencies along with the soft, technical, and digital skills signified by a college degree. That will require instructors to devote more attention to skills-building. It also means that faculty will need to develop new kinds of lower division courses that are more sweeping and interdisciplinary than the discipline-based classes that dominate that portion of the curriculum. Sure, specialized courses have an important place in the upper division, but undergraduates also need broader classes that expose them to how humanists, social scientists, and scientists think and how scholars grapple with climate change, democracy, equality, international relations, justice, merit, gender and race, and other hot topics.

Pedagogy needs to evolve to incorporate the insights of the learning sciences. That means redesigning large-enrollment gateway classes to make them more dynamic, interactive, and participatory. It will also require that institutions assist faculty in incorporating active learning strategies and educational technologies that facilitate annotation, collaboration, text mining, visualization, and novel kinds of student presentations, including digital storytelling and podcasts and the development of virtual encyclopedias, museum exhibitions, and websites. Instructors must introduce more low-stakes formative and authentic assessments into their teaching and provide students with more substantive and timely constructive feedback directed at building their essential skills in communication, analysis, critical thinking, quantifying, and collaboration.

A sense of belonging, we now know, is essential for student success. To create connections, institutions need to place first-year students in a learning community aligned with their career aspirations and expand their access to various cohort programs, including research, community service, and opportunity programs.

Support services are more important than ever, and scaling these services won't come cheap. Still, there are ways to deliver support efficiently and at scale. Colleges and universities need to implement a data infrastructure that allows advisers and instructors to monitor student engagement, performance, and progress in near-real time and triggers nudges and interventions when students fall off track. Schools must establish a tiered system of student support that includes tutoring, peer-led study groups, supplemental instruction sessions, and learning centers in mathematics, science, and writing. Campuses should consider introducing a one-stop student support center to make it easier for students to resolve problems with financial aid, billing, and course registration; adopting a case management approach to advising that allows a single adviser to address multiple issues a student might need to resolve; and appointing a graduation specialist to help students nearing commencement cross the finish line.

In terms of career preparation, the steps that institutions need to take are obvious. Embed career preparation across the undergraduate experience. Establish preprofessional centers in high-demand areas such as the arts, computer science, information technology, prehealth care, prelaw, and public policy. Scale experiential learning opportunities to help students create a record of career-related skills and accomplishments. Also, consider creating a skills transcript to document demonstrated career-related skills.

The simplest, most straightforward solutions to the enrollment, financial, completion, political, and postgraduation employment challenges that today's broad-access colleges and universities confront require campuses to increase retention rates, expedite the time it takes to earn a degree, and prepare students for entry into a meaningful, rewarding career. If degree attainment and credentialing were our only objectives, we could surely do that more cheaply and efficiently. Certainly, we need to think more strategically about the education we provide.

However unequal our system of higher education has become, we still cling (albeit precariously) to the idea that all college students should have the opportunity to work with specialists, authorities, and experts. Let's not compromise that great democratic ideal. Let's not exchange our birthright as scholars for a bowl of porridge. We have it in our power to provide an education that is richer, more immersive, supportive, and effective than what we currently offer. Failure to do so would be a terrible mistake and would expose our pretensions to equity, opportunity, mobility, and deep, durable learning as a sham.

# 1

## Higher Education's Perfect Storm

HIGHER EDUCATION IS IN THE MIDST of a perfect storm. A host of forces—demographic, financial, and political—have converged to disrupt existing ways of doing business. This storm has upset established business models and threatens to bifurcate colleges and universities along multiple dimensions: in admissions selectivity, per student instructional spending, student-faculty ratios, financial aid expenditures, endowment earnings, and college preparedness. The result threatens higher education's democratic role as an engine of opportunity and social mobility.

But this perfect storm has also unleashed a torrent of innovation and experimentation. It has accelerated the spread of online learning and the rise of new approaches to pedagogy: flipped classrooms; problem-, project-, and team-based teaching; service learning; makerspaces; and field- and community-based as well as clinical learning experiences. It has also stimulated the growth of new kinds of nondegree credentials and fueled the emergence of new educational providers that offer shorter or less expensive forms of job training.

The perfect storm is the culmination of a confluence of factors. These range from costs that have consistently risen faster than

inflation (for information technology, financial aid, employee benefits, campus maintenance, and student support services), to stagnant
state and federal funding on a per student, inflation-adjusted basis,
to institutions' inability to continue to shift costs to students and
parents. It is also a product of accreditors who demand more explicit
and transparent learning outcomes, governmental insistence on
greater accountability and cost-effectiveness, and parental and employer pressure to ensure that students graduate with real-world,
marketable skills. Further contributing to the perfect storm are
new entrants into the higher education marketplace. These include
for-profit and nonprofit providers of online education, which offer
career-aligned training at a somewhat lower price point by unbundling the faculty role and replacing professors with low-paid, lower-
skilled coaches, mentors, and graders; nondegree skills academies
that offer short-term training in high-demand fields; and new kinds
of job-aligned credentials offered by corporations and standard-
setting organizations.

Even the most selective, prestigious, and highly resourced institutions are not immune to the impact of this perfect storm. These elite
research universities are under intense pressure to further diversify
their student bodies, extend their global profiles, and prevail in a
competitive arms race for accomplished faculty, top students, reputation, and new revenue streams. This competition takes the form of
ever more selective admissions, star architecture, expensive amenities, and a concerted push into online learning at the continuing, master's, and professional education level. These institutions have established a baseline that other colleges and universities must emulate,
irrespective of the cost.[1]

But the institutions under the greatest stress are the broad-access,
less selective, and less well-funded colleges and universities that serve
the bulk of this nation's undergraduates. These schools are hard-
pressed to offer a range of programs and services comparable to
their wealthier and more prestigious counterparts to a student body
with far greater learning and financial needs. To make matters worse,
these are precisely the institutions that face the greatest competitive

threat from more focused, less expensive, and lower-quality for-profits and their nonprofit imitators.

If these broad-access institutions are to continue to serve as purveyors of a truly well-rounded liberal education and providers of the human capital that an advanced economy needs, then their curriculum pathways, pedagogies, delivery models, and support services need to adapt to a rapidly shifting environment. Many of the strategies adopted by these institutions, however, threaten to dilute the quality of an undergraduate education while exacerbating educational and economic inequalities. These include increased reliance on part-time adjunct faculty, the shedding of traditional liberal arts programs, and low-quality online courses with little instructor presence, interactivity, or constructive feedback.

The traditional brick-and-mortar college or university is not an endangered species. These institutions are, with few exceptions, too valuable to fail. These schools are among their localities' most prized assets and often their communities' largest employers. Altogether, colleges currently employ more than three million people, dwarfing the numbers working in agriculture or for the federal government and almost equaling those working in all information services combined. In addition, higher education is among the greatest contributors to the nation's balance of payments, contributing about $34 billion a year—more than coal or natural gas. These institutions also hold a monopoly over the most trusted job credential, the bachelor's degree, and provide a coming-of-age experience that most graduates regard as among the happiest periods of their lives. But as the economist Irwin Feller has argued, a growing number of colleges and universities have become chronic invalids, facing a gradual erosion of quality and competitiveness.[2]

Popular critiques of American higher education tend to focus on a series of straw men: indifferent or excessively politicized faculty engaged in pointless research; rampant political correctness that stifles free speech; a watered-down curriculum that leaves students without the content knowledge or the proficiencies expected of a college graduate; administrative bloat and country club-like amenities that increase the cost of higher education while doing little or nothing to enhance learning; inflated grades that reward underprepared, coddled, and disengaged students for inferior work; and a rating-fueled pursuit of prestige that has led institutions to chase status by emphasizing buildings, athletics, and expanded program offerings rather than prioritizing student learning.[3]

But higher ed's real problems lie elsewhere: in a high dropout rate that leaves over a third of college students with debt but no degree; in the protracted time to degree that requires most students to pay for an undergraduate education not for four years, but for five, six, or even more; in the gross disparities in funding that leave the fewest resources to students with the greatest needs; and in a lack of transparency about learning, graduation, and employment outcomes that makes it difficult for students and parents to make informed decisions about the most appropriate institution to attend or subject to major in, or, for legislators and policy makers, to gauge the effectiveness of particular institutions, their contribution to social mobility, or their success relative to the composition of their student bodies.[4]

Postsecondary education has never been more valuable, and the penalty for failing to earn a college degree has never been greater. But of all those who enter ninth grade, less than 40 percent wind up with a bachelor's degree. The challenges before higher education are three-fold: to control the cost of a college education without diluting quality; to improve completion rates and close achievement and attainment gaps that exist along the lines of race, ethnicity, gender, and socioeconomic class; and to raise the level of student engagement and ensure that undergraduates obtain windows into future careers and acquire the skills and knowledge expected of a college graduate while also acquiring the critical thinking skills and literacies associated with a rich, robust liberal arts education.[5]

Intensifying these challenges are recent changes in student demographics that have greatly increased the number of nontraditional students who acquire credits from multiple institutions, combine school with work and family responsibilities, and received uneven preparation in high school. Increasingly, these students may also have physical, psychological, or learning disabilities and come from homes where English isn't the first language. Adding to the challenge are stagnating government expenditures on higher education on an inflation-adjusted, per student basis. Successfully addressing those challenges will require the broad-access institutions that serve the overwhelming majority of college students to rethink every facet of the academic experience, from credit transfer policies to curriculum design, major pathways, pedagogies, delivery modalities, scheduling, support structures, and even credentials.

Higher education's problem, however, is not a shortage of ideas; it is, as George Mehaffy of the American Association of State Colleges and Universities has put it, an implementation challenge. Implementing solutions in a cost-efficient manner is higher education's wicked problem—messy, complex, and not resolved with simple answers. But implementation is essential if higher education is to successfully address its current challenges and fulfill its democratic promise.[6]

The most innovative institutions are harnessing design thinking, the learning sciences, data analytics, and educational technology to restructure every facet of the student experience. Solutions include articulation agreements that make credit transfer seamless; curricular pathways that are more coherent, integrated, and synergistic and better connect a college education to a career; pedagogies that emphasize active inquiry, problem-solving, and mentored research, and make experiential, clinical, field, service, and team-based learning a more integral part of the undergraduate experience; block schedules and hybrid course offerings that better serve today's new majority of working students; and "authentic" assessments that are problem- and project-based and mimic real-world job responsibilities. Pacesetting institutions use technology to diagnose gaps in student learning in near-real time, prompt interventions by advisers and learning specialists, provide students with timely, targeted feedback, and increase access to support services outside of normal business hours. These trendsetters use data analytics to isolate and remove curricular roadblocks, target interventions, counsel students about courses to take, and inform decisions about admissions, financial aid, and course scheduling.

Today, however, a host of blockers impedes innovation at scale. The obstacles are many. A tendency to treat each class and each discipline as an independent entity makes it difficult to create coherent, synergistic educational pathways. An incentive structure exists that prioritizes departmental self-interest, discourages cross-departmental and cross-functional collaboration, and impedes adoption of more student-centric forms of scheduling or course delivery. A lack of campus capacity and expertise hinders innovation in areas vital to the future of higher education, such as instructional design, activity and assessment architecture, data analytics, and educational technology acquisition and development. Existing workload policies make it difficult to allocate faculty in untraditional ways that have a great impact on student learning. Classrooms are poorly suited to team- and project-based learning. Legacy technologies cannot accommodate courses with fractional credit, deliver a more outcome-focused education, or support educational experiences that do not conform to a traditional term. Campus information systems are incapable of consolidating information from multiple data silos.

Many of the policies and practices that dominate higher education today are products of a very different world. Ten- and fifteen-week terms, distribution requirements; pedagogies that emphasize lectures, discussion, and cookie-cutter labs; and a tripartite curriculum that consists of general education courses, a major, and electives do not meet many contemporary students' needs. None of these practices are etched in stone; exciting alternatives exist. A growing number of faculty members and administrators have begun to recognize a basic truth: that as our student demographics change and the needs of the economy shift, higher education must change too. By revealing realistic alternatives to conventional practice and offering concrete strategies for institutional transformation, this book offers higher education's diverse stakeholders—faculty, administrators, policy makers, and parents—a path forward.

If higher education is to flourish, it must do several difficult things all at once. It must bring many more students to completion in a timely manner—not just the 36 percent who graduate in four years from a selective four-year private college or university or a flagship public university or the 19 percent who graduate in four years from a non-flagship four-year public university. It needs to make sure that students keep more of their credits when they transfer from one college to another, as more than a third of students do. It has an obligation to help students better manage the tension between college and work now that a majority of students are trying to juggle higher education with a job and family responsibilities. It needs to ensure that college is affordable, not just for those who go to the most highly endowed private universities with substantial financial aid budgets but also for those who attend regional and urban public universities. It should make sure that graduates acquire the essential knowledge and skills that are indispensable for postgraduation success.

The challenge before us is not only to make higher education more efficient and effective, but more equitable, engaging, immersive, interactive, participatory, and well-supported. To accomplish this, we need to take a host of steps that won't be easily accomplished, especially not in a context of resource constraints. Institutions must enhance advising to help students make better-informed choices about the institutions to attend, the majors and other credentials to pursue, and the courses to take. Campuses must make graduation, employment, and earnings outcomes more transparent. Schools need to better align the educations offered by high schools, community colleges, and four-year institutions and institute curricular pathways and pedagogies that are more coherent, outcome oriented, and skills focused and better aligned with workforce expectations and projections. Campuses must also reduce the tensions between school and other demands on students' time, especially workplace responsibilities, and do a better job of identifying students at risk of failure, remediating deficiencies, and providing wraparound support in a scalable, cost-effective manner. Then, too, institutions must expand nondegree options and lifelong learning opportunities to make it easier for working adults to upgrade their skills or retool.

None of these accomplishments is utopian. All are well within higher education's current capabilities. But if these necessary developments are to take place, faculty and other stakeholders need to embrace the urgency of academic transformation, and determined leadership must create the conditions where sustainable innovation can thrive.

It is a sad fact that even at many of the best-funded, most selective institutions, like the ones that I attended and where I taught (Oberlin, Yale, Columbia, Harvard Extension, Pepperdine, the University of Houston, and the University of Texas at Austin), too much education consists of lectures without much interaction and student engagement. Even at leading liberal arts colleges, many students fail to receive the regular substantive feedback, mentoring, and personalized advising that are crucial to academic and postgraduation success. At most institutions, the curriculum consists of a smorgasbord of disconnected courses without much intellectual coherence or clearly defined, granular learning objectives. In the natural sciences, mathematics, engineering, nursing, and even business, weed-out courses and restrictions on entry into high-demand majors persist, preventing many qualified students from successfully pursuing their dreams. Despite distribution requirements that are supposed to ensure a well-rounded education, it's all too easy to graduate without an ability to write or speak clearly and persuasively, produce evidence-based arguments, or demonstrate the level of literacy in the arts, humanities, and social and natural sciences expected of a college-level graduate.

Perhaps the greatest failing of our current educational system is that colleges and universities generally do a poor job of opening students' windows into career possibilities or helping them define realistic postgraduation goals and a path toward achieving those objectives, except for the small minority who enter graduate school or professional programs immediately after earning a bachelor's degree.

Too many graduates flail and flounder for years before falling into a job that may or may not reflect their interests and training.

Among this book's goals is to help institutions clarify the kinds of graduates they seek to nurture and the proficiencies and habits their students need to acquire. This volume lays out cost-efficient strategies that colleges and universities can adopt to build the competencies essential for future success and lay the foundation for a well-rounded professional identity. Like it or not, this nation's colleges and universities, especially its broad-access institutions, must find new ways to increase productivity and absorb reductions in state support while improving retention and graduate rates without compromising quality or rigor. This book offers a realistic, realizable path forward. It lays out practical, pragmatic strategies for driving academic transformation and incorporating evidence-based approaches into everyday practice. The advice it offers grows out of personal experience directing one of the largest, most ambitious innovation efforts in higher education.

Higher education institutions face a choice: play offense, defense, or stand on the sideline. In 2012, the University of Texas System chose to play offense. Its board of regents created the Institute for Transformational Learning to address head-on the key challenges public postsecondary education faces: escalating costs, business models under severe strain, insufficient retention and graduation rates, and uncertain learning and postgraduation employment outcomes. To tackle those challenges, the Institute embraced a three-pronged strategy: building campus capacity and providing consulting services in areas critical to the future of higher education, such as data analytics, competency-based education, and personalized, adaptive learning; helping the system's campuses design, develop, market, and deliver state-of-the-art online programming in areas with high student and employer demand; and implementing the digital infrastructure necessary to consolidate student learning data and provide a more immersive, interactive online experience.

The Institute had a number of genuine successes that included working in partnership with two new medical schools to help design next-generation, competency-based curricula; creating a "Middle School to Medical School" cross-disciplinary biomedical sciences curriculum that attracted national attention; and effectuating a host of initiatives in the realm of health education and cybersecurity. It also worked closely with the Texas Workforce Commission on a statewide credentials marketplace. In directing the Institute, however, I learned a great deal about the barriers to academic transformation and the challenges of sustaining innovation.

Across the country, colleges and universities are establishing centers to drive academic innovation, harness learning analytics, champion technology-enhanced teaching and learning, and provide seed funding for breakthrough educational models. The Institute for Transformational Learning served as a model for such initiatives. Innovation is an iterative process, and I feel confident that the vision the Institute advanced, with its emphasis on mastery and outcomes, well-defined educational pathways undergirded by detailed knowledge maps, personalization of pace and the learning trajectory, interactive courseware with advanced simulations and bilingual content, and microcredentials aligned with the job market, can have a lasting impact on the broad-access institutions that serve the bulk of the nation's students.

Among the lessons I learned is that the mere presence of a vision for the future of higher education is only the first step toward academic transformation. Success ultimately hinges on determined leadership at multiple levels fostering a sense of urgency and possibility, achieving buy-in among diverse stakeholders, developing campus expertise in previously neglected areas, and garnering cooperation among units that historically have not valued cross-functional and cross-disciplinary collaboration. Academic innovation is necessary both as a force for renewal and revitalization and as a response to profound changes in the demographic, economic, and political environment in which higher education operates. To those charged with adapting to this brave new world, this book offers a host of evidence-based ideas and strategies to leverage.

# 2

---

# The Challenges Ahead

MANY OF THIS NATION'S GREATEST challenges—stagnating house-hold income, increasing levels of economic inequality, and intensi-fying political polarization—are directly connected to the failure to create effective pathways to a meaningful postsecondary credential for a sufficiently large share of the population. Never before has a postsecondary credential been more valuable. Not only do most well-paying jobs in today's knowledge economy require a bachelor's de-gree, but also the wage premium over a high school diploma across a lifetime now amounts to more than a million dollars. Currently, just 36 percent of young adults have graduated from a four-year college or university. No other advanced society provides greater financial rewards to college graduates, nor do other societies have nearly as great a gap in income between college graduates and nongraduates. None has a poorer record of bringing students to degree completion.[1]

A distressingly low graduation rate is only one of American higher education's pressing problems. Another is the increasing stratifica-tion of the postsecondary ecosystem. The gap in financial resources, student preparation, graduation rates, and time it takes to complete a degree program across institutions has widened, with low-income students and those from historically underrepresented populations concentrated in the most under-resourced, least selective institutions with the lowest completion rates. Worse yet, it is unclear whether or not the nation's less selective institutions are doing a particularly good job of ensuring that students graduate with the technical and other core skills that they need to flourish in a rapidly churning economy, or with realistic career aspirations and practical plans to achieve those goals.

This book offers pragmatic advice about how higher education can break through the iron triangle of access and affordability, attainment, and quality and bring many more Americans to a high-quality credential and a bright future. A number of innovative institutions are already piloting exciting, cost-effective educational models. The challenge is to scale evidence-based solutions in an environment of strapped financial resources with many blockers to academic transformation.

American higher education is among this society's most successful industries. The nation's best funded, most selective private and public research universities rank among the world's most prestigious and inventive. Nevertheless, American higher education faces an array of challenges. Three overarching challenges stand out. One is to significantly raise graduation rates at the nation's broad-access institutions without diluting standards or rigor. The second is to increase the nation's level of educational attainment by increasing the number of young adults who earn a degree or other credentials with value in the job market. The third is to control the growth of higher education's costs without lowering quality. Failure to successfully address these challenges will inevitably result in significant economic and human costs. The stratification of incomes will worsen; the middle class and working class will continue to face stagnating growth in real incomes; and many talented students from low-income backgrounds will be denied a bright future. Let us look at the major challenges facing higher education in detail.

# The Demographic Challenge

For seven decades, American higher education underwent unprecedented growth, as the share of the population that attended college rose from just 10 percent in 1940 to 56 percent in 2009. After 2010, in contrast, enrollments gradually declined, falling from a record 18.1 million undergraduates to just 15.6 million in 2019, the last year before the pandemic. Undergraduate enrollment is down by nearly 1 million since the start of the pandemic and by nearly 3 million over the preceding decade.[2]

Many colleges and universities, especially small colleges and regional public universities located in the Northeast and Midwest, that are already struggling with enrollment declines face an enrollment cliff—a precipitous falloff in enrollment that is expected to begin in 2025, a byproduct of a sharp decline in birthrates during the Great Recession. It's estimated that during the second half of the decade, enrollments will decline by another 15 percent, although the demographic cliff's impact will vary sharply by geographic region, with enrollment growing in the West, Florida, and Texas, even as it falls in the Northeast, the Mid-Atlantic states, and much of the South. Already, many tuition-dependent institutions, particularly those located in rural areas, are bracing for the looming enrollment decline with layoffs, mergers, consolidations, shuttered majors, shared services, and, in a small number of instances, closures.

Colleges and universities weathered earlier demographic declines by admitting a higher and higher percentage of high school graduates; but with roughly 70 percent of recent high school graduates already enrolling in college, broad-access campuses must look elsewhere: to college stop-outs, working adults, family caregivers, and international students. Many institutions are also adopting aggressive recruitment campaigns, highlighting opportunities to play sports, introducing vocationally aligned majors, and expanding online professional master's degree and job-aligned certificate and certification programs. However, the most obvious response to enrollment declines is also the solution most likely to pay off: raising retention rates. Strategies range from improved onboarding, data-driven and case-management approaches to advising, and one-stop support services to proactive interventions when students are off track and emergency grants to help students meet urgent expenses.[3]

## The College Preparation Challenge

Directly tied to the demographic challenge is a college preparation challenge. Standardized tests suggest that a very high proportion of entering freshmen aren't college-ready. According to the ACT, the testing firm, the percentage of students who met English and math benchmarks in 2019 was the lowest in fifteen years, with just 37 percent meeting three of four College Readiness Benchmarks and 36 percent not meeting any. If this is indeed the case, then it's no surprise that roughly 40 percent of first-time, full-time students fail to graduate from a four-year college and university in six years, and even higher proportions of community college or transfer students never earn a degree. If so, the failure to graduate more students isn't higher ed's fault. Blame should be cast on the high schools, the students themselves, or their families.

It's certainly the case that some students arrive at college with richer vocabularies, greater cultural literacy, and better fluency in writing, and that their preparation for demanding coursework in math, chemistry, and physics is much more advanced. The college preparation gap, however, is, in reality, an opportunity gap. Too often students from lower income communities miss out on opportunities for reasons that have nothing to do with innate ability but rather because of the high schools they attended and the enrichment opportunities they were denied. It's the responsibility of colleges and universities then to rectify these deficiencies and take the steps necessary to help these students fulfill their potential.

At the K–12 level, structural barriers to equality include inequitable levels of funding, unequal distribution of quality teachers, and differences in teacher perceptions of student abilities, as well as gaps in access to advanced coursework, outside-of-school enrichment activities, and other programs (gifted and talented, advanced placement, and early college). To these factors we should add the concentration of all too many low-income and nonwhite students in highly segregated, high-poverty schools, which, in turn, contributes to profound differences in school culture, campus climate, and learning environment—and to differences in opportunities to learn.

The preparation gap doesn't mean these students aren't college material, nor does it imply that these unevenly prepared students aren't motivated or lack a sense of direction or a clear understanding of college's value. Above all, it doesn't suggest that these students are less intelligent or have less academic potential than those who are more advantaged, or that their insights and intellectual contributions are less acute. But it does mean that many of these students start college hampered by factors outside their control. Especially in math-intensive fields, they're struggling to reach first base when some of their counterparts are rounding third. Later in this book, I will lay out a series of strategies for overcoming the preparation gap.

## The Affordability Challenge

American higher education is far costlier than in other countries. All told, the contributions of individual families and government (in the form of government grants, loans, and tax benefits) total about $30,000 per student per year, nearly twice as much as in the average developed country.[4]

Part of the cost difference lies in contrasting conceptions of a college education. The American ideal of a comprehensive institution with dormitories, extensive athletic and extracurricular offerings, campus food services, and health care provisions stands in stark contrast to foreign models, in which most students attend a local institution, live at home, and do not depend on their university for ancillary services. Indeed, the single biggest difference in cost between US and foreign universities lies in spending on non-teaching professionals—not just athletic coaches, administrators, and development officers, but advisers, career counselors, information technology specialists, and mental health counselors, among others—which in turn reflects higher American expectations about the range of services and standard of care that students should receive.

In good times and bad, the net price of a college education has risen steadily, generally faster than the rate of inflation. Between 1997 and 1998 and 2015 and 2016, the net cost of tuition, fees, and room and board rose 69 percent (taking inflation into account) at public universities, over a period when median household earnings actually fell.[5] As the net cost of higher education has risen, an increasing share of the burden of paying for college has fallen on families. Today, one in every five families (and over half of those at the bottom of the income distribution) pays 100 percent or more of their annual income to cover the net price of college (the price after financial aid is figured in). Even at public universities, students from families earning $30,000 and less in twenty-two states face net prices of more than $10,000 a year.[6] Because college costs outstrip their ability to pay, these families need to borrow or use savings to cover tuition bills.[7]

Meanwhile, federal expenditures on research and financial aid have barely kept up with the inflation rate and the growth of college enrollment. Because of competing budgetary demands for primary and secondary education, children's protective services, criminal justice, Medicaid, and transportation, state spending on public higher education on an inflation-adjusted per-student basis has stagnated or fallen in most states.

With the total cost of attendance for the students at the lowest end of the income scale at private colleges and a growing number of public universities reaching $20,000 a year, and significantly higher for middle-income families, tuition increases above the inflation rate may have hit a wall. It is simply unrealistic to expect most families to pay more than their entire yearly income for a year of a college education. Colleges and universities simply must find ways to control costs.[8]

In 1963, the average published cost of tuition and fees at private colleges and universities was $1,011 and $243 at public four-year institutions. Had the published cost climbed at the inflation rate, those figures would have risen to $8,624 at private institutions and $2,076 at their four-year public counterparts. In fact, the posted price of tuition and fees for 2023 had risen to $44,433 at major private nonprofits and $11,541 at major publics.[9]

To be sure, the actual net cost of attendance, including room and board, books, and other expenses, minus grants and scholarships, is not nearly as high as those figures would suggest. Cost of attendance in 2021-2022 averaged $19,250 at public institutions, compared with $32,800 at private nonprofit institutions.[10] Still, this figure is far too high for many families to afford.

Affordability is especially challenging for the lower income students who receive Pell Grants. Fewer than a quarter of public four-year institutions, and only 40 percent of community colleges, are fully affordable for low-income students—that is, financial aid, family contributions, and student wages, plus $300 for emergency expenses, isn't enough to cover the total cost of attendance.[11]

Why has the cost of a college education climbed faster than inflation? This has less to do with the usual suspects—administrative bloat, star architecture, and country club–like amenities—and cutbacks in state spending (which varies widely among states and reflects the business cycle and enrollment) than with other factors. These include rising standards of care (especially evident in increased spending on student support services); expenditures on compliance, financial aid, maintenance, research, and technology; and the cost of establishing programs in emerging fields (such as biotechnology, computer science, data science, and neuroscience).

The great challenge facing higher education is to break the "iron triangle" of higher ed: to increase affordability, quality, and student success all at once. Many of the proposed solutions to the affordability challenge sacrifice quality: through early-college or dual-credit programs where students earn college credits in high school or by awarding substantial amounts of credit for work experience or through fully online programs offered asynchronously or synchronously without a *bona fide* teacher-scholar or much regular, substantive feedback. Another widely touted solution is to tap new markets in order to generate revenue. A growing number of institutions view online professional master's programs and non-degree certificate programs as cash cows that can subsidize undergraduate education. But, as we shall see, the simplest solution to the affordability challenge is also the most straightforward: increasing retention and completion rates. At a time when roughly two out of every five undergraduates fail to earn a degree in six years, there is substantial room for improvement.

## The Student Loan Challenge

To fill the gap between the financial aid they're offered and the full cost of attendance, over 70 percent of students who receive a bachelor's degree take out loans. In 2020, these students each borrowed an average of $28,400 through federal and private loans. In addition, in 2017–2018, parents took out federal PLUS loans averaging $16,542 to help pay for the education of 800,000 undergraduates.[12] In the absence of student loan forbearance, these debts significantly delay attainment of the key markers of adulthood: marriage, childbearing, and home ownership.[13]

The financial aid system is extremely difficult to navigate, and without help, many prospective students and their families simply give up. In 2020, over 800,000 students who would have qualified for need-based federal aid failed to fill out the Free Application for Federal Student Aid (FAFSA).[14] Also, award letters are, much too often, so misleading and opaque that students and families find it difficult to calculate how much they will pay or owe after receiving financial aid.[15]

Despite executive actions to provide repayment relief to student loan borrowers—including a multiyear repayment pause, an easing of penalties for loans in default, easier access to income-based repayment programs, and easier access to public service loan forgiveness and loan discharges—many loan recipients struggle to repay their debts. Before the federal government froze repayments of student loans in 2020, a million Americans annually defaulted on their loans.[16]

Loan repayment weighs heaviest on students from low-income backgrounds who struggle to pay off unmanageable levels of debt. Also, even though white students make up a majority of borrowers, Black and Latinx students take on larger amounts of debt to finance their education, and these debts make it harder to build intergenerational wealth, thereby exacerbating the racial and ethnic wealth gaps and making it more difficult for Black and Latinx families to fund their own children's education. Prior to the pandemic, Federal Reserve data indicated that 20 percent of Black borrowers and 23 percent of Hispanic debt holders were behind on their payments, compared to just 6 percent of white student borrowers.[17]

## The Completion Challenge

In 2007, Barack Obama pledged to make the United States the world leader in college attainment by 2020, promising to increase the percentage of young people who hold an associate's degree or a bachelor's degree from 40 percent to 60 percent. "I want us to produce eight million more college graduates by 2020," then presidential candidate Obama declared.[18] A decade later, the figure had climbed to 46 percent, far from President Obama's goal. Indeed, at that rate of progress the United States would not reach the 60 percent goal for at least two more decades. The proportion of high school students who enroll in college has shot up, but the proportion who complete a degree has remained flat, with a million students dropping out each year. Worse yet, the gap between the educational attainment of African Americans, Hispanics, and children from low-income families and affluent whites has widened rather than narrowed. The cost to society of the high dropout rate is enormous. Two of every five students who leave college without a degree default on their student loans.[19]

According to the National Student Clearinghouse Research Center, 54.8 percent of those students who entered college in 2010 had completed a degree or certificate within six years. These figures include part-time and transfer students who are often excluded from other studies of graduation rates. Even at four-year institutions, nearly two out of every five students fail to receive a bachelor's degree after six years, leaving most with debt and little of the economic advantages that come from having a college diploma.[20]

College completion rates, however, vary widely along racial and ethnic lines. On average, white and Asian students earn a college-level credential at a rate about 20 percentage points higher than Hispanic and Black students do. White and Asian students completed their programs at similar rates—62 percent and 63.2 percent, respectively—while Hispanic and African American students graduated at rates of 45.8 percent and 38 percent, respectively.[21]

Socioeconomic class, too, is a major source of division. Rich and poor students don't merely enroll in college at different rates; they also complete it at different rates. Among those from the most disadvantaged families, just 14 percent had earned a bachelor's degree, on average—that is, just one out of four of the disadvantaged students who had hoped to get a bachelor's do so, on average. Among those from the most advantaged families, 60 percent had earned a bachelor's—about two-thirds of those who had planned to.[22]

Despite large gains over the past two decades in the number of people enrolled in colleges and universities, completion rates have been slower to catch up. Without a doubt, part of the reason is the set of challenges low-income students and those who are first in their family to pursue a degree face once they reach college, including financial stresses, inadequate advising, and uneven high school preparation. Yet even if one looks only at the low-income students who score in the top quarter on standardized mathematics tests, one discovers that these students' chance of graduating is no greater than that of a wealthier student in the second quartile of math scores.[23]

The inability of four-year institutions to graduate two-fifths of their students is a tragedy of criminal proportions. Failure to graduate from college exacts substantial costs. The financial cost is especially noticeable. The pay gap between high school and college graduates continues to deepen, doubling from a 50 percent premium in 1980 to 111 percent today. College graduates are not only richer, but happier and healthier than those who do not earn a postsecondary degree. They also lead more fulfilling lives. Not surprisingly, students who come from low-income families are especially likely to drop out, primarily for financial reasons. Here, it is important to note that most students who leave college do not do so for academic reasons. Most are in good academic standing at the time they withdraw and many have nearly completed a degree. While a fifth of students drop out during the first two years, a significant number withdraw after they have earned 90 or more credit hours.

There are, of course, many reasons why a student might drop out. For those from low-income backgrounds, a family or financial emergency or a shift in work schedules can lead to a decision to withdraw from college: over half of those who left college without a degree reported that they found it difficult or impossible to balance academics with their work and family responsibilities. Nearly 40 percent said that they dropped out for financial reasons, because they couldn't afford their education or lacked financial support from their family or because the opportunity costs in foregone earnings were too great. However, more than a quarter attributed their decision to drop out to a lack of academic motivation or preparedness.[24]

Many completion problems, though, are institution related and can be successfully addressed. These include the inability to apply transfer credits obtained at a community college or from another four-year institution to general education or major requirements or the accumulation of excess credit hours due to poor advising or a change in majors, extending the time to degree completion and tacking on extra costs in the process. Later pages in this book will describe proven strategies that regional comprehensive universities and other institutions that serve the bulk of students can use to significantly raise their graduation rates without diminishing quality or rigor.

## The Transfer Challenge

Even though a majority of undergraduates start at a community college and aspire to a bachelor's degree, and even though four-year schools would benefit from an influx of new students, barriers to transfer student success include delays in credit evaluation, transfer credits denied or only accepted as electives, and inequities in financial aid allocations. Also, four-year institutions generally fail to recruit transfer students or provide them with sufficient post-enrollment academic or social integration support.

Earning credits from multiple institutions is now the norm. Approximately 45 percent of those who earned an associate's degree and 67 percent of those with a bachelor's degree attended more than one institution. Yet even though transferring from one institution to another is commonplace, credit transfer is still a difficult process, with students losing on average 43 percent of the credits that they had previously earned. Worse still, even when courses do transfer, many count only as electives, and do not apply to general education or major requirements.[25]

What, then, should be done? To reduce credit loss, four-year campuses need to sign articulation agreements with feeder institutions that specify which courses fulfill particular requirements. Faculty need to better align two- and four-year college curricula to ensure that community college courses count toward degrees. Degree maps need to spell out a clear pathway to a degree. Another promising option is to co-enroll students into a community college and a bachelor's degree–granting institution. Some public university systems and state legislatures have gone even further, mandating a common numbering system, course titles, and course coverage in the lower-division general education curriculum to expedite credit transfer. A few systems require colleges to identify community college courses that automatically apply toward a high-demand major. Of course, the problem with these approaches is that they only work within a particular system or geographical region.

The Interstate Passport offers a promising approach to transferring courses from one institution to another across state lines.[26] Rather than focusing on specific courses, the Passport asks institutions to identify the competencies or mutually agreed-upon learning outcomes that courses build. Then participating institutions can better decide which courses meet their general education requirements.

Another transfer challenge involves awarding credit for life experience, for example, through military or corporate training or practical workforce knowledge. As it is, evaluation of such experiences tends to be arbitrary, inconsistent, and unpredictable. To make matters worse, institutions that depend on tuition revenue and enrollment have few incentives to grant credit for learning that takes place outside their campuses.[27]

The transfer challenge isn't restricted to credit transfer. As students move between institutions, many experience transfer shock, a dip in grades, and a reduction in academic momentum. A significant number of transfer students drop out during or immediately after the first year. To minimize transfer shock, institutions need to make sure that transfer students have equal access to financial aid and the classes they need to graduate. Campuses must also dispel damaging stereotypes that stigmatize transfer students as less academically prepared. The fact is that transfer students make up the majority of those graduating from many urban and regional public colleges and universities.[28]

Also, campuses need to think more intentionally about transfer students' challenges and needs and the barriers to transfer student success. Every policy—from application, admissions, and onboarding to the awarding of financial aid and course registration and major requirements—should be reviewed from the perspective of transfer students. Four-year institutions should provide special transfer student orientation sessions and ensure that credit transfer evaluation takes place quickly. In addition, they should encourage transfer students to take advantage of bridge programs and boot camps, which will require schools to make admissions decisions earlier and conduct transcript evaluation more quickly.

Special programs targeting transfer students can make a big difference. A dedicated orientation program for transfer students, providing transfer-specific information, can build a sense of community and contribute to a sense of belonging. Bridge programs and boot camps can better prepare students for academic success. A transfer student support center, a one-stop resource center for transfer students can also help. Special sections of high-demand/high-DFW courses targeted at transfer students can make a big difference, too. (A high-DFW course is one where students frequently make a D or F or withdraw.) Proactive outreach efforts and peer mentoring programs can connect transfer students to campus and provide practical advice.

There's every reason to think that the number of transfer students will rise in the years ahead, as more students seek affordable education options that offer more flexible scheduling and more employment-focused programs. Since bachelor's degrees remain essential to supporting a middle-class family, four-year institutions have a moral and political obligation to do more to recruit and welcome transfer students and take active steps to ensure that these students succeed.

## The Equity Challenge

In the mid-2010s, Yale University spent $117,473 per student on instruction and student services plus another $12,856 for academic support. It served 12,336 students with a student–faculty ratio of 6:1. Roughly 75 percent of its classes have fewer than twenty students. That same year, Ohio State University spent $18,870 per full-time equivalent (FTE) student on instruction and student services and $1,969 for academic support. It served 51,864 FTE students and had a student–faculty ratio of 18:1. Thirty percent of its classes have less than twenty students. Meanwhile, per FTE student spending on instruction and student services at Cal State Long Beach was $7,735 plus another $1,507 for academic support. It served 30,271 students with a student–faculty ratio of 24:1; 22 percent of classes are smaller than twenty.[29]

This country's system of higher education is highly stratified with resources inversely distributed relative to student needs, defined in terms of the students' family income, high school preparation, class rank, average college board scores, and transfer status. And the situation is worsening. Over time, there has been growing inequality in resources per FTE student. Ironically, students at the most selective institutions pay a much lower proportion of the cost of their education.

The wealthiest, best-prepared students are most likely to attend a well-resourced institution, while those from low-income backgrounds are concentrated in community colleges or unselective four-year institutions with the lowest graduation rates. To make matters worse, the vast majority of high-achieving low-income students (whose grades and test scores place them among the top 4 percent of US students) do not apply to a selective institution. These well-qualified students will pay more to attend a less selective school, where they will receive less support and have a lower chance of graduation.[30]

Alongside economic disparities are racial inequalities. At the top 500 universities, whites comprise 70 percent of students, although they represent only 57 percent of the college-age population. Meanwhile, as Black and Latinx students have swarmed the halls of open-access colleges, whites have fled them. White students have declined from 68 percent to 49 percent of students at open-access colleges, while Black and Latinx students have grown from 26 percent to 45 percent.[31]

The highly stratified nature of the nation's college system harms even the best-prepared students from affluent families, who feel intense pressure to compete for admission to top-tier institutions. The competition for admissions, in turn, results in high school students who engage in an array of athletic, service, and other extracurricular activities not out of personal passion but to build up their qualifications. It also drives grade inflation and has apparently contributed to the growing number of well-off students who seek accommodations for learning disabilities.

But we mustn't delude ourselves: Economically disadvantaged students are the ones who suffer most from the inequities that pervade American higher education. A disadvantaged student with top-half scores has a lower chance of earning a college degree than an advantaged student in the bottom half of test scores. Worse yet, low-income students, irrespective of their abilities and potential, disproportionately attend colleges with the fewest resources. As a result, few of these students receive the kinds of support or enrichment activities that lead to secure well-paying jobs.

Expressed in statistical terms: a Black student with above-median 10th-grade math scores is 22 percent less likely than a white student to earn a college degree and 43 percent less likely than an Asian student. Latinx students with above-median math scores are 46 percent less likely to earn a degree than a comparable white student and 78 percent less likely than an Asian student. The Georgetown University Center on Education and the Workforce describes the implications of these statistics in blunt terms: "Equally talented students don't get the same chance to be all that they can be."[32]

Equity needs to be more than a catchphrase. Equity-mindedness requires institutions to focus first and foremost on the barriers to academic success that function in discriminatory ways. These include recruitment practices that fail to target students from lower income and underrepresented backgrounds as well as admissions policies that downplay work experience and distance traveled. Then, too, there are the obstacles to community college transfer, pedagogies and assessments that heighten stereotype threat, and practices biased against part-time, commuting, and older students.

We know how to address the equity challenge. Institutions need to identify and address barriers to equal opportunity, including high-DFW weed-out courses, course unavailability, impediments to credit transfer, and complicated degree requirements. Faculty need to embrace course designs, pedagogies, and assessment strategies that support equity, including approaches that are interactive, participatory, inclusive, experiential, and inquiry-, problem- and project-based. Campuses must implement a tiered system of academic support, including access to bridge programs, tutoring, study groups, science and math learning centers, and supplemental instruction sections of roadblock courses. Above all, colleges and universities need to ensure financial support for students from lower income backgrounds that covers the full cost of attendance. Equity may not be everyone's assigned job, but it's everyone's responsibility.

# The Learning Challenge

In its annual report for 1930, the Carnegie Foundation for the Advancement of Teaching announced the results of its Pennsylvania Study of college student learning. Its conclusion: "College students learn practically nothing, that seniors within a month are nearly as ignorant as freshmen, and in some important fields even more so." The product of a study of some forty Pennsylvania colleges over a seven-year span and several thousand students, the report reminds us that concerns over learning at colleges are longstanding.[33]

How much learning takes place in college? Given the absence of reliable measures about how much students study or retain, we still don't know the answer to this essential question. However, the limited evidence we do have prompts concern. Two widely publicized studies make two sweeping claims. The first is that most college students devote much more time to their social life than to academics and spend, on average, half as much time studying compared to their counterparts in the 1960s. One survey of 3,000 students reported that these undergraduates devote about three-quarters of their time to socializing, working, and sleeping, and just 16 percent to studying or attending class. The second claim, based on a 2011 analysis of the results of the Collegiate Learning Assessment, a standardized test that purports to measure students' critical thinking, analytic reasoning, and writing skills, is that after two years in college, 45 percent of students showed no significant gains in learning, and that after four years, 36 percent showed little change.[34]

These profoundly disturbing findings have been hotly contested. Other research suggests that time spent studying has not declined nearly as much as the earlier study suggested, and that the claims that 45 or 36 percent of students showed no significant learning gains are not justified by the data.[35] Nevertheless, concern about the quality and rigor of undergraduate education is well taken, especially in light of evidence of significant grade inflation. A 2012 study of grades at 135 colleges and universities over seven decades found that As represent

43 percent of all letter grades, an increase of 28 percentage points since 1960 and 12 percentage points since 1988, with Ds and Fs comprising less than 10 percent of all letter grades.[36] An A became the most common grade around 2000. At Harvard, the average GPA now stands at 3.8, up from 2.8 in 1966.[37]

More than a decade after the publication of *Academically Adrift*, the landmark study by Richard Arum and Josipa Roksa that questioned college's contribution to student learning, we still don't know whether students are learning as much as they should during their college years. What does seem clear is that academic rigor and expectations about homework and outside-of-class study time and writing vary widely across courses, fields, and even institutions. Without a doubt, colleges and universities should define their learning objectives with greater precision, better assess whether students actually achieve those learning goals, and be held accountable by accreditors for ensuring that the education they provide is effective and successful.

## The Return on Investment Challenge

The rising cost of a college education has prompted many students and families to ask whether college is worth the expense. Although the cost of tuition, fees, room and board, and other expenses are steep, the return on investment is substantial. Students who complete their bachelor's degree make more than $1 million—75 percent more on average—over their lifetime than those who don't. In addition, college graduates are healthier, more civically engaged, less likely to be unemployed, and more likely to be in a stable relationship.[38]

In general, more education means higher earnings, even though there are some exceptions. About 28 percent of those with an associate's degree earn more than their bachelor's degree holder counterparts. There are also some jobholders without a college degree who earn more than some college graduates, but their numbers are diminishing. It's estimated that eight out of ten jobs will require some postsecondary education by 2030.[39]

Return on investment is largely determined by where undergraduates go to school, what they major in, and what degree they receive. Still, it's important to recognize that too many degree programs fail to provide a payoff. According to one recent study, in over a quarter of degree programs in Massachusetts, graduates earn less than high school graduates and must work for 20 plus years to recoup their education's cost. Altogether, a fifth of all graduates fall into this category.[40]

Clearly, this society needs greater transparency in program outcomes and earnings, much better academic and career advising at the high school as well as at the college levels, and smoother pathways into advanced education and training. We must break down the barriers that separate high school from college and higher education from job training and the workforce. The answers exist and include more apprenticeships, job shadowing, and internships.

## The Political Challenge

Even though a college degree has never been more valuable economically, a sizeable portion of the public (Democrats as well as Republicans) questions whether a college education is worth the price. An overwhelming majority of adults believe that college tuition is too high and that colleges and universities are failing to provide necessary workplace skills. Both Democrats and Republicans complain that higher education prioritizes research over teaching and the liberal arts over career preparation. Both worry that professors are bringing their political and social views into the classroom. A majority of both parties believe that it is more important to allow people on college campuses to speak freely than to guard students from objectionable ideas.

Other complaints fall along predictable party and ideological lines. Republicans are more likely to view colleges as liberal bastions indoctrinating students with radical ideologies and to see colleges as overly concerned with shielding students from offensive views.

Republicans are also more likely to criticize affirmative action. Many on the right condemn institutions for rising costs, declining rigor, and diminishing academic standards, and for embracing political correctness, sidelining great works of Western literature and intellectual thought, and failing to instill basic knowledge and skills. Meanwhile, many on the left denounce the neoliberal university that functions like a business rather than being treated as a public good, and critiques the deprofessionalization of academic labor, with adjuncts increasingly replacing tenured faculty, and the drift toward vocationalism and away from a view that colleges should provide an enriching intellectual experience rooted in the humanities.

There is the litany of criticism that regularly appears in books and newspaper editorials. There's the view that the tenure system—rather than promoting free intellectual inquiry, diversity of thought, or rigor in grading students—is a job protection scheme for inactive scholars and incompetent teachers, while much of the actual teaching and grading is done by adjunct instructors and graduate students.[41] Then, there's the complaint that academic standards and rigor are declining, evident in grade inflation, reduced requirements for reading and writing, and the proliferation of courses that pander to immature undergraduates, while education is becoming depersonalized with the expansion of online learning.

When campuses offer credit-bearing courses on Harry Styles, we shouldn't be surprised that the curriculum is regarded as frivolous and trivial. When a campus like my alma mater, Oberlin, pits itself against a longstanding local business, don't be shocked to discover that even the most liberal townies turn against the campus.

Many criticisms of higher education are exaggerated or misplaced. The critique of tenure as a lucrative sinecure for life is occurring at the very moment when an increasing share of teaching is conducted by those off of the tenure track, with negative consequences for students, and when most universities have instituted mechanisms for post-tenure review.[42] In terms of academic standards, the fact is that we lack valid and reliable measures of what students are learning, both currently and in the past (in the age of the "Gentleman C").

But there are areas in which concerns are surely warranted. This includes the number of college graduates who hold jobs that do not require a degree or jobs that are unrelated to their field of study. According to one recent national poll from 2018, 40 percent of college graduates are underemployed, holding jobs that do not require a bachelor's degree.[43] The political question that needs to be posed and answered is how can colleges and universities do a better job of advancing social mobility, equity across lines of race and income, and workforce capabilities?

The biggest political challenge to higher education comes less from political ideologues or worries about political indoctrination, trigger warnings, the policing of microaggressions, or outrage over social justice warriors run amok than from a diminishing faith among broad segments of the public in the power of higher education to transform lives, open doors, and open minds. It's that loss of faith that gives traction to the recent political attacks. Even though a college education pays off in terms of higher earnings, better job opportunities, enhanced health, and greater civic engagement, worries about higher education's return on investment add fuel to the argument that American society needs to embrace faster, cheaper—and less rigorous and well-rounded—paths into the workforce.

If colleges and universities are to obtain stable public support and retain a high degree of autonomy in matters relating to admissions, curricula, hiring, and research, then these institutions must demonstrate that they place a priority on undergraduate teaching, produce graduates who are well prepared for the workplace, engage in meaningful research, and contribute directly to local and regional economies.[44] They must also demonstrate the ways they serve their locality and region, for example, by supporting local schools and making purchases from local businesses. Otherwise, a skeptical public will continue to doubt whether American higher education is keeping up its end of the compact that predicates public support on proven public benefits.

## The Postgraduation Challenge

During the Great Recession, a host of newspaper and magazine articles, novels, and movies promoted a popular meme: failure to launch. These works depicted college graduates' difficulty in making the transition to a responsible, self-sufficient adulthood. Possessing unrealistic expectations about their personal future, yet lacking much internal motivation, these financially dependent young layabouts lived in their parents' basement and were portrayed as entitled, selfish, and fearful of intimacy and commitment.[45]

Pejorative views of youth have a long history, but the difficulty that many young adults have in entering the job market is not a myth. In 2018, well after the end of the Great Recession, 23 percent of those ages 25 to 29 were living in their parents' home, up from 17 percent in 2007, just before the onset of the economic downturn. A significant majority of graduates leave college feeling unprepared to get a job after graduation. Two-thirds doubt whether they graduated with the skills needed to succeed in the workplace, and half do not believe that their major will lead to a well-paying job.[46]

Lacking realistic career ambitions or a practical plan to achieve their goals, many young people flail and flounder for years before falling into a job that too often is not connected to their training or interests. Many find themselves in a job for which they are overqualified or which does not make use of their college training. Fully half of humanities graduates say that they wish they had chosen another major in college.

A college is not a vocational training school, but four-year institutions could certainly do a better job of opening windows into career opportunities and preparing graduates to pursue jobs in their area of interest. As it is, students rarely visit their campus career services office until their senior year; once there, these students rarely receive the kinds of practical advice or guidance, mentoring, and connections that might help them find appropriate employment.

Among business leaders and human relations specialists, there is a perception of a serious disconnect between higher education and the needs of today's workforce. Many are convinced, wrongly or rightly, that recent degree holders lack the communication and collaboration skills expected of a college graduate, let alone the specialized technical skills demanded by many jobs. One recent survey found that companies rated only 26 percent of college graduates as very well prepared in writing and considered only 22 percent qualified in critical thinking.[47] At a time when many businesses are cutting back on in-house professional development training, many industry leaders blame colleges and universities for a perceived lack of qualified job applicants.

The pressure from legislators, parents, and students themselves for colleges and universities to do a better job of preparing graduates for the workplace is not misplaced, but doing so successfully will require much more than expanding career services. It will require institutions to take a more proactive role in exposing undergraduates to career options and equip them with the range of skills, including the digital and interpersonal skills, needed to acquire a job and to function effectively in today's workplaces. It also involves expanding access to internships and providing more opportunities for undergraduates to create a meaningful record of skills and accomplishments. Making job market preparation an institutional priority will greatly ease the tangled and twisted path to a successful adulthood.

———

The many challenges facing American higher education can no longer be ignored or evaded. The college-going population consists in increasing numbers of the students that higher education has too often failed. Students, in growing numbers, are older, employed, and attending part-time. Many have care-giving responsibilities. A substantial number are financially independent, first-generation, and transfer students. At a growing number of institutions, the business model is broken. States are likely to impose caps on tuition increases and admittance of out-of-state students at public institutions, while demanding greater accountability for learning and employment outcomes. Less selective private institutions have found it difficult to increase net tuition and fees above the inflation rate.

Many seemingly simple solutions—like cutting the number of administrators or closing under-enrolled departments—are impractical or undesirable. Most administrative positions exist in order to provide essential services, meet government mandates, or generate revenue; meanwhile, shuttering departments not only damages faculty morale but harms perceptions of an institution's quality and financial health. Without better solutions, resource-strapped institutions face a gradual deterioration of educational quality if they cannot find a way to raise revenue and control costs.

Higher education's perfect storm is deeply disruptive, but it also brings with it many opportunities. It has revealed many underserved student markets domestically and internationally. It has underscored the importance of lifelong learning in a rapidly churning economy in which the average American adult will hold eleven jobs in three different career fields. It has opened the eyes of many faculty members to apply insights drawn from the learning sciences to make teaching more effective and efficient. It has also alerted faculty to the innovative ways that digital technologies can potentially cut costs while offering a more immersive, engaging, and personalized educational experience. It is encouraging institutions to experiment with new student success strategies, including one-stop student service centers where students can readily access help with advising, career services, financial aid, and writing; data analytics to optimize admissions, course scheduling, financial aid allocations, and interventions with at-risk students; and new curricular and pedagogical models that are more skills-focused, experiential, and career-aligned.

We are at one of those once-in-a-lifetime moments of ferment when fundamental transformations are possible. Certainly, academic transformation will not take place easily or without substantial resistance. But faculty roles are already evolving, and new kinds of educational professionals (including instructional designers, educational technologists, assessment specialists, and academic and nonacademic coaches) are already assuming a more prominent role in designing, developing, and delivering courses. The broad-access institutions that will thrive will be those that are nimble, adaptable, and willing to experiment; that are open to accepting credits from other institutions, including military, corporate, and nonprofit training programs; and that embrace a new educational vision that is personalized, flexible, career-aligned, technology-enhanced, data-driven, and emphasizes active and experiential learning.

# 3

---

# The Shifting Higher Education Landscape

THE HIGHER EDUCATION LANDSCAPE is shifting under our feet as
new providers, delivery modalities, and credentials challenge established practices. Curriculum design, pedagogy, assessment, instructional staffing, academic calendars, course schedules, student support services, and transcripting are all subject to radical rethinking.
We are, in short, in the midst of a once-in-a-generation transformation of the postsecondary education ecosystem. A new educational
landscape is gradually emerging, far more diverse but also far more
stratified than the one it is replacing.

After a prolonged period of seeming stasis, when the postsecondary educational ecosystem grew to become more uniform and standardized, the postsecondary ecosystem is now undergoing a series of
seismic shifts. A host of new educational models coexist and compete
for students, including competency-based approaches that award
credit based on demonstrated mastery of essential skills and knowledge rather than seat time or credit hours; earn-learn models that
combine classroom-based learning and practical work experience;
and scaled, lower cost, fully online, self-paced, self-directed models
that are more career-aligned than their predecessors. There are new

pedagogies that emphasize inquiry, active learning, and problem solving that promise to more effectively and efficiently build essential academic and workplace skills. New delivery modes, including asynchronous and synchronous online, hybrid, low-residency, accelerated courses, claim to make an education cheaper and faster while maintaining quality. There are new kinds of certifications including badges, professional certificates, specializations, MicroMasters, and nanodegrees, some of which can stack into traditional degrees.

New models of student advising and support that are technology-enabled, data-driven, proactive, and holistic are being put into practice. Alternatives to the traditional tripartite curriculum design, consisting of a general education core, a major, and elective courses, are undergoing testing. There are new instructional staffing models that replace traditional faculty with course mentors, coaches, and dedicated graders; new academic calendars with multiple start dates and shorter terms; course schedules that allow students to compress their time on campus; new approaches to grading; and new transcripts that provide inventories of all the skills that students acquire, irrespective of where those skills are learned.

A series of developments converged to drive these innovations. One is the enrollment crunch, which has led campus leaders to push for reaching new sources of students by adding more online and hybrid courses, increasing the number of graduate students and adult learners, re-enrolling college stop-outs, offering short-term microcredentials and certificates, expanding opportunities for students to earn credits during vacation breaks, making it easier for transfer students to enroll, and working with businesses to make college tuition an employment benefit.

Financial stresses have also prompted institutions to diversify revenue streams, broaden the markets they serve, expand their reputations and reach, and encourage entrepreneurship. Another factor driving innovation has been the intense pressure from students, parents, and legislatures to demonstrate the marketable skills and return on investment that campuses offer. As I will describe below, competition from a host of new competitors—boot camps, skills academies, apprenticeships, and fully online providers—has been yet another major spur to innovation.

Not all the forces for change, however, are a product of demographics and economics. Innovation is also driven by advances in the science of learning that hold out the promise of making learning deeper and more durable, and by a faith that new technologies can create learning experiences that are more immersive and engaging and can identify students who are at risk of failure and then prompt timely interventions to keep them on track to graduation. Increasingly vocal demands for equity, too, are leading institutions to do more to bring more undergraduates to completion, help more students succeed in demanding STEM (science, technology, engineering, and mathematics) disciplines, and better prepare degree holders for the workplaces of today and tomorrow.

Among the great challenges facing faculty is ensuring that these new models do not undercut the most basic element of a meaningful education—the rich relationships between knowledgeable instructors, students, and their peers—and do not bifurcate the postsecondary educational system, in which the most college-ready students will receive a robust liberal education while students from first-generation, low-income, and underrepresented populations receive vocational training that leaves them without the skills and knowledge necessary for personal advancement.

Many highly touted innovations threaten to severely erode educational quality. These include asynchronous online programs and computer-based instruction that offer little substantive interaction with a teacher-scholar or classmates; certificate and credentialing programs without reliable measures of quality or return on investment; and training programs and career and professional preparation that demote the arts and humanities as well as the communication and critical thinking skills that these disciplines cultivate.

An exchange in Lewis Carroll's *Alice's Adventures in Wonderland* should remind us of the importance of having clear goals and priorities as higher education evolves and the postsecondary eco-system shifts. The exchange begins when Alice asks the Cheshire Cat for directions:

> "Would you tell me, please, which way I ought to go from here?"
> "That depends a good deal on where you want to get to," said the Cat.
> "I don't much care where—" said Alice.
> "Then it doesn't matter which way you go," said the Cat.[1]

Without a firm sense of the purpose of a college education and the knowledge and skills that graduates should possess, there is a real danger that higher education's democratic promise will diminish. A college education isn't and shouldn't be the only route to a steady, well-paying job. But it does provide the most reliable path precisely because it offers a far wider array of skills—cognitive, social, digital, and technical—and a greater capacity for adaptation than the alternatives that are emerging.[2]

———

The tsunami sweeping across the postsecondary education ecosystem is, in large measure, a product of the Great Recession that began in late 2007 and was the most severe financial downturn since the Great Depression. Even after the financial crisis ended, its impact persisted.[3] One effect of the Great Recession was to throw a harsh spotlight on the cost of a college education and the debt burden this placed on students and their families. Even before the onset of the downturn, student debt had already reached a record high; the financial crisis significantly exacerbated the debt repayment problem. At the same time, the recession threw institutional finances into disarray, reducing endowment returns, alumni giving, and state appropriations.

To sustain enrollment, private nonprofit institutions were forced to raise tuition discount rates—the net tuition and fees charged after awarding scholarships and grants—to unprecedented heights. This, in turn, posed an existential threat to many small, less selective private colleges that were highly dependent on tuition. Public institutions faced a different financial challenge. To offset cuts in state appropriations, public universities were forced to raise tuition at an unparalleled rate, shifting much of the burden of paying for college onto students and their parents.

Another consequence of the Great Recession was that students began to question the value of a traditional liberal arts education. When asked why they are going to college, an overwhelming majority of students say that the main reasons were to obtain financial independence, a well-paying job, and a satisfying career—a sentiment echoed by most parents. As a result, there has been a growing demand that colleges provide students with marketable skills tightly aligned with the job market. Students responded to the financial crisis by seeking vocational and preprofessional majors in business, engineering, and health care, turning away from majors in humanities disciplines such as English, history, and the foreign languages. More students than ever viewed the general education requirements as a distraction, a box-checking exercise, or an obstacle to be overcome rather than as the foundation of a well-rounded education—with the result that humanities departments' enrollment and number of majors plunged as more students acquired general education credits in high school or at community colleges.

Perhaps the most far-reaching consequence of the financial crisis was that it placed issues of access, affordability, and student success front and center in national discussions about higher education. Traditional colleges and universities found themselves under intense pressure to demonstrate the value of the education they offered, enroll more students from underrepresented groups, radically improve graduation and postgraduation employment outcomes, and reduce attainment gaps. There was also a growing sense that if the United States was to remain a world leader in attainment of postsecondary credentials, it needed to guide many more young adults to a bright future and institute new forms of credentialing and certification.

In 2011 and 2012, toward the end of the Great Recession, higher education as we knew it appeared headed toward a precipice. MOOCs, the massive open online courses from Stanford, MIT, and Harvard that attracted more than 100,000 enrollees, held out the prospect of a handful of institutions providing "the best courses from the top professors" to students across the world for free.[4] Indeed, one disrupter, Sebastian Thrun, co-founder of the MOOC provider Udacity, predicted that "in 50 years, there will be only 10 institutions in the world delivering higher education."[5]

Thomas Friedman, an influential *New York Times* columnist, described MOOCs as the beginning of a "college education revolution."[6] Suddenly, it seemed possible to make college-level courses by the world's preeminent scholars available for free to anyone, anywhere. Critics quickly dismissed the MOOCs as video textbooks which did little more than disseminate content. Persistence rates proved dismal, and the student experience impersonal and unsupportive, with participation largely limited to asking questions, taking quizzes, and participating in discussion boards. The hype was over as the trough of disillusionment was reached. MOOCs came to be viewed as a failure and disappointment.

Meanwhile, for-profit universities, with little competition from existing brick-and-mortar institutions, attracted 10 percent of all US college students by tapping into the fastest growing segments of the student population: working adults, family caregivers, and low-income students seeking a convenient path toward a degree with marketable skills. Radical innovation was in the air as a host of transformational educational models suddenly sprang up. There was Minerva University, which sought to become the first elite liberal arts institution founded in a century, offering its students an international experience by living in one of seven global cities while participating in highly interactive online seminars, for a tuition of $10,000 a year. There was the University of the People, a tuition-free online university that offered disadvantaged students around the world open courseware and volunteer faculty. Then, there was the University of North Texas at Dallas, with a nontenured, non-research-oriented faculty offering a narrow range of career-aligned majors.

In the years since, MOOCs still flourish and, for the first time, generate a significant amount of revenue. But they have pivoted to a new financial model. Rather than serving undergraduates, MOOCs offer corporate training and advanced, career-aligned instruction for a fee to degree holders seeking to upgrade their skills. Minerva University, the University of the People, and the University of North Texas at Dallas continue to attract students. Nevertheless, MOOCs' pivot meant that higher education's existential crisis coming out of the Great Recession was over. The most radical forces for disruption had faded.

Meanwhile, for-profit universities came under fierce scrutiny from government regulators for deceptive marketing and recruitment practices, high rates of student debt, and notoriously low graduation and employment rates. Many were charged with violating the "gainful employment rule," which states that career education programs must "prepare students for gainful employment in a recognized occupation" in order to be eligible for federal student aid, and many for-profits were forced to forgive debts and go out of business. For-profits' enrollment plummeted.[7]

Other hyped innovations failed to gain traction. Highly touted personalized, adaptive commercial software failed to live up to its promise of providing students with a highly effective, individualized learning experience. Free and low-cost undergraduate options, like ASU's Global Freshman Academy, failed to find a substantial audience. Even open educational resources—free digital textbooks— failed to gain much traction.

The failure of MOOCs and for-profits to disrupt higher education produced a great deal of malicious pleasure and gloating among academic professionals at traditional institutions. Still, the higher education ecosystem had undergone a sea change. Online learning gained a degree of legitimacy even before the pandemic, with a third of all students now taking at least one fully online class and a majority of online students enrolled in traditional brick-and-mortar institutions.

At the same time, the for-profits offered nonprofits a number of lessons. First, there are large markets of students who had been poorly served or unserved by the traditional higher education establishment, including college drop-outs (now known as "stop-outs" or "degree completers"), older students, working adults, and family caregivers. These students offer a large potential market for existing institutions. Many of these students seek an education with a clear value proposition that conforms to the needs of their busy lives. A second lesson is that students' educational trajectories need to be "process analyzed" to determine why students flounder and drop out. Fine-grained learning analytics can be used to identify the pinch points and barriers to graduation so that they can be addressed head-on. A third lesson is that too many students fail to graduate due to inadequate advising, mentoring, coaching, tutoring, feedback, and timely support. Additional support can bring many more students to completion. A fourth lesson is that the cafeteria-style curriculum with unlimited options does not serve many nontraditional students well. Time is generally the enemy of graduation, and wasted credit hours contribute significantly to low graduation rates. Additionally, a fifth lesson is that online education can be delivered at scale through a combination of master courses that can be taught by a variety of instructors or delivered in an asynchronous, self-paced, self-directed format. Scale, in turn, allows institutions to invest in new kinds of educational technologies and student support services.

The rise and fall of the MOOCs and the for-profits taught brick-and-mortar institutions yet another lesson: campuses need to shift their focus from access to retention and completion, and they need to demonstrate the added value of the face-to-face education that they offer. One takeaway was especially important: if high-quality content had become a commodity available to anyone with an Internet connection, then traditional institutions had to offer things that could not be offered by a MOOC or a no-frills provider, things that justified a much higher tuition. Those things, many agreed, were rich, personal relationships with faculty and classmates, extensive mentoring, personal attention, comprehensive student support services, active learning, a vibrant campus life, and a wealth of experiential learning opportunities including mentored research, internships, and clinical-, field-, community-, and team-based learning experiences. In other words, MOOCs contributed to an educational revolution, just not the one that their proponents anticipated.

These massive online courses inspired many faculty members to integrate new pedagogies and technologies into their teaching. The MOOC example also led a growing number of faculty to experiment with new forms of online learning: synchronous as well as asynchronous, with electronically assisted social experiences in which students could interact in digital hangouts and participate in group projects.

Curiously, few faculty showed any interest in a very different conception of a MOOC. When the term MOOC was first coined by Dave Cormier of the University of Prince Edward Island in 2008, the acronym referred to a very different educational model than the kind offered by Stanford, MIT, or Harvard. It rested on the principles of "connectivist" pedagogy—that knowledge is not something to be transmitted, but rather constructed by networks of individuals who participate in a process of collaborative discourse and knowledge building. The original MOOC rejected a transmission model of education in which information is disseminated primarily through lectures. Instead, by sharing information and ideas, asking and answering one another's questions, aggregating content, and collaborating on joint projects, MOOC students became participants in a community of professional practice. The first connectivist MOOC, which attracted 2,200 participants, demonstrated the radical potential of online education to create learning communities that transcend national borders. This is certainly a model of education that others should emulate.

When we think about how higher education is evolving, there's a tendency to fixate on the most obvious changes, such as the advent of test-optional admissions or the rapid acceptance of online learning. But transformation is taking place across virtually every domain, and the trends most likely to leave a lasting imprint aren't those that the higher education press often emphasizes. It's essential, therefore, to distinguish between fleeting fads or evanescent innovations and developments whose impact will last.

Over the past decade, every year has seemed to bring a new craze. After MOOCs' advent, there was a fascination with coding for all: teaching students to master a programming language in order to build websites and applications. Breaking down a problem into individual steps was supposed to train students to think logically and creatively, but in practice no one needs to know coding in order to use a computer. Then came interactive courseware and personalized adaptive software that feature rich multimedia, sophisticated simulations, built-in remediation, and embedded assessments, along with the promise to increase and accelerate learning. Unfortunately, the vision of personalizing education proved to be beyond the technologies' capabilities and few students found computer-based learning particularly engaging.

Other highly hyped innovations of the past decade included augmented and mixed reality, educational gaming and game-based learning, gesture-based computing, the Internet of Things consisting of "smart," Internet-connected objects, learning relationship management systems, lifelong learning, makerspaces, robotics, smart objects, virtual assistants, virtual worlds, and wearable technologies. More recently, there was enthusiasm over blockchain, chatbots, microcredentials, modularized and disaggregated degrees, 3D printing, and artificial intelligence and machine learning–powered text and image generators.

To be sure, some innovations did catch on, such as data analytics and open educational resources, though not to the extent that their champions anticipated. But most innovations went through the Gartner hype cycle, a five-phase pattern that begins with a technology trigger followed by the peak of inflated expectations, the trough of disillusionment, and, in a few instances, a plateau of productivity.

How, then, is the face of higher education changing? Let's begin with the most readily observable shifts before moving on to the broader themes that underlie the transformation of the postsecondary landscape. One noteworthy development is the pronounced shift in student interest away from the humanities toward more vocationally and professionally oriented fields with better job prospects. In recent years, a slew of humanities jobs have dried up. There was a glut of lawyers and a sharp decline in employment in newsrooms, book and magazine publishing, many nonprofits, and, of course, the academy itself. Strikingly, just 28 percent of humanities graduates without an advanced degree found work in a field closely related to their training. Only about 40 percent said they'd major in the same field, a much lower proportion than those who majored in science, math, or engineering. A similar percentage said that their education failed to prepare them for life.[8]

Another remarkable development is the growing gender divide in higher education, with colleges now enrolling six women for every four men. The gap in graduation rates is even wider, with 67 percent of women eventually earning a degree versus just 60 percent of men. These figures represent a stark reversal of the pattern half a century ago. As recently as 1970, men accounted for 57 percent of college students and a majority of those earning master's degrees, doctorates, and professional degrees. Today, women outstrip men in graduation rates from master's and PhD programs, as well as from law and medical schools—a development that is likely to have profound consequences for marriage, family formation, childbearing, and child-rearing. Women, much more than men, recognize that a college degree is essential to success in today's postindustrial economy, where educational credentials and advanced skills are a prerequisite for acquiring a stable, middle-class income. Men, who have failed to recognize that market signal, now account for 70 percent of the recent decline in college enrollment.[9]

Yet another salient shift is the increasing reliance on instructors outside the tenure system, including adjunct faculty, practicing professionals, lecturers, clinical faculty, postdocs, and graduate students, as well as new kinds of nonteaching educational professionals such as instructional designers, educational technologists, assessment specialists, academic and nonacademic coaches, and writing and teaching center professionals. Indeed, much of what's commonly called "administrative bloat" involves the increasing number of service-providing professionals. According to some estimates, adjunct faculty, lecturers, postdocs, and graduate students hold about three-quarters of all instructional positions. This development, which allows faculty to devote more time to research, scholarship, and advanced instruction, provides institutions with flexibility and cost savings, but it also leaves many instructors without the protections or benefits accorded to tenured faculty.

Although community colleges have the highest percentage of adjuncts, who make up about four-fifths of the faculty at those institutions, instructors outside the tenure system are responsible for much of the teaching at all kinds of institutions. At four-year universities, tenure-track and tenured faculty make up about a third of instructors, with graduate students, postdocs, and full-time lecturers doing much of the teaching performed by part-time adjuncts at community colleges.[10]

Reliance on adjuncts is not a new phenomenon, initially surging in the 1970s and arousing a response in the 1980s. In fact, the first statement on contingent faculty from the American Association of University Professors appeared in 1980, calling out the contradiction between institutional and professional ideals and the grim realities of adjunct life. Contributing to the increased reliance on instructors outside the tenure system are an oversupply of prospective faculty members as a reserve army that can be easily drawn upon; fluctuating enrollment, which makes staffing flexibility very attractive; shifts in institutional spending priorities away from instruction and toward executive-level salaries, financial aid, information technology, research centers, and student support services; and treating service courses—especially freshman composition, lower division mathematics, and foreign language instruction—as commodities that don't require tenurable faculty.[11]

The status quo isn't sustainable. Wage increases, better benefits, access to professional development and research, grant, and staff support, greater participation in governance and curriculum decisions, scheduling preferences and parking privileges, office space, renewable contracts, strengthened protections for academic freedom, and an "adjunct-to-full-time" process are among the possible remedies. Already, reliance on part-time adjuncts is declining, even as the number of full-time nontenured lecturers increases. However, resolving the cost versus quality challenge in a context of highly constrained resources won't be easy.

Other noteworthy changes include the rapid expansion of online professional master's and certificate programs as a potential revenue source; a more intensive focus on federally and commercially funded research, patents, licensing, technology transfer, and revenue-producing ancillary services as ways to fund institutional operations; and an explosion of wealth among the most selective private institutions that ignited an amenities and student services arms race that has placed severe financial pressure on less well-funded, selective institutions. There has also been a shift in the financing of higher education, with the burden increasingly falling on students and parents, often in the form of loans and a growing tendency for students to sort themselves among institutions according to affluence and college readiness, defined in terms of high school grade point average, college board scores, and access to Advanced Placement courses.

In the United States, the term "innovation" tends to carry positive connotations. But when applied to higher education, one must be wary. Certainly, some of the changes that are taking place in higher education are for the good, especially the growing emphasis on students' academic and postgraduation success. But other trends—such as the increased reliance on adjunct faculty or the tendency at tuition- and enrollment-dependent institutions to eliminate traditional liberal arts programs—are undoubtedly for the worse.

So, what, then, are the underlying shifts that are transforming higher education? First of all, the higher education landscape is growing more segmented, differentiated, and competitive. We are witnessing an intensifying stratification among higher education institutions in terms of mission and resources, with less selective institutions increasingly unable to sustain a comprehensive liberal arts curriculum and relying more heavily on part-time adjunct faculty.

The higher education market has always been diverse. In the past, it included correspondence schools, normal schools, vocational schools, liberal arts colleges, land grant universities, and various academies and seminaries. Today, in addition to the public and private research universities and liberal arts colleges, there are technology institutes, historically Black colleges and universities, tribal colleges, regional comprehensives, urban publics, community colleges, religious colleges, military academies, fully online universities, and institutions specializing in the arts and health care. Private and public, religious and secular, for-profit and nonprofit, residential and fully online—the higher education ecosystem not only includes a diverse array of institutions and approaches, but also curricula that range from those firmly rooted in the liberal arts to those that are more practical, vocational, applied, or career-oriented.

Not only is the higher education marketplace increasingly differentiated, but it has also grown more competitive and stratified. More and more students now apply to and enroll in institutions outside their locality or region, resulting in a more competitive national marketplace. At the same time, colleges and universities have become more stratified in terms of their financial resources, facilities, student-faculty ratios, graduation rates, ranges of programming, and student qualifications. Increasingly, students with the highest high school grades and standardized test scores have gravitated away from local institutions to those that are more highly ranked and resource-rich. In other words, the same kinds of inequalities that characterize the nation's distribution of wealth and income can be found among colleges and universities.

The result is a higher education ecosystem that is increasingly divided between the haves and the have-nots: between those institutions that are extraordinarily selective and highly resourced, those that are highly or moderately selective, and those broad-access institutions that admit over half of the students who apply. Those latter institutions, which enroll roughly 80 percent of all undergraduates, not only attract the most students with the greatest academic needs, but they are also the most resource-constrained and tuition-dependent. In other words, higher education, which thinks of itself as an engine of economic opportunity and upward mobility, tends to reproduce and reinforce the country's class structure. It relegates the students who received the most uneven high school education to the most under-resourced universities and community colleges. Common beliefs—that admissions to elite campuses is meritocratic, that campus diversity is genuine and extends equally across all institutions, that college is a melting pot, and that campus life is a democratic, egalitarian experience—turn out to be myths, perhaps true to a limited extent, but actually quite misleading.

Even within many individual colleges and universities, serious inequities exist. In about three-quarters of the top 25 public universities, admission into the majors with the biggest payoff—computer science, economics, engineering, finance, and nursing—is restricted. The result is to reduce the number of students who earn majors in those fields by 15 percent, exacerbating racial and ethnic disparities. Why do departments impose such restrictions? Capacity constraints are a factor, but so is a desire to raise a department's rankings.[12]

A second major development is a proliferation in educational options. No longer do colleges and universities exercise a monopoly on access to advanced education. Programs for dual credit/early college allow students to earn college credits in high school. Military crosswalks award credit for military training. For those uninterested in college, apprenticeship opportunities, though still limited in availability, are expanding. More and more community colleges offer applied bachelor's degrees, typically in areas not served by four-year colleges and universities.

At the same time, new providers have entered the postsecondary education marketplace. Tech firms like Google and Amazon offer industry specializations and career certificates in fields that include construction management, digital marketing, e-commerce, financial analysis, IT support, project management, public sector data analytics, financial analysis, and sustainability analysis. In some cases, these courses can translate into college credit. Museums and foundations, too, including the American Museum of Natural History and the Gilder Lehrman Institute of American History, are entering into graduate education, alone or in partnership with existing institutions. Meanwhile, new pathways into the job market are proliferating, including boot camps and academies that offer short-term, nonde-gree, and career-aligned skills programs, although the value of the training offered remains unclear.

Yet another key development is an increasing focus on skills and outcomes. A skills-based approach to learning is intended to give students analytical tools and the disciplinary, digital, social, and technological skills that will better prepare them for a rapidly changing workforce. Champions of skills-focused approaches tend to speak of various twenty-first century literacies that students need to acquire. These include multimodal communication skills, involving the ability to communicate effectively in oral, written, and digital forms; literacy skills, that is, the ability to evaluate the reliability and accuracy of information acquired through various media; civic skills, such as the ability to resolve conflicts and behave in a civil manner; critical thinking skills, including the capacity to analyze, evaluate, synthesize, and think contextually; and computational thinking, that is, the ability to translate data into information and solve complex problems.

A focus on skills and outcomes has some real plusses. It can encourage institutions to focus on skills gaps and prompt instructors to take steps to remediate and rectify disparities in proficiencies, performance, and equity. It can also lead instructors to integrate more active learning into their classes and adopt assessments that require students to apply the skills and knowledge they've acquired to solve authentic, real-world problems. However, in general, the heightened stress on skills and outcomes has not been matched by rigorous and systematic efforts to assess whether those skills and learning objectives have been met. Without well-defined metrics, rubrics, and outcome measures, a skills focus is more a matter of rhetoric than of substance and runs the risk of downplaying the importance of content and knowledge acquisition.

Another major development that is reshaping the higher education ecosystem is the propensity of campuses to grow: to add new programs, expand student services, hire more nonteaching professional staff, and enroll more students, if possible, whether to generate revenue or in response to political pressure. A host of factors are driving growth, beginning with the perceived need, in a competitive marketplace, to emulate aspirational peer institutions and improve campus rankings. As the wealthiest institutions strive to outshine their competitors, they raise the bar for all campuses. At the same time, market-driven competition forces less selective and less well-resourced institutions to enhance their brand and emulate institutions higher up on the food chain.

Also contributing to campus growth is the emergence of new fields of study. While it's easy to poke fun at programs in esports, cannabis studies, and viniculture, most of the new programming is in areas that will play an important role in the economy in the years to come. These include programs in brain science, computer science, data analytics, information technology, logistics, and arts, technology, and emerging communications—the latter is a field that encompasses interactive game design, computer animation, user interface design, and digital and new media arts. As fields of study are expanding, so too are student and parental expectations about the facilities, services, and programming that an institution should offer; the needs of increasingly diverse and financially disadvantaged student bodies that require more support and services; and the obligations to comply with government regulations and avoid legal liability.

Growth can, of course, be good or bad. When community colleges confer bachelor's degrees in technical fields, this innovation can serve local labor force needs and improve graduates' job and earnings prospects—assuming that the degrees are in high-demand fields with high earnings potential. But such an initiative can also result in mission creep, redirecting resources away from higher priorities and diverting faculty from their existing responsibilities out of a misplaced desire to raise an institution's status.[13]

Under intense pressure to control costs while meeting rising expenses—for information technology, financial aid, enrollment management, student services, benefits, utilities, and compliance with government mandates—institutions have been forced to become much more entrepreneurial. This has led to increased spending not only on development and contract research, but also on continuing education and a host of ancillary programs, including summer camps and facilities rentals. It has also led to a proliferation of centers, institutes, and research initiatives.

The propensity toward growth is especially striking in Texas, which recently opened six new medical schools at Sam Houston State University, Texas Tech University, and the Universities of Houston, North Texas, and Texas at Austin and Rio Grande Valley. Another way for universities to enhance their reputations and expand their reach is by opening branch campuses. Texas examples include the University of Houston in suburban Katy and Pearland, Texas A&M University in San Antonio and McAllen, and the University of North Texas in Dallas. Meanwhile, the quest for new markets has led some campuses to establish branch campuses not only in their own regions, but also in other states, including Pittsburgh-based Carnegie Mellon University in Moffett Field, California; Philadelphia-based Drexel University in Sacramento; and Boston-based Northeastern University in Charlotte (North Carolina), London, San Francisco, Seattle, and Silicon Valley. Even more striking is the number of institutions that have opened international branch campuses at sites as remote as the United Arab Emirates, Qatar, Malaysia, and India. From 50 such international branches at the end of the 1990s, the number rose to 215 in 2015 (excluding for-profits that also have campuses outside the United States). Growth, not focus nor institutional distinctiveness, has become an essential part of many institutions' DNA.

Of course, institutional expansion is expensive, and adding a more diversified curriculum, new facilities, and expanded services (let alone new campuses) adds significantly to the cost of higher education. Indeed, I would argue that mission creep is among the most important explanations for why tuition and fees have consistently risen faster than the rate of inflation. That is not to say that campuses shouldn't have established branch campuses, instituted a host of new programs, or replaced spartan gymnasia, dormitories, dining halls, and outdated laboratories with snazzier or safer or more accessible facilities. Nor is it to assert that growth has been driven largely by an empire-building impulse (though there has certainly been some of that). Growth also reflects campuses' embrace of a more entrepreneurial ethos. It's essential to recognize that the very definition of a college or university is undergoing a profound transformation. No longer just an educational institution, a college or university is now like a small (or not-so-small) city, with its own health services, police force, research centers, transportation services, sports and entertainment complexes, and much more. There are those who believe that campuses should have retained a much narrower focus, but, in my view, such an approach would have been a recipe for long-term decline.

Let's turn to the specific changes occurring in the higher education ecosystem, beginning with new providers. Competing with traditional brick-and-mortar two-year and four-year colleges and universities are a host of new entrants. Attracting the most students are scaled, lower-cost, online universities, of which the largest are Western Governors University, Southern New Hampshire University, and Grand Canyon University. Like the for-profits, these nonprofits offer a limited number of self-paced, technology-enabled, workforce-aligned programs. Costs are radically reduced by disaggregating the traditional faculty role and standardizing courses. Subject-area specialists design courses in conjunction with industry advisers, while coaches or course mentors monitor student engagement and progress, and a separate group of graders evaluates student work.

Defenders of this approach argue that a self-paced, self-directed model makes sense for older students with complex lives, many with previous college experience. But critics consider these programs as little more than twenty-first century versions of a correspondence course, since students are left to learn largely on their own and the rigor of the assessments is unclear. Under this model, students receive no actual instruction from a professor, nor do they have regular, substantive interactions with a faculty member or even with classmates.

Other new entrants into the postsecondary education ecosystem include "career accelerators," which are skills academies that offer short-term training in high-demand fields, such as coding, data analysis, and supply chain management, and technical skills certification courses, like those in cloud data engineering, database development, machine learning, and web applications offered by Amazon, Google, and Microsoft. In fact, most of the students who embrace these accelerated programs are already degree holders. Such programs meet a genuine need; employers need employees who can step in and use the software that undergirds their business, like Google AdWords and HubSpot for marketing, Epic for electronic health records, Workday for HR, Zendesk for customer service, ServiceNow for IT management, Atlassian for product and project management, Xero for accounting, MuleSoft for application development, and Splunk for data analytics. Since most colleges and universities do not teach such skills, other providers have stepped up to fill the vacuum.[14]

Other examples of alternative providers include the unaccredited business and technology skills courses and tutorials offered by LinkedIn Learning (previously known as Lynda.com) and Udemy and the relatively inexpensive but unaccredited entry-level, self-study courses offered by companies like StraighterLine, whose classes carry "college equivalency" recommendations from the American Council on Education (ACE) and the College Board's Advanced Placement Program, and which are accepted by a small number of mainly online institutions. Such courses may also serve as preparation for the CLEP exams, the standardized tests administered by the College Board that provide a mechanism, at some schools, for earning college credits by demonstrating command of a particular subject area without taking an actual college course.

Then, there are corporate universities, in-house academies that focus on leadership development, business management, and technical skills training. Corporate universities, once associated with McDonald's Hamburger University and Ringling Bros. and Barnum & Bailey Clown College, have multiplied in recent years. Although corporate universities have existed for decades—General Motors established a technical training center in 1919—their numbers have grown rapidly in recent years, doubling from about 1,000 in 1997 to 2,000 in

2007, doubling again between 2007 and 2011, and now exceeding 4,200. Their goals are to instill a corporate culture, disseminate the company's strategy, provide tailored, proprietary professional development and skills training, and strengthen a company's human capital. These training programs, of course, pose a competitive threat to many existing master's programs, especially those in business.

Next, let's look at the new educational models that are taking hold. A growing number of institutions are experimenting with nontraditional education pathways that hold out the prospect of a faster, more affordable route to a credential or career and that provide many on-ramps and off-ramps that allow students to stop out, reenroll, and continue their academic journey across a lifetime. Here are a few of the most important new educational models that have recently emerged.

- **Integrated high school–community college–four-year university pathways**: Currently, the pipeline to a postsecondary degree is quite leaky. In Texas, just 20 percent of eighth graders ever receive a postsecondary credential of any kind. In other states, the figure is scarcely higher. The leaky pipeline has many causes, but one is especially significant: inadequate connections between the education students receive in high school and community college and that provided by four-year institutions.[15]

  One recent answer to this disconnect is to allow high school students to take courses for college credit. In the past, this option was largely limited to Advanced Placement and International Baccalaureate courses, but a new option has recently emerged: early-college or dual-enrollment programs. Today, more than 2 million high school students in at least 47 states are enrolled in early college courses on a community college campus, in their high school, or online. Such programs provoke a litany of criticisms, including that many of the high school enrollees are not prepared for and their instructors are unqualified to teach college-level classes; that the rigor of assessments—unlike that of AP tests or CLEP exams—is suspect; and that most students enrolled in these programs would be better served by taking AP courses. But it is also the case that high school students who take dual-credit courses, including youth from low-income households and underrepresented groups, are more likely to go to college, earn a degree, and graduate in fewer years.

Even when students earn college credits in high school or community college, many discover that four-year schools are unwilling to accept credits earned elsewhere or count these credits only as electives. Part of the solution to the community college transfer challenge lies in improvements in articulation agreements that assign common numbers to general education and gateway courses to guarantee transferability. But a growing body of research suggests that such agreements are insufficient in themselves. Why is this the case? Because there are mismatched expectations and divergent learning objectives in high schools, community colleges, and four-year institutions. Nominally identical courses too often fail to cover the same material or evaluate student performance according to identical standards. To address the problem of credit loss, a number of states have instituted "Field of Study Curricula," which are sets of courses that fulfill both the four-year institution's general education requirements and the lower division requirements in a particular major.

- **Competency-based models that emphasize demonstrated mastery of essential knowledge and skills rather than seat time or the accumulation of credit hours**: A competency- or mastery-based curriculum awards credit based on mastery of essential knowledge and skills rather than seat time or credit hours. In practice, the programs that adopt the competency-based education label tend to emphasize credit for prior learning and a self-paced, self-directed approach to pedagogy, but a mastery approach need not be online or self-directed. Advantages of a competency-based curriculum include clearly defined learning objectives, an emphasis on project-based skill-building activities, and rigorous assessments of mastery. By awarding credit for prior learning and allowing students to demonstrate mastery at any time, this approach can expedite time to completion.

But such a competency-based approach is subject to many justified criticisms. Too often, students lack adequate interaction with faculty members or peers, fail to receive sufficient feedback from subject matter experts, and do not get the kind of guidance and support taken for granted by students in more traditional programs. Questions have also been raised about the rigor of the assessments. If competency-based education is to become a credible alternative to a more traditional approach, then there must be multi-institutional agreement on the learning objectives and how mastery is certified. A possible model is the Interstate Passport, a multistate agreement that makes it easier for students to transfer credits from one institution to another. This interstate compact identifies the learning outcomes that must be attained in lower division general education courses if the courses are to be eligible for transfer.

- **Earn-learn models that integrate paid internships, on-campus work, or community service into a college education**: Most students work, so it makes sense to ensure that a student's work life complements what they learn in class.[16] However, only a small number of institutions formally integrate work into undergraduate education. Earn-learn models take a wide variety of forms, ranging from tuition-free models in which every student is given a campus job (a model pioneered by Berea College) to co-op models where students alternate between academic coursework and internships (a model that Drexel and Northeastern Universities exemplify).

  Earn-learn pathways combine an academic curriculum with relevant work experiences. The goal is to blend the strengths of a traditional academic experience with career exploration, job training, experiential learning, and real-world professional, technical, and soft skills development. Work colleges provide reduced or free tuition in exchange for work on campus or in the surrounding community. Currently, there are nine federally designated work colleges. To gain federal recognition as a work college, a school must create a supervised work program, make it integral to its curriculum and mission, and require all students to perform at least five hours each week of on-campus work.[17]

The most formal and oldest earn-learn model is cooperative education, which combines paid employment and formal study as a requirement for graduation. In certain instances, students alternate terms of academic study and paid internships; in other instances, each week is divided between time spent in the classroom and on the job. Prime examples of cooperative education are found at Drexel and Northeastern Universities. Another way that some institutions integrate work experience into undergraduate education is through a practicum, a field or clinical experience where a student typically works under the direction of a field or clinical supervisor and has the opportunity to apply theory to professional practice. Practicums are most common in such preprofessional fields as social work or nursing.

- **Scaled online degree programs that cut costs by disaggregating the traditional faculty role**: The fastest-growing segment of undergraduate education consists of fully online programs that cater to those who have had some college experience and who seek a degree in a vocational subject. In an effort to make a college degree cheaper and faster to attain, many of the new models blur the divide between education and training, rely heavily on adjuncts and coaches rather than traditional faculty, and dispense with many of the accoutrements of a traditional university campus: not just dormitories, student unions, and wellness centers but also laboratories and physical libraries.

The most radical versions—pioneered by Western Governors University and Southern New Hampshire University's competency-based College for America—let students study at their own pace and award credit for skills earned outside the classroom. The appeal of their industry-aligned model is obvious, given its explicit connection between education and employment and students' desire for a more effective and less costly alternative to traditional college. But the perils are also readily apparent: these might be digital diploma mills or trade schools for the digital age that offer a watered-down educational experience, lacking direct contact with a credentialed scholar or with classmates.

Other new educational models are also gaining traction. Among these are the following:

- **Military crosswalk programs**: These programs grant academic credit for training received during active duty.
- **Stackable models**: These models disaggregate courses into modules that can be combined (or stacked) into a degree.
- **Prior learning assessments**: These assessments award college credit for life experience based on a test such as a portfolio assessment. Credit by exam is not new; the College Board has offered CLEP (College Level Examination Program) exams since the late 1960s. The US Department of Defense DSST (Defense Activity for Non-Traditional Education Support) also assesses prior learning. CLEP and DSST are standardized, high stakes, multiple-choice tests.
- **Hybrid models that combine online education and physical spaces**: Online education works well for some students, but not for others. Unfortunately, many of those who are poorly served by online courses are precisely the students who need the most help: the less proficient students, often younger students, without high levels of motivation or effective time management and study skills. One attempt to address this is to provide these students with the support they need to earn a degree: an academic and life coach, a course mentor, study

spaces, and a community of peers. PelotonU offers an example of this approach. Its staff meets biweekly with first-year students in a dedicated space. By partnering with Western Governors University and Southern New Hampshire University, it seeks to provide a debt-free path to graduation. 2U students enrolled in online programs at Georgetown and USC use space at any WeWork location to take tests or meet with study groups. The physical spaces provide learners with access to technology, academic advising, tutoring, career counseling, and a supportive community.

- **Applied bachelor's degrees**: Many students want a degree with a clear value proposition. Some 23 states now allow community and technical colleges to award applied bachelor's degrees to meet local workforce needs and provide a more affordable option to nontraditional students. Typically, this kind of degree is labeled as a Bachelor of Applied Science, to distinguish it from a Bachelor of Arts or Sciences. Among the degrees offered are ones in radiologic and imaging sciences, electrical and computer engineering technology, film, television, and digital production, medical and health service management, and physician assistant studies.

- **Plus degrees**: These are bachelor degrees that rethink the traditional division between the arts and sciences or that supplement traditional liberal arts majors with marketable skills. Examples include Stanford's now abandoned CS+ degrees that linked computer science with humanities fields; the University of Texas at Dallas's Arts and Technology degree programs that combine the visual arts, music, and narrative with new computing and media technologies in such fields as animation and game design; Brigham Young University's Humanities Plus initiative which helps students develop a skill set that will be identifiable and attractive to employers; and Boise State University's job skills courses in design thinking, digital marketing, and introduction to app development.

- **Stackable credentials**: Currently, there are over 1 million nondegree credentials offered by about 60,000 providers—corporations, nonprofits, skills academies, MOOC platforms, and academic institutions. These digital badges, certificates, and licenses are supposed to denote mastery of essential competencies, but given the often-confusing jargon and a lack of clarity about outcomes, the value of these credentials is opaque. At this point, there's no easy way to know what employers think about these various records of achievement or whether they'll be accepted for credit toward a college degree.[18]
- **Accelerated models**: These models, which take advantage of the students' prior learning in Advanced Placement, International Baccalaureate, or early-college or dual-credit courses or in the military and employment, include three-year degree programs and four-year bachelor's and master's programs. In addition, a year-round schedule that includes summer classes and intersession courses can compress time to degree and potentially cut the cost of a higher education by as much as 25 percent without any reduction in rigor.
- **General studies, campus extension, degree completion programs**: A small number of elite campuses offer bachelor's degrees to nontraditional students, typically working adults who have already acquired some college credits, through their schools of continuing education or extension services. Some programs, like Harvard University's and Columbia University's, are largely in-person; others, like Georgetown University's bachelor's degree completion program, are online. Some offer a wide range of majors; some simply offer a general studies or liberal arts degree. But these degrees are labeled in ways that make it clear that they aren't equivalent to the campuses' more renowned undergraduate programs, and they don't provide access to the parent institution's standard services or cocurricular or extracurricular opportunities. Far

less expensive than their campuses' standard undergraduate offerings, these continuing ed and extension programs do provide a broader range of students the opportunity to take classes from some of the same faculty who serve these institutions' other undergraduates. But the diversity of such students and their access to scholarships, rates of completion, and postgraduation outcomes remain uncertain. It's also unclear whether these programs, despite their relatively low price, are essentially moneymakers for their campuses or whether they do significantly expand access to a high-quality education to groups who have been historically excluded from such institutions.

- **A distributed campus presence**: The assumption that a campus should have a single physical location is gradually giving way to the idea of a distributed campus presence. International campuses, extension centers, campus storefronts, extension centers, and co-located multi-institution campus centers have grown increasingly common and are some of the ways that colleges and universities are expanding their brands. The idea of a distributed university presence is not new. Many of these academic outposts represent an updated version of the concept of extension services introduced by the 1914 Smith-Lever Act, which connected land grant universities to communities across their states. Motivations for a distributed presence vary widely. Some of these programs aim to give students a base from which to undertake internships. Others provide online students with a space for face-to-face advising, tutoring, and networking. Still others seek to ease transfer from a community college to a four-year institution, and others intend to produce a critical mass of educational options, often in a medical center.

One of the most notable and controversial aspects of the new educational landscape is the appearance of "embedded for-profits," companies that assume functions previously performed in-house.

Perhaps the most striking example involves the outsourcing of actual coursework. Harvard Extension School, for instance, is launching a coding boot camp taught by Trilogy Education Services; somewhat similar programs are offered by Georgia Tech, University of Pennsylvania, University of California at Berkeley, Northwestern, UCLA, University of North Carolina, University of Texas, George Washington, and Rutgers in collaboration with commercial partners. Meanwhile, Google developed the curriculum and instructional materials for introductory courses on computer science, data science, and machine learning that will be delivered at four-year institutions, as well as an information technology support certificate offered at more than 25 community colleges.

"Smart partnerships" certainly serve a useful function by providing start-up funding and expertise in areas where cash-strapped institutions lack expertise and internal capacity. But such collaborations can also exact a steep cost. To launch online degree programs, many institutions have partnered with online program managers (OPMs) or their à la carte competitors, who assume responsibility for marketing the programs, managing enrollment and student registration, staffing help lines, and, in many cases, designing and delivering courses. In exchange, the OPMs typically require long-term contracts which are exceedingly difficult to terminate and take anywhere from 50 to 70 percent of revenue. Nor is the cost purely financial. The corporate partners often own any data and leads that the programs generate. In addition to running online programs, embedded for-profits have taken on other responsibilities such as managing an institution's data analytics infrastructure and helping to implement new technologies. In some cases, such partnerships make sense. But given the lack of transparency about costs and contractual obligations, it's hard to know whether institutions would do better to augment their internal capacities in areas ranging from marketing and enrollment management to coaching, data analytics, portfolio management, badging, and course design, development, and delivery.

We are in the midst of a profound historic transformation in the postsecondary education ecosystem. A new educational ecosystem is gradually emerging that poses a particular risk to the regional comprehensive institutions and community colleges that educate the vast majority of college students. These institutions are threatened, on one side, by scaled, lower-cost, fully online universities, and, on the other, by the allure of accelerated, affordable nondegree credentialing programs. If these institutions are to successfully compete in a context where there are stagnant public resources and limits on parents' and students' abilities to pay while also bringing students to academic and postgraduation success, then it is essential that they better understand and emulate the example of the university pacesetters, which are reengineering every aspect of education to help students succeed in the classroom and beyond.

# 4

---

# Lessons from the History of American Higher Education

THE GOLDEN AGE OF AMERICAN HIGHER EDUCATION does not lie in the distant past. It exists within living memory. Colleges and universities in the wake of World War II came to be viewed as essential for national security, economic growth, and social mobility. As a result, the states and the federal government invested substantially in increasing access to a college education, and unprecedented numbers of high school graduates flocked to colleges and universities. Mass education was soon succeeded by near-universal higher education.

Starting with the 1944 G.I. Bill of Rights, government investment in higher education soared. Surging post–World War II federal support for university research was followed by the enactment of the 1958 National Defense Education Act, which provided the first federally funded grants and subsidized loans for college students, and later by the 1965 Higher Education Act, which expanded need-based grants and loans and created work-study jobs and outreach and support service programs for students from low-income backgrounds. Thanks to these initiatives, undergraduate enrollments increased 45 percent between 1945 and 1960, then doubled again by 1970.

At the same time, the number of colleges and universities climbed by 70 percent, as city campuses run by local school districts were converted into state urban universities, and a number of YMCA-affiliated institutions became private universities.[1] States further increased access by transforming teachers colleges into regional comprehensives and greatly expanding the number of community colleges and extension campuses while establishing dozens of public university systems and coordinating boards to oversee and manage the booming higher ed sector. Meanwhile, major state universities grew dramatically in size, increasing enrollment from between 3,000 and 6,000 before World War II to 20,000, 30,000, 40,000, and even more by the mid-1970s.[2] The number of instructors increased especially fast, from just 110,885 in 1949 to 954,534 in 1988.[3]

Perhaps most impressive was the growth in state and federal spending. State spending rose from $4 per every thousand students to $10 between 1960 and 1975, while federal research grants quadrupled. The share of campus budgets funded by the states climbed from around 20 percent in 1945 to about 35 percent thirty years later. Federal spending, too, grew dramatically. Between 1965 and 1975, direct federal support for colleges and universities increased 259 percent. Indirect support, largely in the form of guaranteed federal loans, grew from $128 million to $4.2 billion in 2001 dollars.[4]

Three legacies grew out of this golden epoch in the history of higher education. First, research universities became vital partners in the emerging government-corporate complex. Building on foundations laid during the 1950s, applied and contract research became central to research universities' finances. Although defense research attracted the most attention from campus protesters, other forms of research—medical, scientific, and social scientific—also fundamentally altered Tier 1 institutions' priorities, staffing, and business models. As more and more institutions pursued Tier 1 status, these universities, too, made applied and contract research central to their mission, often at the expense of their teaching responsibilities.

Second, as universities grew in size and function, the student experience became increasingly impersonal, feeding student discontent.

Today's calls for 360-degree, comprehensive, holistic, one-stop support structures represent a reaction against the fact that large numbers of students feel a deep sense of disconnection from their professors and the institution itself. It was during the 1960s that students for the first time spoke of being reduced to mere numbers. Now, an army of professional advisers and student service and academic support professionals who staff growing career centers, disability and psychological service centers, and tutoring and writing centers are needed precisely because earlier forms of mentoring and caring proved wholly inadequate and unresponsive.

Third, even as access to higher education expanded, new forms of stratification emerged. Ironically, it was during the 1960s that this country institutionalized certain profound and persistent inequalities in campus resources and reputation. California's master plan, which at the time was held up as a model for expanding access to advanced education, has become, in retrospect, a system of hierarchy and exclusion by relegating the Cal State universities and community colleges to seemingly permanent second- and third-class status. Research grants and contracts greatly advantaged their recipients, while other institutions, especially community colleges, lagged far behind in per-student instructional expenditures.

———

When I speak of the post–World War II years as higher education's golden age, it's important not to overstate subsequent years' fall from grace. This nation's investment in higher education, financial and in other ways, remains impressive. A college degree is still widely viewed as the prerequisite for financial success, and the lifetime payoff is $1 million more than the earnings of a typical high school graduate. Even as tuition has increased, enrollment at four-year institutions remains very high, and applications to selective institutions far exceed the number of available seats. Nor did most tenured or tenure-track faculty suffer financially even during the Great Recession and the pandemic. Unlike many other workers, faculty salaries actually increased.[5] In absolute dollars, state and federal spending on colleges and universities, including on financial aid, has never been higher. Research expenditures have soared in recent years, rising tenfold in inflation-adjusted terms between 1980 and 2010, and American research universities continue to dominate international rankings. Meanwhile, a new market for professional master's degrees and certificate programs opened up, with the number of master's degrees conferred rising 60 percent between 2000 and 2014.[6]

That said, real problems remain. The undergraduate graduation rate remains too low, and the time it takes to obtain a degree is too long. Resources are highly concentrated among a relatively small group of institutions. Fewer than 300 of the 1,364 four-year institutions accept less than half their applicants. Just seventeen schools accept less than 10 percent of those who apply, and another twenty-nine campuses admit between 10 and 20 percent of applicants. In stark contrast, over half of all the nation's colleges and universities accept more than two-thirds of applicants.[7]

There are other causes for concern. Total enrollment has declined for over a decade. Competition from alternative providers has picked up. At the same time, the leading US universities struggle to maintain their preeminence in the face of mounting foreign competition. Three-quarters of the 335 US universities in the global top 2,000 have seen their rankings decline. At the same time, the growth of scientific research at European and East Asian universities exceeds that in their American counterparts. Another measure, international student enrollment, should also spark concern. For five straight years, international student enrollment has dropped. Since international students account for roughly a quarter of universities' tuition revenue, any losses on this front carry a significant economic impact.[8]

Let's view these indicators not as false flags but as a call to action. The trend lines are worrisome, and we ignore signs of a relative weakening of the nation's colleges and universities at our peril. The economist Richard Vedder's words, while pointed and even harsh, are not wrong: "too little learning is going on, and there is a significant mismatch between student vocational expectations and labor market reality . . . Not a particularly uplifting story, but one needing to be told."[9]

---

Beginning in the mid-1970s, a series of historic shifts transformed higher education. The bachelor's degree became a prerequisite for a growing number of steady, middle-class jobs as the knowledge economy grew and the industrial economy stagnated in the face of mounting foreign competition and soaring energy costs. At the same time, state support for higher education fell in per-student, inflation-adjusted terms even as inflation raised colleges' costs. Campuses compensated by dramatically raising tuition—or instituting tuition for the first time, such as within the City University of New York and the University of California systems. To compensate for rising costs, many campuses, led by Harvard, adopted a "high-tuition, high-financial aid" model, in which, in theory, high tuition for more affluent students would subsidize the tuition of those from lower income backgrounds. In practice, however, rising costs led to a heightened reliance on student loans and parental debt, ultimately sparking calls for debt cancellation and free college. Average student debt in 2021 dollars rose from $5,060 in 1975 to $31,100 in 2021.[10]

Meanwhile, student interests shifted away from the liberal arts, and especially the humanities, toward pre-professional and more vocational and technical fields of study, such as business, engineering, and nursing. In other words, the "vocationalization" of higher education was half a century in the making. So, too, was the academic job crisis, as more and more campuses introduced doctoral programs and flooded the PhD market, creating a reserve pool of labor that could serve as adjunct or contingent instructors. In short, the academy's increasing reliance on instructors off the tenure track didn't emerge overnight. In the pointed words of NYU's Clay Shirky, "The faculty has stopped being a guild, divided into junior and senior members, and become a caste system, divided into haves and have-nots."[11]

By the time that the Great Recession emerged in late 2007, it was clear that higher ed had reached a crisis point. There was a mounting sense that higher education's business model was broken and that the growth in tuition and student debt was unsustainable. And yet, despite fervent calls for disruptive alternatives—MOOCs, skills academies, and fully online education—and for cost-cutting, most colleges and universities continue to function pretty much as normal. Students and their families responded in contrasting and contradictory ways, with a growing number of students applying to the most highly ranked and well-resourced institutions, convinced that they offered the best pathway to future success, while others downsized their aspirations, enrolling in a less expensive public university rather than a private institution or attending a two-year school rather than going directly to a four-year institution. Alternatives to traditional providers didn't benefit nearly as much as radical innovators predicted, in part because the overwhelming majority of undergraduates preferred an on-campus experience and partly because most were convinced, quite rightly in my opinion, that they were more likely to achieve their goals at a more traditional institution. As costly as a college education can be, it still provides the single most reliable path to a stable, rewarding career, and the in-person experience provides the motivation, structure, discipline, and support that most students need to succeed academically.

This may not be higher education's golden age, but it is certainly the golden age of histories of higher education. There are sweeping surveys like Roger L. Geiger's magisterial *American Higher Education since World War II* (the sequel to his *The History of American Higher Education: Learning and Culture from the Founding to World War II*) and John Thelin's *A History of American Higher Education*. There are novel interpretations like David Larabee's *Perfect Mess* or more focused studies like Jonathan Zimmerman's *Amateur Hour* on college teaching and Matthew Johnson's *Undermining Racial Justice* on the racial integration of higher education. These works reveal an analytical acuity, theoretical sophistication, topical and chronological range, breadth, and depth of research that matches or exceeds the very best studies of the past.

Which presents us with an irony of, shall we say, historic proportions: even as the history of higher education achieves new heights, the academy as a whole is awash in ignorance of its own history. In the culture wars, history is often deployed as a weapon targeted at one's adversaries—resulting in oversimplification and sweeping overstatement. But a more nuanced understanding of history is of enormous value, providing insights that can be acquired in no other way.

When it comes to knowledge about higher education's history, most academics are aware of a few historical landmarks: Harvard's founding in 1636; the Morrill Acts of 1862 and 1890, establishing land-grant colleges; the formation of the American Association of University Professors in 1915; and the enactment of the 1944 G.I. Bill of Rights. But most know remarkably little about key historical themes involving academic freedom, coeducation, racial integration, and the development of tenure. Few, I suspect, realize that tenure only became near universal at four-year institutions in the 1960s. In 1935, fewer than half of a sample of seventy-eight well-known universities had instituted formal tenure policies, and Rice University only did so in 1962. Few academics today realize that tenure was viewed by administrators largely as a fringe benefit that could strengthen faculty recruitment as well as be a mechanism for weeding out unproductive faculty.

Thanks to works like Ellen Schrecker's *No Ivory Tower: McCarthyism and the Universities*, faculty recognize that anti-Communist hysteria led Cold War administrators to demand that faculty sign loyalty oaths and fired and blacklisted those who refused. But far fewer know about the gay purges during the 1940s at the Universities of Texas, Wisconsin, and Missouri, resulting in Texas in the dismissal of ten faculty members and fifteen students and the forced resignation of the campus president for supposedly harboring a "nest of perversity."[12]

Ignorance of higher education's past carries many deleterious consequences. It blinds us to the fact that many of today's most highly touted innovations—including technology-enhanced learning; personalized, adaptive learning; and three-year degrees—are simply updated versions of ideas promoted in the past. It also encourages the illusion that colleges and universities can't, won't, or shouldn't change. In actuality, despite the superficial appearance of continuity—a facade that colleges and universities have done their best to perpetuate in their architecture, ceremonies, discourse, and regalia—higher education has undergone recurrent shifts in mission, organization, and operations in order to adapt to altered circumstances. Equally important, it helps us recognize that today's flash points—over academic freedom, admissions policies, campus unrest, curricula, diversity and inclusion, pedagogical practice, a practical versus a liberal education, student learning and motivation, and town-gown relations—have a long history.

Academics also need to recognize that many of the challenges campuses face today—including motivating students and providing for their welfare and well-being—were familiar issues at American colleges from their inception and that students have driven many of the most important transformations in the history of American higher education, not just the abolition of the policy of *in loco parentis* and parietal regulations, or the institution of course evaluations, but others, often unintentionally (like the imposition of letter grades) or indirectly (such as the development of electives). Every generation's reformers believe that they had the solution to higher education's failings—only to see their dreams of transformations dashed.

It is easy to think that the history of higher education is irrelevant to the challenges that today's colleges and universities face. After all, in 1870, just 50,000 men and women attended college—just 1.7 percent of the college-aged population. Today, in stark contrast, 20.5 million (57 percent female and 17 percent African American, Hispanic, Asian, or Native American) attend a postsecondary institution. That's over 40 percent of eighteen- to twenty-four-year-olds.

Historical illiteracy is not a victimless crime. It has real-world consequences. Scholars need to know why past efforts to technologize or personalize higher education generally failed; why, roughly every twenty years, activists have had to echo their predecessors' calls for equity and inclusion; and why seemingly commonsensical innovations, like John Dewey's proposals for more hands-on, authentic, civically engaged learning have yet to be realized. Knowing American higher education's history can not only keep us from repeating past mistakes, it can lay bare the processes that transform the academy and reveal the deeply embedded assumptions that inhibit many well-intentioned reforms. Even more importantly, this history can remind us of the principles and values we need to sustain.

So what, then, are elements that every academic and especially every educational reformer ought to know? For one thing, that the American system of higher education has, since the early nineteenth century, differed dramatically from the European institutions that inspired it, and this distinctiveness helps explain both the system's strengths and failings. In stark contrast to their international counterparts, American colleges and universities exist in a highly competitive marketplace, with each campus vying for resources, students, and prestige. From the early nineteenth century onward, colleges' survival depended on their ability to attract students and donations, which, in turn, hinged on their reputation. The college rankings, combined with a slowdown in population growth, have intensified competition among colleges and universities, which are under intense pressure to expand their offerings, improve their facilities, and enhance their appeal to students and donors. An entrepreneurial spirit, as the historian David F. Labaree has shown, has driven campuses to grow, raise their research profile, groom facilities and grounds, and strive to improve their reputation.[13]

American institutions were also distinctive in their belief that every college graduate should be exposed to the liberal arts and have a solid grounding in the humanities. To that end, almost all institutions of higher learning require undergraduates to fulfill distribution requirements or complete a core curriculum that ensures that even the most vocationally focused students take classes in literature, history, and other liberal arts disciplines. Then, too, American colleges and universities were unique in striving to combine three very different traditions: that of the English college, with its stress on teacher–student interaction (embodied in the Oxbridge tutorial) and a robust campus life; the German research university, with its emphasis on original scholarship and graduate programs; and a distinctively American commitment to universal access, even for students who in the past wouldn't be considered college-ready. The United States is the only society that assumes that the overwhelming majority of individuals should attend college. For better and worse, a college credential has become a prerequisite for a middle-class standard of living.

American colleges and universities are distinctive in other respects, for example, in their emphasis on campus life beyond the purely academic. College-going in the United States, in stark contrast to institutions elsewhere, is as much a coming-of-age experience and rite of passage as it is an educational experience. The "college experience"—a mixture of casual socializing; participation in clubs, organizations, and intramural sports; attendance at intercollegiate sporting events; and Greek life—is a big part of college's attraction. It's why many alumni consider the college years the best years of their lives. This nation's campuses are also unique in their range of responsibilities. In addition to its instructional and research missions, colleges are drivers of workforce preparation and regional economic development; providers of health and counseling services, dining facilities, dormitories, clubs and organizations; and purveyors of sports and entertainment.

So, what else should academics know about higher education's history? If any single overarching theme can be said to run through the recent history of higher education, it is the ambiguities of progress. Superficially, the history of American higher education looks like a textbook example of progress or, as it was put in the 1950s and '60s, modernization. This seemed self-evident in the democratization of access; the diversification of student bodies; the opening of doors to previously underrepresented racial, ethnic, religious, and low-income groups; expanding opportunities for women; and the gradual broadening of the curriculum. According to this Whiggish formulation, elitism and exclusivity gave way to democratic access; a narrow, rigid, and dated curriculum to breadth and choice; regimentation, paternalism, and expectations of deference to a recognition of student autonomy; and pedagogies emphasizing recitation and rote memorization to discussion, lab work, and active learning. Adding weight to this overly sanguine perspective are quantitative measures that underscore higher education's success: the ongoing growth in the number of tenured and tenure-track professors and the increase in research expenditures, scholarly publication, and research productivity.

But any fair-minded account reveals reverses as well as advances. Alongside the increase in postsecondary degree attainment, the growth in enrollments and endowments, the remarkable success of colleges and universities in making a degree a prerequisite for a middle-class livelihood, and in extending their values and modes of thought across the culture, there are also well-founded concerns about American higher education's cost, stratification, uncertain learning and employment outcomes, adjunctification, and, above all, inequities that relegate far too many talented students from African American, Hispanic, and low-income backgrounds to the least selective, most under-resourced institutions. The unhappy fact is that graduation rates at broad-access institutions haven't budged in recent years, that enrollment of students from low-income and other unrepresented groups has stagnated, and that the pipeline from a community college to a bachelor's degree remains incredibly leaky.

Historic advances often come with a cost, and several examples underscore progress's ambiguities. For example, the rapid growth of community college opened doors to higher education that had previously been closed, but the rise of the community college was also part of the emergence of a hierarchically differentiated higher education system that intentionally diverted those deemed less qualified to separate institutions from which only a small minority ever succeeded in earning an associate's degree, let alone a bachelor's degree. Another example: the professionalization of the faculty meant that students nationwide encountered *bona fide* subject matter experts, but as the professoriate professionalized, the faculty, as a whole, grew more distant and detached from students, with professional staff assuming many of the faculty's earlier nonacademic functions. A third example: the long-term decline in the number of the liberal arts colleges—the historic exemplars of a conception of higher education that emphasizes close faculty-student interaction, intensive mentoring, the development of the whole student and cultivation of well-rounded graduates—means that a spur, inspiration, and model of what educational quality looks like is, alas, slowly disappearing.[14]

As an alternative to excessively linear and teleological narratives of progress, we might instead view American higher education's history through other lenses: First, as a series of distinct, transitional moments when institutions underwent change across multiple dimensions in response to a variety of pressures, including the needs of an evolving economy, drives for professionalism, demands for access, campus unrest, and the success of journalists, novelists and Hollywood moviemakers in making college fashionable, prestigious, and making campus life alluring, but not for academic reasons. Second, as a history of contestation and conflict, in which various stakeholders have continuously struggled over the purpose, curriculum, pedagogies, access, and affordability of individual institutions and higher education as a whole—a tussle that persists today over admissions policies, financial aid, requirements, online learning, and above all, how best to realize higher education's democratic possibilities. Third, as a history that situates the evolution of higher education within the main currents of American history, including the shifts from an agricultural and mercantile economy to an industrial economy and to a service and knowledge economy, the development of large, complex, systematic bureaucratic organizations, and the federal government's ever-expanding reach.

Higher education is many things: a sorting mechanism; a contributor to human capital formation; a major source of basic and applied research; a driver of local and regional economic growth; a provider of employment, entertainment, health care and cultural enrichment; and, yes, an educational institution. But we mustn't forget higher ed's primary purpose: human development (or what our predecessors called "character formation"). For the overwhelming majority of undergraduates, and not just those at residential campuses, college is, first and foremost, a coming-of-age experience and a rite of passage. It provides a controlled environment in which most young people separate from the natal home, experiment with more mature and intimate relationships, begin to define their adult identity, and, parents hope, embark on a vocational path.

At their best, colleges and universities do much more than build skills and knowledge; indeed, their primary value lies in exposing undergraduates to diversity, the rich realms of culture, and the intellectual life. It also does something that some partisans incorrectly confuse with political indoctrination: it gives students a vocabulary and intellectual framework with which to make sense of the world. Concepts like intersectionality, implicit bias, and stereotype threat are, in a sense, the successors to the ideas that earlier generations of college students drew from Freud or the Frankfurt School. Foucault is, in a sense, the successor to Herbert Marcuse, Edgar Z. Friedenberg, Michael Harrington, and Theodore Roszak, whose impact on the baby boom generation was immense.

———

According to my reading, the history of American higher education is best understood in terms of a series of pivot points or watersheds, each the byproduct of the intersection or conjuncture of three forces: evolving societal and economic needs, changes in the makeup of the student body, and shifts in colleges' mission and responsibilities. One such transitional moment took place in the late nineteenth century. Many of the defining features of higher education today—distinct disciplines and departments, majors, and credit hours—are products of this era when American colleges and universities underwent profound changes in the face of two major societal challenges.

The first challenge was to meet a rapidly evolving industrial economy's need for formally trained experts in rapidly expanding fields that included business administration, engineering, evidence-based

medicine, and science-based industry. To meet the need for technical instruction, the college curriculum broadened and faculty became
more professional. Hard to believe, but as late as the 1870s, there were
still individual professors who taught everything from classics to engineering. Now, colleges turned to disciplinary specialists.

The second challenge was to create a more structured pathway into
adulthood for ambitious or affluent young men. In the early nineteenth century, young men's lives were extraordinarily unpredictable. Youth was a period when a young man moved repeatedly
between the natal home and independent living elsewhere, and
from one apprenticeship or job to another. There was no clearly
defined or well-demarcated pathway to advancement and success.
Consequently, many young men experienced their twenties and
early thirties as a period of intense anxiety and uncertainty. Sound
familiar?

A redesigned college experience offered a solution to both challenges. During the late nineteenth century, the modern concept of a
career materialized, in which formal training was followed by entry
into a profession, which was then succeeded by a sequence of ascend-
ing positions within that profession. College became the entryway
into professional life. The effort to smooth the path to a secure adulthood extended to the extracurriculum, as colleges and universities
assumed oversight over activities—from competitive athletics to
campus publications and clubs—that had previously been organized
and run by students themselves. It is not an accident that as youth no
longer was a true odyssey of discovery, colleges created alternative
rites of passage, which, however demanding, like football, were constrained by adult oversight and adult-defined rules.

Today's colleges face very different challenges than their late-
nineteenth-century counterparts. Indeed, the older conception of a
career, in which one devotes a lifetime to a particular professional vo-
cation, has increasingly broken down. That reality imposes an imperative on today's colleges and universities. Our institutions need to
do a better job of preparing students for success in the high-demand
knowledge economy, the creative sector, technical and technology

industries, and occupations involving advanced analysis and management of data in which career paths are neither obvious, well-trod, or secure.

To call out these sectors is not to dismiss the importance of the liberal arts or the fields that have attracted the largest numbers of students over the past half century, such as communication, education, finance, hospitality, human resources, marketing and sales, nursing, and social work. But we must recognize that college students need better employment options than the jobs most of our graduates take. That means preparing many more graduates for the fast-growing jobs in artificial intelligence, computer science, environmental science, information security, machine learning, materials science, multimedia design and production, neuroscience, user interface design, web and application development, and the many areas in the biomedical sciences, like biostatistics, epidemiology, virology, and health informatics.

Almost all of these fields require additional education and experience beyond a bachelor's degree, but colleges need to lay the foundation that students need. How can we do that? Too often, the answer is ludicrous. Teaching all students to code does little to prepare them for the world of work or the new economy (unlike, say, offering training in Excel or project management or technical writing or fluency in a foreign language). Without in any way belittling the societal value of underpaid applied positions like medical coder, massage therapist, paralegal, phlebotomist, ultrasound technician, or health, nutrition, or fitness coach, a four-year college degree should open the door to something more.

Here are some strategies. Ensure that more students, especially more diverse students, attain the prerequisites for success in fields that require facility with advanced mathematics and statistics. Diverse fields now require facility with computational and algorithmic thinking, statistics, and the derivation of meaningful patterns in data sets, but only a small minority of our students attain a viable level of competency in these areas. Currently, if students haven't mastered calculus in high school or their freshman year, many STEM majors are unattainable. Might it not make sense to offer targeted programs and supplemental instruction sections and boot camps to ensure that larger numbers achieve competency in advanced mathematics?

Insert more authentic learning experiences and more making and doing opportunities into major pathways. Many employers in high-demand fields want evidence that a graduate can actually perform a particular job. The answer is to make project-based learning and internships an integral part of the major requirements so that a student can assemble a portfolio and a competency transcript. Also, place practicing professionals in the classroom. In computer science, a technologist-in-residence program can introduce timely topics into the curriculum, like Agile design, blockchain, distributed systems, and web development. Biomedical science programs might develop partnership arrangements with nearby medical schools, health science centers, and biotech companies to introduce majors to the breadth of opportunities within the health professions.

In addition, it's essential to address pipeline issues head-on. To bring more undergraduates who are women, African American, and Latinx into high-demand fields, reach out to students in closely related fields and forge interdisciplinary partnerships. Let's again take the example of computer science, where undergraduates who are women or are people of color are sorely underrepresented. Many undergraduates in biostatistics, emerging media, and statistics would benefit from greater engagement in computer science. The answer: create new entry points into the computer science major and minor, introduce these students to working professionals who can serve as mentors, give them early experience in project building with real-world data sets, and expose these undergrads at early stages of their college careers to programming and data analytics while underscoring the application of computer science in health care, education, and other fields that these students often find more engaging than coding.

Much as late-nineteenth-century colleges and universities recognized that student engagement and alumni loyalty required a vibrant campus life to build a sense of belonging and connection, we too need to reimagine the college experience for a generation that is far less interested than its predecessors in the traditional trappings of student life: football, fraternities and sororities, and homecoming. Intensifying this challenge are the growing numbers of commuting students who must balance their studies with work and caregiving responsibilities and can spend only limited time on campus. However, the contours of a new brand of campus life are already visible in student-organized international food fairs, take-a-professor-to-lunch programs, welcome week activities for new and returning students, pop-up concerts in classroom buildings and dining halls, and cocurricular student engagement activities that integrate visits to museums and performance venues into academic classes.

In the pandemic's wake, we need to produce future-proofed graduates who are also automation-proofed and recession-proofed. If we are to prepare our students for the post-COVID economy, then we need to ensure that they acquire certain hard skills, for example, in design, data literacy, project management, and research methods, as well as the so-called soft skills of judgment, abstraction, empathy, leadership, critical thinking, entrepreneurialism, emotional intelligence, and cross-cultural competence.

The first industrial revolution substituted machine labor for hand labor and water and steam power, and eventually fossil fuels and electricity for human and animal power. Today's economic revolution promises to augment the human mind with artificial intelligence, virtual reality, computer technologies, digitization, advanced data analytics, and self-monitoring smart machines. Ready or not, the time has come for our institutions to discuss how to better prepare students for this brave new world. This is an economic environment that holds out great promise but also a milieu from which far too many individuals risk being excluded for lack of the proper skill set.

———

Familiarity with the history of American higher education should serve to remind academics that many of today's challenges were familiar issues at American colleges from their inception. For example, from American higher education's earlier days, institutions have been preoccupied with motivating students and providing for their welfare and well-being. Somewhat similarly, the history of new educational technologies is largely a history of unrealized promise, littered with flawed techno-fads: overhead projectors, slide projectors, reading accelerators, B. F. Skinner's "teaching machines," film strips, educational television, videotapes, multimedia CDs, Second Life, PowerPoint slides, chat rooms, and clickers. All promised to revolutionize learning. None succeeded. Given this history, one must ask: Will today's personalized, adaptive software, virtual and augmented reality, and educational games be any different? These innovations certainly won't if they replace human interaction with programmed learning that consists of little more than skills and drills or edu-tainment and provides little in the way of substantive feedback. But technology can, of course, be used differently: to promote inquiry, enhance collaboration, offer case-based or challenge-based learning experiences, and above all, to give students opportunities to create digital stories, audio tours, annotated texts, virtual encyclopedias, and a host of other projects.

Above all, an understanding of history should awaken us to the fact that claims that higher education is in crisis are nothing new. Virtually every decade over the past century has produced books with such titles as *Higher Education in Crisis* (1995), *The Education Crisis* (1988), *Campus Unrest* (1970), *The Big Squeeze: Crisis on the Campus* (1946), and *Crisis on the Campus* (1900). The concerns have certainly shifted, but the belief that higher education is faced with impending calamity continues.

The key question, as the economist Irwin Feller has suggested, is whether this time is different: whether a confluence of factors—a long-term decline in per-student state funding, a rise in net tuition, stagnating federal funding of academic research, and the increasing costs of information technology, support services, shifts in student behavior, and compliance with government mandates—have combined to fundamentally threaten higher education's business models.

There is reason to think that yes, this time is different: that tuition and institutional expenses cannot continue to rise at the rate they have; that levels of student and familial debt have reached their limit; and that alternative providers and alternative credentials pose an unprecedented threat to higher education's monopoly over educational credentialing.[15]

And yet, I view history as ultimately reassuring. American higher education is currently in the midst of a profound moment of transition as it wrestles with its many challenges involving completion, cost, equity, and finances. But this is only the latest in a series of similar transitions. I feel confident that if campuses remain true to their guiding principles—democratic access, a relationship-rich education, and curricula that balance a liberal and a career-ready education—then they will successfully weather today's storms as they have successfully addressed past crises.

# 5

A Learner- and Learning-Centered Vision
for the Future of Higher Education

FOR ALL THE TALK ABOUT THE NEED to provide faster, cheaper, more convenient, and flexible paths into the workforce, most high school graduates still want an education that resembles a traditional on-campus college experience. But how can we afford to provide the vast majority with something like the education that the most privileged students who attend highly selective liberal arts colleges or private universities and flagship campuses or who participate in public universities' honors programs receive?

This challenge resembles the problems of access, affordability, and quality confronting the nation's health care system. Higher education must break this iron triangle, the notion first advanced by William Kissick in 1994 that there is an inevitable tradeoff among cost, access, and quality. Colleges and universities must increase affordability and access, quality, and student success all at once.

Colleges must provide an education that features more of the high-impact, educationally purposeful practices that are associated with higher rates of student engagement and academic and postgraduation success. This will require colleges to offer an education that is more immersive, participatory, and experiential, and that provides expanded opportunities for mentored research, internships, and field-, community-, and project-based learning. This education also needs to be more skills and outcomes oriented, and our campuses need to do a better job of ensuring that graduates acquire the communication, quantitative, critical thinking, and technical skills; cultural literacies; and competencies in the natural, life, and social sciences that we associate with a college graduate. Colleges must also provide more mentoring, scaffolding, and proactive academic and nonacademic advising and support than most students currently receive. In addition, colleges need to place many more undergraduates in a learning community, research cohort, or preprofessional interest group to cultivate a sense of belonging and connection and to embed career preparation across the undergraduate experience. And campuses must do all these things in a context of pinched resources and with students who require more support and aid than those in years past.

Creating a more learner- and learning-centered college or university is not a mission impossible. It turns out that the most effective, efficient solution to higher education's financial challenges is to increase retention and completion rates while reducing time to degree completion. Achieving these goals, however, will require the broad-access colleges and universities that serve the bulk of undergraduates to rethink their curricula, pedagogy, faculty roles, and support structures. It will also compel institutions to think more intentionally about their learning objectives, obligate departments to operate collaboratively, and require faculty to think of themselves in new ways: as learning architects and mentors, as well as teacher-scholars.

Meeting these challenges will also require institutions to create the data infrastructure that will allow advisers and faculty to identify, in near real time, students who are disengaged or off track and intervene proactively; that will help departments schedule courses at times that better meet the needs of today's post-traditional students who commute to campus and juggle academics with work and caregiving responsibilities; and that will identify curricular bottlenecks and inequities in student performance in essential gateway courses. Fine-grained data about student engagement, persistence, and performance can also help faculty better understand their students' learning needs and strengths, adjust their pedagogy accordingly, and bring more students to academic success.

Addressing today's learning challenges will require a technical infrastructure capable of supporting the kinds of online and hybrid learning that need to take place in the twenty-first century—an infrastructure that can support a wider range of activity and assessment types and that can facilitate more robust social, networking, and collaborative learning activities. A next-generation online experience must be able to support personalized, modularized, gamified, variable-paced learning; support advanced simulations and interactives and deliver high-fidelity, transmedia learning content on the go, in class, and in the field; support a broad range of assessment types, including those that are case-, challenge-, and team-based; connect students seamlessly to a community of care consisting of faculty, instructional facilitators, tutors, peer mentors, and advisers; and gather "click-level" data on student engagement, persistence, pace, performance, and other variables to improve an understanding of a particular student's learning needs and strengths and adjust the curriculum and pedagogy accordingly.

The challenges, however, are not exclusively or even primarily technological. The challenges are multidimensional, involving institutional policies, curricula, pedagogy, and services. Let's start with policy changes that are essential if colleges and universities are to remove institutional barriers to student success. These include the following:

- a more proactive admissions process, in which institutions identify, in cooperation with local school districts, prospective enrollees and preemptively offer them admissions spots plus financial aid or co-enrollment with those who decide to attend a local community college;
- a more robust onboarding process that provides new students with a degree plan, an adviser, and information about campus services;

- a transfer process that reduces delays in transcript evaluation, minimizes credit loss, and ensures course availability;
- the elimination of overly complicated degree requirements; and
- the adoption of practices like block scheduling and expanded availability of hybrid and online courses to better meet the needs of commuting and part-time students and those who work or are caregivers.

Another major challenge is curricular. Too many students find today's curricula insufficiently engaging (particularly at the foundational level), incoherent, irrelevant, and lacking in a clear value proposition. In addition, too few curricular pathways offer many windows into future careers. Many students would benefit from a very different curricular model: a clearly delineated, structured pathway consisting of synergistic courses with well-defined learning objectives. Such a curriculum would be developmental by design, with a careful sequencing of courses to build skills and competencies and open many windows into future career options. However, collaborative design of the curriculum, especially across departmental lines, remains extremely rare.

For institutions, a bloated, fragmented curriculum is extremely costly, featuring many low-enrollment, highly specialized boutique courses. Such a curriculum diverts faculty from participating in the high-impact practices, like supervised research and project-based learning, that can transform student lives. Yet optimizing the curriculum is extremely difficult, since it raises sensitive issues about workload, instructional staffing, and faculty autonomy in course design.

Were I king, I'd urge faculty members to think much more intentionally about the learning outcomes they expect of a college graduate. I consider some of those learning objectives to be self-evident. At the college level, illiteracy isn't the inability to read and write; it's more insidious. It's mathematical and statistical, financial, geographical, historical, psychological, cultural, sociological, psychological, and scientific. It's innumeracy, ahistoricism, ethnocentrism, and essentialism and other forms of conceptual, analytical, and cognitive distortion.

To encourage breadth, most colleges and universities require undergraduates to fulfill a series of distribution requirements, which, typically, can be met by dozens if not hundreds of departmental courses. These are usually discipline-based surveys or more narrow and specialized courses. As a result, few students graduate with the sweeping civic, cultural, social scientific, mathematical and statistical, and scientific knowledge and skills that are the hallmark of a liberal arts education.

Wouldn't it make more sense to rethink lower division offerings and make them broader, more interdisciplinary, and better aligned with our learning aims? Thus, a course on social scientific literacy might introduce undergraduates to the methods that social scientists use to collect, evaluate, and analyze qualitative and quantitative data; to the interpretive frameworks that these scholars use to understand observed facts and behavior and other social phenomena; to the tools and techniques that social scientists use to transform data into useful information; and to how social scientific data, findings, and theories are used (or misused) in policy formulation; in clinical, educational, and therapeutic interventions; and in personal life. Somewhat similarly, a course on the frontiers of science that is modeled on a mandatory core curriculum class offered by Columbia University might look at artificial intelligence and machine learning; the brain and behavior; cosmology; evolutionary biology; global climate change; and quantum mechanics, while introducing students to scientific methods.

The humanities, in turn, would benefit from introductory courses that cover the enduring issues that these disciplines deal with—aesthetics, divinity, ethics, evil, free will, and moral and political philosophy—and those that are more timely, such as reparations for past injustices, structural and systemic inequities and biases, and what the current generation owes to the future, as well as the methods and interpretive frameworks that the humanities use to examine texts, artworks, music, photographs, and other forms of creative expression.

We also need to update pedagogy. Currently, faculty have no sufficiently strong incentives to alter their instructional approaches, nor do instructors receive the support from course designers, instructional technologists, and assessment specialists that would help them redesign their classes. Lacking clear measures of student engagement or learning outcomes, or a reward structure that values teaching innovation, faculty have few inducements to apply the emerging lessons of the learning sciences to curricular and course design, pedagogy, or assessment.

Certainly, instructors need to adopt techniques that have been shown to enhance student learning and engagement and to adopt more formative assessments that will help them identify and remediate content and skill deficiencies, close achievement gaps, and build on students' prior knowledge and skills. Campuses need to do a better job of helping instructors redesign their classes to make them less faculty centric and more dynamic, engaging, inclusive, immersive, interactive, participatory, and learner and learning centered. Institutions need to do a better job of supporting faculty to incorporate more hands-on learning, group work, and inquiry and project-based activities into their courses. Improving pedagogy needs to be a top institutional priority.

In addition to strengthening instructional practices by adopting evidence-based active learning pedagogies, institutions need to integrate other kinds of learning experiences into their course inventory: classes that do not rely largely on lectures or even discussion. Studio courses, clinicals, field- and community-based and service learning, makerspaces, earn-learn experiences (such as co-ops), mentored research, and supervised internships offer proven ways to better engage students and prepare them for life postgraduation. Other kinds of learning experiences can also be valuable. These include communities of inquiry—interdisciplinary groups of students and faculty who jointly investigate a major societal challenge, such as pandemics in world history or societal inequalities. They also include solver communities—teams that devise solutions to the real-world problems faced by a local community or a nonprofit organization.

Another key challenge is to improve mentoring, advising, and academic and nonacademic support services. Even at the most selective, best-endowed institutions, most students rarely receive the kinds of intensive, timely, substantive, and constructive feedback they need to truly master essential skills. Instructors need better training and support if they are to provide the actionable advice that students need. Students, especially the first-generation college-goers who constitute a growing share of the undergraduate student body, need more personalized learning support and greater professional academic and career advising than they currently receive. A tiered approach to academic advising and mentoring holds great promise. To better meet students' academic needs, this approach combines access to tutors, peer mentors, organized study groups, learning support centers (typically in the areas of foreign languages, math, science, and writing), and designated supplemental instruction sections.

To better address nonacademic challenges, a case management approach has demonstrated promising results. A care coordinator can help students navigate difficult transitions, including changes of major or transfers to or from another institution. A life coach can help students tackle financial problems, family emergencies, and shifts in job schedules. Greater use of peers and near peers—as tutors and as leaders of study sections, team-based learning experiences, and supplemental instruction opportunities—can augment student support and feedback while expanding on-campus employment, a proven contributor to student success.

Then there's a need to embed career preparation throughout the undergraduate experience. Many students would benefit from systematic exposure to career options and formal assessments of their strengths and interests. Undergraduates also need to become familiar with the skills that particular occupations require and develop a realistic path toward entering into these careers.

To be sure, other steps can further contribute to affordability and student success. These include better curricular and course alignment among high schools, community colleges, and four-year institutions; and exploratory majors or meta-majors to open windows into particular fields of study. Four-year degree plans prior to the first semester, participation in a learning community, and ready access to emergency financial aid can also make a big difference in raising graduation rates and reducing time to degree completion.

Can we break through the iron triangle in ways that are cost-effective and financially sustainable? Yes. But the task won't be easy, for the steps we need to take are anything but business as usual. Three key barriers to tackling higher education's cost, quality, and student success challenges include initiative fatigue, an absence of accountability, and, perhaps most important of all, diffusion of responsibility. When everyone is collectively responsible for addressing critical challenges, the "bystander" effect kicks in: no single group takes ownership of a problem. The results are inertia, finger-pointing, and buck passing. But affordability, quality, student success, and employability aren't someone else's problem. These are a collective challenge that deserves all the attention faculty, staff, and campus leaders can muster.

William Gibson, the essayist and author associated with a science fiction genre known as cyberpunk, once said, "The future is already here—it's just not very evenly distributed."[1]

In thinking about higher education, there's much truth to that iconic statement. Isolated examples of successful initiatives abound across higher education, but they are insufficiently publicized and, consequently, rarely imitated. In the pages that follow, I will offer proven, practical steps that campuses can take to improve students' academic outcomes and postgraduation success. As we shall see, the process of institutional change cannot be imposed from the top down, nor can it be accomplished one instructor or department at a time. It is a collective action problem that requires a coordinated institutional response. If colleges and universities are to innovate, all stakeholders must embrace a shared vision, develop a sense of urgency, recognize the opportunities that innovation will open up, and contribute to a broader process of institutional transformation. This can be done—indeed, it must be done—if our colleges and universities are to successfully meet the needs of a shifting student body.

# 6

---

# Thinking outside the Box

AMERICAN HIGHER EDUCATION LARGELY CONFORMS to a series of conventions. These include the fixed-length semester, two or three standardized start dates, the credit hour, the course, distribution requirements, academic departments, department-based majors, and letter grades. Under this model, a typical course is worth three credit hours—with three hours of contact with an instructor and six hours devoted to outside-of-class study. An associate's degree requires a student to accumulate 60 credit hours; and a bachelor's degree, 120. About a third of a student's academic experience consists of general education courses to ensure breadth, roughly a third in a major to guarantee depth, and a third in electives to facilitate student choice. In other words, like a matryoshka doll (those nested Russian dolls of decreasing size placed one inside the other), a college education is nested inside a series of boxes.

To borrow the language of the educational historian Larry Cuban, these conventions constitute the "grammar" of higher education.[1] Today, many of these conventions are subject to severe criticism, especially from online providers, whether for profit or nonprofit. A number of these criticisms are well taken: that the current model fails to serve nontraditional students with complicated lives well, or to focus sufficiently on learning and employment outcomes. These boxes, we are told with some justification, are not designed to meet student learning needs, but rather, reflect other priorities: faculty interests, research concerns, cost, enrollment considerations, flexibility, and the like. This one-size-fits-all structure also discourages cross-discipline collaboration and prevents many students from progressing according to their individual pace. Yet with a few notable exceptions, this structure persists. Higher education remains firmly encased within its traditional boxes.

What if we were to think outside those boxes? If we were no longer forced to think in terms of courses, credit hours, semesters, or traditional degrees, then we could free ourselves to imagine other possibilities. Instead of organizing students' academic experience around stand-alone courses, we might envision other kinds of learning experiences that are more experiential, immersive, and project oriented, alongside shorter modules and skills-based workshops. We might supplement traditional degrees with other kinds of credentials, including badges, specializations, and certifications. We might substitute more integrated career pathways or interdisciplinary or individualized programs of study for traditional department-based majors. Ditto for the fixed-length semester. Once we break away from the notion of a quarter or semester, we can envisage more flexible term lengths that better conform to students' learning needs, whether accelerated or slower paced. We need to recognize that many students who are not ready for an exam on October 15 might succeed on November 1. We can also consider more flexible start dates.

Too often, we find ourselves trapped inside an educational paradigm and fail to see alternatives or to appreciate their advantages. Many of the roughly 40 percent of students at four-year institutions who never graduate might well benefit from different, more flexible approaches to higher education.

Most colleges resemble one another in their physical landscape, architecture, organizational structure, institutional calendar, faculty hierarchy, curricular and extracurricular offerings, and even their mission statements. Sociologists use the term "isomorphism" to describe these similarities, which are a product of shared norms, professional socialization, accreditation and regulatory pressures, and parental and student expectations. Mid-tier colleges and universities are especially prone to isomorphism as they seek to emulate the sector's leaders.

As a thought experiment, we might ask how campuses might change if they were to become truly learner- and learning-centered institutions that placed student needs and aspirations first. They'd embed career preparation across the college experience. They'd provide more advising and mentoring and offer better support services. They'd better address students' basic needs for food, housing, health care, child care, and transportation and better handle the unpredictable disruptions that all too frequently interrupt students' education. They'd provide wrap-around academic and nonacademic supports, including intensive, personalized academic, financial, and career advising and ready access to supplemental instruction. They'd eliminate obstacles to timely completion, including outdated or irrelevant graduation requirements and arbitrary barriers to transfer.

The educational model we have embraced, which consists of a smorgasbord of disconnected courses coupled with very limited advising and mentoring and graduation requirements that can be met in multiple ways without much attention to learning and skills outcomes, works well for some students, but certainly not for all. It maximizes options, flexibility, and serendipity but makes little effort to help students or their families understand the purposes of a college education that goes beyond career preparation.

We are at one of those rare moments of fluidity when it is possible to think outside the box. Many instructors are experimenting with alternatives to high-stakes examinations, including frequent low-stakes assessments and a multi-tiered assessment ecosystem that ranges from recurrent checks for understanding (to monitor lower level thinking skills, such as recall) to performance-based assessments (which involve application, analysis, and evaluation), and team- and challenge-based activities (to assess creativity and problem-solving abilities). Such an approach has the beneficial side effect of discouraging students from punctuating long periods of disengagement with unhealthy cramming for exams.

Such approaches alter the traditional instructional staffing model and, to a certain extent, the role of an instructor. Faculty, in such contexts, demonstrate skills less apparent in conventional classroom environments. In team-based courses, faculty must serve as learning architects, mentors, and instructional scaffolders, as well as content experts and providers of feedback and evaluation. Generally, such classes are augmented by a robust online experience and the faculty members are assisted by one or more instructional facilitators. Such an approach can allow a faculty member to work with more students than in a typical "small" class, but with far fewer than in a large lecture hall, while ensuring that the students engage in active learning and receive the substantial feedback they need to hone their skills and competencies.

One of postmodernist thought's key insights is that many practices that seem natural or inevitable are anything but. Many of higher education's boxes are constructs, reinforced by tradition and custom. Many may well have outlived their usefulness. Let's take advantage of this moment of fluidity and reimagine education not as it is, but as it might be.

———

Of all the boxes that colleges and universities need to rethink, the most important, in my view, involves the design of the curriculum. When I look at the curricula at various colleges and universities, and compare it to the requirements-free education that I encountered at Oberlin in the early 1970s, I am struck by how detailed and prescriptive general education has become.

Harvard, in 1900, had only one required class for graduation: a single course in rhetoric and composition. Today, in stark contrast, at the University of California, Santa Cruz, an undergraduate must fulfill requirements in the following fifteen categories: Cross-Cultural Analysis, Ethnicity and Race, Interpreting Arts and Media,

Mathematical and Formal Reasoning, Scientific Inquiry, Statistical Reasoning, Textual Analysis and Interpretation, Environmental Awareness, Human Behavior, Technology and Society, Collaborative Endeavor, Creative Process, Service Learning, Composition, and Disciplinary Communication. Each category is important. Sure, it would be possible to nitpick, check for omissions and call for an even longer list. After all, Santa Cruz does not require courses in history, a foreign language, or government, nor are students mandated to take courses that ensure that they encounter masterworks of art, literature, music, philosophy, or moral and political theory. Nothing guarantees that students will attend a concert, a dance performance, a play, or an opera, or visit a museum.

Also missing are requirements that students are exposed to various forms of pedagogy: collaborative, experiential, field-based, immersive, inquiry-based, integrative, multidisciplinary, project- or problem-based, research-based learning or learning through making or doing. Nor is familiarity with modes of interpretation and methodology explicitly required, such as those grounded in particular disciplines or in the latest currents of cultural studies, such as critical race theory, feminism, Marxism, postcolonialism, postmodernism, poststructuralism, or semiotics. Then, too, there are no explicit requirements that students take a seminar, a lab, a practicum, a proseminar, a tutorial, or a performance class, or that they develop social emotional skills (including relationship skills, social awareness, empathy, and responsible decision-making) or learn about the job market and career possibilities or acquire marketable skills.

I mention all this not to pick on a particular university, or to call for a lengthier and more comprehensive list of requirements, but rather to prompt reflection on the nature of general education today. We might ask: Do these institutional requirements reflect a coherent philosophy of education or a consensus about educational goals, or are the requirements best understood as the product of political negotiations? Are the requirements reasonably easy to navigate, or do they make it difficult for students to graduate in a timely manner, especially those who transfer from community colleges? Are the general education (gen ed) requirements generic, or do they speak to a particular institution's identity and distinctive mission? Does the gen ed curriculum actually ensure that students acquire the breadth of knowledge, the command of skills, or the habits of mind that are expected of a college graduate, or does it consist merely of box-checking?

I know firsthand how hard it is to achieve consensus about institutional requirements; and given the number of stakeholders and interest groups involved, it's amazing that the faculty reach any agreement at all. Over the past few years, many institutions have reconsidered their gen ed requirements. Sometimes, this reconsideration is driven by the reaccreditation process. At other times, it is a branding exercise, as a private institution seeks to make a name for itself in today's highly competitive higher ed environment. In still other instances, it involves repackaging and relabeling an existing curriculum, to give the requirements a contemporary sheen. In still others, curricular redesign serves as an excuse for reducing the number of required courses in foreign languages, the natural sciences, and mathematics. But in many instances, a review of the gen ed portion of the curriculum is a serious endeavor, motivated by a desire to give the lower division experience more coherence, thematic unity, and relevance, and to provide a clearer rationale for the courses students must take.

Certain themes run through gen ed redesign within institutions that take this exercise seriously. First of all, instead of concentrating general education during the first two years, the requirements are dispersed throughout the entire undergraduate experience. Students often must fulfill a writing-within-the-discipline requirement and complete a capstone course or senior project. Then, too, these institutions typically require students to participate in a number of outside-the-classroom activities. These range from required attendance at lectures and performances to more ambitious requirements that may include experiential learning, an internship, or international or intercultural exposure. Then there are requirements that students engage in applied learning. This may include a service-learning or civic engagement activity, a global or cross-cultural learning activity, a collaborative problem-solving project, or a creative activity.

In redesigning their gen ed curriculum, colleges and universities have generally settled on one of a number of popular strategies. Some have adopted a competencies or literacies focus: instead of emphasizing specific bodies of content, the curriculum is redesigned around skills, modes of inquiry, and twenty-first-century literacies (critical thinking, financial literacy, information literacy, second-language proficiency, scientific and technological literacy, media literacy, data fluency, citizenship and empowerment, wellness, and communication across borders).

Others have adopted a career preparation focus: by requiring courses on work and the workplace, a field experience, an internship, and a project that demonstrates the student's creativity, problem-solving acumen, and ability to apply skills, the institution seeks to produce job-ready graduates. Perhaps the most widely publicized example is at the City University of New York's Guttman Community College in its first-year Ethnography of Work course, which gives students the opportunity to investigate a range of careers and understand the job market and the nature of work into today's highly volatile economy. Students also acquire ethnographic skills involving research design, observation, and interviewing; examine workplace and work-life challenges; and participate in a work-placement program.

Still other campuses have adopted a thematic approach: for example, Northern Illinois University organizes its core curriculum around themes such as health and wellness, social justice and diversity, and sustainability. Yet another approach emphasizes real-world relevance: undergraduates are required to take a cluster of courses that tackle a grand challenge, a big question, or an enduring or contemporary issue from the perspective of multiple disciplines. By addressing real-world problems through an interdisciplinary lens, institutions hope to help students understand the multidimensional nature of problem-solving.

Let me suggest several alternative approaches that might help meet the needs of today's extraordinarily diverse students who have their own goals and interests. One is a pathways approach in which faculty create a structured "vertical" in certain high-demand fields of study. This approach requires faculty across disciplines to work together to design a more coherent, synergistic curriculum for students who wish to become accountants or engineers or physicians or social workers or teachers, with each course contributing to the production of a well-rounded professional. The University of Texas Rio Grande Valley experimented with a biomedical sciences pathway that included courses in the history of medicine, the literature of pain and illness, medical ethics, representations of the body, and other humanities and social sciences courses that sought to nurture professional identity formation, with a goal of producing health professionals well versed in the full range of knowledge and skills we expect of a doctor or nurse. Even though a pathways approach can be very difficult to implement, it has the great advantage of offering students a more cohesive, coherent, synergistic, and intentionally designed roadmap to a degree and a postgraduation career.

Given the fact that many institutions find it exceedingly difficult or impossible to agree on a uniform gen ed curriculum, why not let interdisciplinary groups of faculty devise their own gen ed tracks? Harvard's Humanities 10 and 11 and its Social Studies 10 courses, Yale's Directed Studies program, and Purdue's Cornerstone certificate program exemplify such an approach. Under this model, groups of faculty create their own ideal lower division curriculum. This approach has proven to be quite successful, attracting a lot of undergraduate interest. Typically, these initiatives offer sweeping introductions to classic texts and frameworks of analysis courses that give motivated students a rigorous way to meet key requirements that goes far beyond disciplinary-based introductory courses.

A handful of liberal arts colleges—like Hiram College, with its Urgent Challenges Curriculum—now offer general education pathways that underscore and reinforce the school's distinctive institutional identity. Arthur Levine's Bradford Plan for a Practical Liberal Arts

Education pioneered this approach. It combined the application of liberal arts skills through internships, applied minors, study of work and workplaces, senior projects, and "outside-the-classroom" cocurricular activities. Although Bradford College ultimately succumbed to debt and declining enrollment, it demonstrated the possibility of designing a curriculum around a collective vision.

Another option is to let individual students design their own lower division educational pathways, an approach instituted, with some variation, at Amherst, Bennington, Brown, Hampshire, Sarah Lawrence, Smith, and Wesleyan. Viewed by its proponents as a way to affirm students' freedom, creativity, and individuality and produce agile, independent thinkers, this approach is often regarded skeptically by those who doubt that students receive the kind of active advising and faculty engagement they need if they are to achieve curricular breadth and tackle difficult and unfamiliar courses outside their comfort zone.

An alternative to explicit requirements is to offer students opportunities to acquire special skills that can be denoted on their transcripts. These might involve certificates in data analysis, design, project management, research methods, sustainability, or even career preparedness (which might involve workshops in etiquette, job-search techniques, leadership, presentation skills, and résumé writing).

My own preference is to let a thousand flowers bloom. Interesting ideas abound. Much as the economy has embraced customization and individuation, might it not make sense to give students options within a broad set of expectations? I find it ironic that a generation of faculty who began their studies during the 1970s and 1980s, when many requirements were eliminated, are now exiting institutions that have imposed requirements not radically dissimilar to those they rebelled against.

If we think outside the conventional boxes, we can see how we might enhance the quality of the education we offer. Faculty recognize that students' communication skills benefit greatly from substantial amounts of writing. But many faculty members limit the amount of assigned writing because drafting comments and grading is too time-consuming. But one can imagine other ways to give students more opportunities to write while ensuring that they receive valuable feedback. These might include peer or near-peer feedback, using carefully designed rubrics, or even a degree of autofeedback. Breaking free from legacy models liberates us by expanding our options. We might blur the lines separating the campus from the outside world by integrating more experiential learning into educational pathways, whether in the form of internships or e-internships, clinical or field experiences, or service learning, and further blur the line between high school and postsecondary education by integrating foundational courses tightly aligned with college expectations into secondary school.

The boundaries between face-to-face and digital learning, too, might blur. Instead of relegating one modality to knowledge transfer and the other to active learning, we would ensure that both the online and face-to-face components of a class involve highly interactive forms of learning. Formalized course-sharing and cross-registration arrangements (modeled perhaps on the way that the Big Ten Academic Alliance collectively offers over a hundred less commonly taught languages) greatly expand student access to specialized courses while keeping education affordable.

## Rethinking the Curriculum

Read virtually any college mission statement and you will discover that it resembles a vision put forward by Harvard's dean of the faculty, Henry Rosovsky, in 1976. In his words, a college graduate "must be able to communicate with precision, cogency and force" and "should have achieved depth in some field of knowledge" and have a "critical appreciation of the ways in which we gain knowledge and understanding of the universe, of society and of ourselves." As he later added, "an educated person" was someone who has an "informed acquaintance" with literature and the arts, history, social and philosophical analysis, science and mathematics, and foreign languages and culture.[2]

Do we truly produce graduates who can write well, speak clearly and compellingly, or grasp statistics? Or who have a basic understanding of the frontiers of science or a familiarity with world literature or the visual and performing arts? Or who can think like a historian or a social scientist or natural scientist? Or who can effectively collaborate in highly diverse groups? If we do, it's less a product of a concerted plan than serendipity. That's why I think we need to incentivize faculty to offer courses that are broader and less discipline specific than those typically offered in the lower division.

What if we were to embrace the notion that a key purpose of the lower division undergraduate curriculum was to teach undergraduates to think like a humanist, a social scientist, and a natural scientist? In 1959, the British scientist and novelist C. P. Snow published a hugely influential book entitled *The Two Cultures*. In that volume, he argued that intellectual life in the West was divided into two mutually antagonistic subcultures: one rooted in the arts and humanities, the other in science and engineering. Snow expressed a deep concern about what he saw as a widening gulf of misunderstanding and mistrust, of suspicion and distrust, between scientists and nonscientists. In Snow's view, humanists and scientists existed in separate cultures that have "almost ceased to communicate at all."[3] Science conceived of itself as dispassionately objective, while the humanities and arts emphasized sensibility, values, and the influence of culture. The breakdown in communication between the sciences and the humanities was vividly illustrated by a controversy that erupted after the mathematical physicist Alan Sokal revealed that an article he had published in the humanities journal *Social Text* in 1996 was a hoax. To Sokal, this incident revealed the lack of "standards of intellectual rigor in certain precincts of the American academic humanities."[4] This charge provoked an outcry from many humanists.

The gap between the sciences and the humanities carries profound social and intellectual consequences. On the one hand, science and technology, without a humanistic understanding of aesthetics and ethical values, risks becoming mere scientism: soulless, antisocial, and lacking an awareness of human values. Likewise, the humanities without an understanding of contemporary science is impoverished indeed; it is necessarily ignorant of the most recent conceptions of causality, interactivity, and representation.[5]

A humanistic understanding of human life cannot leave science aside. After all, science is central to cultural self-understanding. Students in the arts and humanities benefit enormously from learning the language, methods, and concepts of science. One of the academy's aims must be to encourage science students to contemplate the legal, ethical, social, and philosophical implications of cutting-edge scientific research into fields such as genetic engineering, new reproductive technologies, and animal and human experimentation. At the same time, students outside of science, technology, engineering, and math (STEM) fields need to learn the language, methods, and concepts of science. All students, in turn, need to understand that scientists and humanists wrestle with many of the same fundamental questions, even as they rely on distinctive methodologies, languages, and traditions. We must, in short, bridge the divide that separates the humanities and STEM majors, and ensure that both groups understand the scientific method, the nature and limits of scientific knowledge claims, and scientific ethics. One perspective is incomplete without the other.

Much hand-wringing has been done over this cultural divide— which is, of course, part of a larger fragmentation and specialization of human understanding. Yet despite widespread concern about the chasm separating the sciences and the humanities, gaps in learning have in fact widened and proliferated. Among the challenges we face is to ensure that all undergraduates achieve a basic literacy in the arts and humanities, the social sciences, mathematics, and the brain, life, natural, and physical sciences. That will require campuses to rethink their requirements, their curricula, and their pedagogies.

———

Let's begin by considering how we might ensure that all of our graduates achieve a viable level of scientific literacy. I think it's fair to say that much of the general public today feels ill equipped to assess the reliability or significance of scientific findings or make sense of how these fit into a larger portrait of nature's evolution and workings. Scientific understanding has become a matter of faith: it doesn't rest on genuine knowledge or understanding. It requires the public to defer to scientific authority, a difficult task in a culture suspicious of elites claiming special expertise. We need to make sure that all college graduates, not just those in STEM fields, are capable of reading and understanding articles in newspaper and magazine science sections, can intelligently evaluate recommendations made by doctors and medical scientists, and can assess public policy debates involving science.

Americans once revered science and scientists. That, I think it's fair to say, is no longer the case. Many people do, but a substantial number don't. Nor is scientific skepticism confined to religious fundamentalists or the conspiracy minded. Retractions, fudged data, conflicts of interest, irreproducible results, shifting theories, and highly publicized disagreements, compounded by the pandemic, all reinforce distrust. So, too, does the all-too-common tendency of scientific and medical authorities to move beyond agreed-upon facts in making policy recommendations. Vaccine hesitancy, climate change denial, and a belief in the efficacy of unsupported alternative medical treatments are just a few of the by-products not only of American culture's profound mistrust of expertise, but of the perception among some that bias, political and otherwise, has infected and tarnished science and medicine.

I, for one, am increasingly convinced that one or two introductory courses in biology or geology is not the best way to instill scientific literacy. We need a different approach. Such an approach must acknowledge up front that suspicion of science has deep historical roots. Scientific racism and Eugenics are just two examples of how science has served as a tool for justifying and perpetuating social distinctions and discriminatory policies that rest on pseudoscientific understandings of race, ethnicity, gender, and class. There are similar examples from the history of scientific medicine, which includes wrenching examples of grotesque surgeries and disparate treatment of pain and illness rooted in ideas that were subsequently repudiated. In other words, science mustn't be fetishized. It is vulnerable to group-think and bias.[6]

Instilling scientific literacy within nonscience majors requires, I believe, a multitrack approach that combines an understanding of the scientific method and the nature and limits of scientific claims and hands-on experience in scientific inquiry. Students must understand, first, that science is not simply a body of knowledge—it's a methodology that depends on evidence, observation, experimentation, the development and testing of falsifiable hypotheses, and revision. Scientific conclusions and insights are provisional, and open to questioning, refutation, and modification. The scientific community is collectively responsible for evaluating scientific conclusions and correcting errors. Students must understand that one of science's most distinctive features lies in its willingness to question and test all scientific claims. Students need to be introduced to scientific reasoning and the scientific method, the difference between scientific and nonscientific thinking, and how the scientific community seeks to avoid bias and wild speculation. Students must also learn about scientific ethics, and the various ways that scientists seek to avoid error and maintain research integrity. It's essential that they understand that fabricating, falsifying, or misrepresenting research data is *verboten*, that human subjects must give informed consent before taking part in a research project, and that scientists must publicly acknowledge conflicts of interest and recognize their responsibility to respect people's privacy and confidentiality.[7]

––––––

Let's turn to the way that colleges and universities might strengthen the teaching of mathematics. According to Robert Parris Moses, the civil rights hero who helped organize the 1964 Mississippi Freedom Summer project that registered thousands of Black voters and who died in 2022 at the age of 86, mathematics is itself a civil rights issue, "a passport to full citizenship for disenfranchised people" and an issue of "justice and equity." In today's data- and technology-rich,

STEM-oriented society, those without quantitative and statistical literacy, he believed, were relegated to the back of another bus.[8]

Civic equity and access to advanced employment ultimately hinge on mastery of math. But in California as recently as 2019 just 34 percent of students overall, and 18 percent of Black students and 20 percent of Latinx students, met or exceeded the state's math standards. California isn't alone. In 2015, just 25 percent of twelfth-grade students nationwide performed at or above proficiency level in math, according to the National Assessment of Educational Progress. It's not surprising, then, that math requirements turn out to be the single biggest academic barrier to graduation. In 2017, 110,000 of 170,000 undergraduates placed in remedial math never, ever fulfilled the math requirement for an associate's degree. According to one study of community college students, 50 to 60 percent of disparities in degree completion is driven by which students are placed in remedial math classes.[9]

Yet despite over thirty years of math education reform and the steadfast efforts of reformers like Bob Moses and his fellow MacArthur "genius" Uri Treisman, we have not yet figured out how to bring all students to a minimum viable level of mathematical understanding. Since math is a "promoter of possibility," we must do better.[10]

Why aren't high schools and colleges more successful? According to one school of thought, this is because traditional math instruction turned off many students by stressing rote memorization of "'meaningless formulas' and procedures; along with being boring, it was disconnected from students' lives and experiences."[11] From this perspective, the answer lies in rethinking math pedagogies and redesigning math pathways. Innovators assert, first of all, that quantitative literacy requires not simply memorization and the mechanistic application of a set of procedures and formulas, but conceptual understanding and mathematical reasoning, which can only be achieved through inquiry, discussion, collaborative problem solving, and the conceptual understanding that can be achieved by asking students to formulate explanations.[12]

Another guiding principle is that math instruction should engage students in meaningful and authentic tasks that utilize real-world problems and everyday situations to help students master key math concepts, tools, and techniques. A third principle is that effective and engaging teaching requires math instructors to improve their ability to explain, illustrate, and lead inquiries, discussions, and projects that involve real-life issues. A fourth principle is that math curricula should align with students' interests and prospective majors, with science-focused students on a track that leads from algebra to calculus; those in the social sciences instead introduced to data science and statistics; and those in the arts, humanities, and applied fields to quantitative reasoning.

We shouldn't be surprised that in today's highly polarized political environment, pedagogy itself has become embroiled in conflict. Critics charge that the new "new math," with its emphasis on thought processes and written and oral communication and its shift away from teacher-directed instruction downplays the importance of mastering the step-by-step procedures that are essential to mathematical problem solving, substitutes estimation and thinking strategies for actual computation, and devalues the importance of memorization and practice and creates the illusion that there are no right or wrong answers. Many fear that this approach will create a two-tiered system that will exclude students from low-income backgrounds from opportunities in STEM fields.

Without embroiling myself in this dispute, I do think it's fair to say that in today's world, numeracy is about as important as competence in reading and writing. How, then, can we best achieve much higher levels of quantitative and statistical literacy? One exciting strategy that a growing number of math instructors have pursued is to link math and social justice issues. These instructors have sought to engage students and demonstrate math's relevance by studying racial and class disparities, crime and incarceration, inequalities of wealth and income, gerrymandering and ranked-choice voting, immigration, the distribution of disaster aid and college entrance exam scores, the relationship between campaign spending and votes received, and environmental issues using algebraic functions, data visualization techniques, mathematical modeling, and statistical methods.[13]

Using math as a window into social realities is sometimes derided as "woke math," and there can be no doubt that there are instances when this approach devolves into discussions of power, identity, and oppression rather than actual math instruction. The noted historian of education, Diane Ravitch, then in her conservative phase, regarded "social justice mathematics" (or what she dismissed as "ethnomathematics") as anathema, a fusion of political correctness and lax educational standards, and a shameless, bald-faced attempt to bring an explicitly political agenda into the classroom.[14]

Does this pedagogical approach help students master math? We simply don't know. Is teaching math through a social justice lens creating a two-tiered system, in which affluent students learn "college prep math" while those from low-income backgrounds learn "real-world math" that ill prepares them for success in advanced college STEM courses? Again, we don't know. In the end, the efficacy of this approach is an empirical question that requires randomized controlled trials.

At stake in today's controversies over math education is a fundamental concern over equitable access to many of the fastest growing fields. After all, students who lack a solid background in calculus and statistics are not only closed out of programs in business analytics and financial technology, engineering, epidemiology and health informatics, machine learning, and the quantitative social sciences, but even medical, dental, and nursing school.

Among the bitterly contested debates today are questions like these: Should all students be exposed to advanced mathematics, or should there be different pathways for those who do not intend to enter math-intensive fields? Will differentiated math tracks—with one path leading to calculus and another to statistics and culturally relevant mathematics—become "pathways for students of color" that reinforce racial and class-based inequalities? Underlying these controversies is an even bigger issue: Is it possible to bring many more students, not just those gifted in mathematics, to an appropriate level of competence? Are some students simply more talented in math and should they be placed in more demanding math classes, while other students aren't "math persons," and would benefit from a different pathway better aligned with their interests? Society doesn't expect all students to be equally talented in art, music, or athletics. Should we expect all students to become proficient in math and statistics?[15]

There can be no doubt that many Americans find math difficult and anxiety inducing. According to one widely reported statistic from 2009, 17 percent of the general population has high levels of anxiety involving mathematics. Anywhere from 3 to 7 percent are thought to suffer from a math-specific learning disability like dyscalculia.[16] This is the math equivalent of dyslexia, and those with dyscalculia find it difficult to grasp number-related concepts, perform accurate math calculations, and reason and problem solve with numbers or statistics. Dyslcalculia, however, doesn't explain gaps in math performance in the general population, which appear to be more a matter of the quality and forms of instruction and deeply embedded attitudes and beliefs. This has led math education reformers to the conclusion that math achievement can be raised through better teaching, mindset training, extra attention, and a more relevant and culturally responsive curriculum.[17]

So, what does this mean for colleges and universities? Our campuses need to recognize that fluency with quantification, probability, statistics, and data is essential. Facility with analytics, data mining, data visualization, informatics, and probability isn't a luxury. It's necessary. A college graduate should be able to locate and understand data sources; derive meaningful information from data; interpret data visualizations (including graphs and charts); critically assess, analyze, and evaluate statistical claims; and recognize when data are misrepresented.

Also, colleges and universities should infuse numeracy and statistics across the curriculum. Just as writing is too important to be left to one or two courses in rhetoric and composition, so, too, math is too important to be left to a few introductory math classes. Many disciplines outside math are well equipped to incorporate mathematics and statistical analysis into many of their classes. Even humanities courses can integrate computational thinking, data mining, data visualization, geospatial analysis, time series network analysis, provenance, data privacy, 3-D digital reconstructions, and simulation modeling into their classes. Institutions should offer more opportunities for students to take discipline and career-aligned courses in applied mathematics. These include classes in biostatistics, climatology, computational modeling of behavior, computational social science, epidemiology, finance, genomics, investment analytics, materials science, medicine, risk management, and supply chain analysis.

Wellesley College's Quantitative Reasoning Program makes an assertion that I think we should all embrace: "The ability to think clearly and critically about quantitative issues is imperative in contemporary society." While it may not be literally true that "quantitative reasoning is required in virtually all academic fields . . . [and] most every profession," as the Wellesley website claims, the fact is that in an increasingly data-driven society, the ability to analyze data, statistics, and charts and graphs is a key component of critical thinking. Mathematical illiteracy imposes a glass ceiling that limits possibilities and potential. We mustn't echo Teen Talk Barbie, with its dismissive catch phrase: "Math class is tough." Yes, math is tough but it's also vital. As Galileo quite rightly observed in 1623, the book of nature is written in the language of mathematics.[18] Quantitative literacy needs to become a shared responsibility that permeates the curriculum.[19]

––––––

Let's examine next how we might introduce students to social science thinking, not by taking an introductory course in anthropology, political science, psychology, or sociology, but by a broader, more intentional focus on social science methodologies and approaches to understanding. Our goal would be to combat various kinds of unsophisticated, naive, simplistic thinking that are applied to public policy and personal decision making and expose undergraduates to the kinds of errors in cognition, reasoning, and logic that occur widely but often subconsciously—or worse yet, are used to manipulate and exploit.

Social scientific illiteracy, I am convinced, is as malign as scientific, quantitative, and cultural illiteracy. Yet apart from requiring students to take a class or two in a social science discipline, our institutions tend not to think of the disparate social science courses as efforts to introduce students to the errors in thinking that grow out of social scientific ignorance and the inability to apply core social science concepts, methods, and analytical techniques systematically.

It's one thing to accept certain scientific findings largely as an act of faith. After all, very few highly educated adults are truly able to grasp the foundations of contemporary scientific thought about cosmology or quantum mechanics, let alone astrophysics, molecular or computational biology, or neuroscience. Yet social scientific thinking does not require acts of faith. Undergraduates, irrespective of major, are fully capable of replicating key psychological experiments, conducting data analysis, undertaking anthropological, economic, geographical, historical, and sociological research, and testing and applying concepts drawn from political science, sociology, and related fields. All are able to understand causation, correlation, sampling, and selection.

This isn't to imply that the social sciences are easier than the natural or physical sciences, but rather that social science methods and modes of interpretation are more accessible. To this, you might well say: Isn't that what lower division social science classes already do? In a few cases, the answer is certainly "yes"—though even then, there's an unhealthy tendency to fragment social science knowledge and skills by discipline instead of addressing key topics more holistically. Here, I'd simply like to suggest that rather than relying as heavily as we currently do on introductory courses in specific social science disciplines, we consider offering one or more broader courses that teach students how to research, think, analyze, and apply findings like a social scientist.

Such a course would introduce lower division undergraduates to social science research methods—to how social scientists collect, evaluate, and analyze qualitative and quantitative data. It would expose students to archival research, comparative research, ethnographic research, experimental research, participant observation, and survey research. It would also introduce students to social science theory, the interpretive frameworks that social scientists use to understand observed facts and behavior and other social phenomena, and to data literacy, and the tools and techniques that social scientists use to transform data into useful information. It should also examine the application of social science insights into public policy and everyday life; the challenges, limitations, and complexities of gathering and analyzing data; and how social scientific data, findings, and theories are used (or overhyped or misused) in policy formulation and in clinical, educational, and therapeutic interventions.

Since academics are trained in specific fields, the idea of teaching a more synthetic approach to the social sciences strikes many as repugnant—as superficial, artificial, and unsophisticated. As disciplinary specialists, most only feel comfortable teaching within specific disciplines and fear that they can't do justice to the breadth and depth of related areas of study. That's a point well taken. But I suspect that much of the reluctance grows out of the bad name that the more holistic approach practiced in K–12 social studies has offered. Too often, I fear, those K–12 courses devolve into bull sessions about current events or a superficial mishmash of subjects that require deeper levels of understanding.

However, as fewer and fewer students major in the social sciences, we need to ensure that undergraduates who concentrate in business, communication, computer science, engineering, mathematics, and the natural sciences acquire a familiarity with social science vocabulary, methods, theories, applications, and schools of interpretation. A more broad-based approach to lower division social sciences education might offer a side benefit: convincing more students to major in one of the social science disciplines. Certainly, something is lost when we confront texts without the scaffolding offered by a particular discipline, which brings its own methodology, vocabulary, subject matter, and agenda. But something is also gained by such an approach. Such a course is interdisciplinary by design. Instructors become active participants in the learning process, rather than simply serving as subject matter specialists. Above all, the skills most prized by the liberal arts—critical inquiry, research, analysis and interpretation, and theorizing—become central to the learning experience.

In a democracy, social science literacy isn't an extravagance. Informed and responsible citizenship requires all of us to be able to attain a level of civic, economic, historical, and sociological understanding that allows us to critically evaluate the research and theories that undergird policy decisions. Then, on a more personal level, economic, psychological, and sociological insight is essential if we are to achieve greater self-understanding, fathom why people act as they do, better manage our behavior and emotions, and make more informed decisions.

All of us need to think like a social scientist, replacing naïve, everyday thinking with a more social scientific approach. Distribution requirements are not enough. We need to think historically, spatially, computationally, and cross-culturally. We need to think like an anthropologist, an economist, a political scientist, a psychologist, and a sociologist. If that's indeed the case, then we must think harder about how to ensure that all of our graduates achieve a viable level of social science literacy and achieve an acceptable degree of methodological, theoretical, and analytical sophistication.

―――

In a later chapter, I will discuss in depth how to better engage the mass of undergraduates in the humanities. Here, I will touch on the challenge, which is exemplified by an email message that I received from an unnamed correspondent. This person shared a memorable quotation from the Nobel laureate Ernest Rutherford: "That which is not Physics is stamp collecting."[20] In other words, that which isn't science is a trivial and inconsequential waste of time.

Bored out of his mind by box-checking introductory courses in the humanities, my correspondent wrote: "To many STEM students the truly 'Great Books' were written by Physicists and Mathematicians." He added: "A deep study of literature will not get you through a decent course on Differential Equations. Facile speech doesn't get you through Physical Electronics." Those words give vivid expression to a deep divide between those who value creative writing and the arts and those who attach the greatest importance to scientific inquiry.

How might we bridge this divide? Several strategies suggest themselves. These include courses that speak to existential and developmental issues such as gender, ethnic, racial, and sexual identities, love and intimacy, tragedy, and death and bereavement; and classes that address enduring moral, philosophic, and political issues involving aesthetic judgment, divinity, justice, equity, the good society, and life's meaning. Students would also benefit from classes that connect the humanities and the professions—for example, healthcare classes on narratives of pain and illness, the history of disease, and representations of the body, or business-related courses on the history of capitalism or global languages and cultures, or technology-aligned humanities classes on the arts, humanities, and emerging communication technologies, humanizing technology, ethical issues in technology, and gender and technological change.

A lower division curriculum that largely consists of discipline-based introductory courses is simple to offer. Indeed, many of these classes can be offered cost-effectively by adjuncts, postdocs, or even graduate students. But in my view, this approach fails to achieve its purported objectives: to ensure that every student acquires a grounding in the liberal arts, grasps essential findings of the humanities and the social and natural sciences, and achieves cultural and quantitative literacy. Let's reaffirm a commitment to a well-rounded education by rethinking and reconceptualizing these courses and making sure that they produce the well-rounded college graduates we aspire to nurture.

# 7

---

# From Teaching to Learning

OVER A DECADE AGO, ALFIE KOHN, a widely read educational commentator perhaps best known for his critiques of standardized testing and homework, published an article with the provocative title "It's Not What We Teach; It's What They Learn." Teaching typically involves knowledge transmission. Learning, by contrast, involves conceptual understanding and skills acquisition. It's high time to recognize that teaching only matters insofar as it contributes to student learning.[1]

I, for one, have encountered teachers who adopted very different pedagogical styles and approaches. I've come across effective and ineffective lecturers—some who were disorganized or droned in a monotone and others who captivated my attention and enthralled. I've run into discussion leaders who dominated the conversation or treated students rudely and insensitively and others who had a talent for drawing even the shyest student out and encouraged us to elaborate on classmates' statements. To be sure, the best college teachers I had tended to share certain common characteristics. They inspired. They entertained. They motivated and engaged. They were charismatic and often quirky. They were passionate about their subjects. They were memorable. However, they didn't fit a single mold. Some were authoritative. Others were touchy-feely. Some modeled the intellectual life. Some altered students' worldviews. Others instilled confidence in their students. Some enchanted listeners with intriguing stories.

Not all of us can be such teachers. But all of us can teach better and more effectively. We mustn't forget, our primary interest should not be in teaching per se, but in student learning and development. Entertainment can contribute to effective teaching, but it isn't synonymous with learning.

It's my view that the most effective college teachers aren't sages on the stage, nor are they guides on the side. They're learning architects whose goal is to help students master essential content and skills, instill a sense of agency and empowerment, help students think like a scholar within a particular discipline, and produce critical thinkers who are self-directed, self-regulated learners. All of us can become learning engineers. As we'll see, the attributes of effective teaching are not a trade secret. They involve skills that can be acquired: clarity, organization, and, above all, thinking intentionally about course design, pedagogy, and activity, assignment, and assessment design.

Learning requires foundational knowledge—and that implies memorization of essential terminology, content, and concepts. But deep, durable learning depends on more than memorization. It involves processing information, practicing skills, and solving problems. It also requires the acquisition of higher order thinking skills—the ability to explain, analyze and interpret, generalize, and synthesize—as well as the ability to apply knowledge and skills in new and novel contexts. Most important of all, deep, durable learning requires engagement, motivation, and active involvement in the learning process.

As I will explain in greater detail, there are four pillars that underlie effective teaching. The first is motivation. Students need to be motivated if they are to engage, persist, and master a topic or skill. The second is engagement. An instructor must capture students' attention and sustain their focus. Engagement can be cognitive, appealing to their curiosity and interests; it can also be emotional, social, and cultural. Enthusiasm, humor, passion, eye contact, and identifying students by name are essential. The third pillar is empathy. Instructors must build relationships with students; convey their passion for the subject; be attentive to students' interests, needs, confusions, and goals; instill confidence; and encourage risk-taking. Effective teaching is about building connections and a sense of community. It's about rapport. Rapport helps reduce the sting of failure; it gives students opportunities to grow and develop intellectually.

The fourth pillar is active student participation or involvement or engagement in the learning process. Students frequently resist the idea of the active learning classroom. Many regard it as a waste of time. After all, active learning is much more demanding than sitting passively. It's also difficult for the instructor, who must cede responsibility to students. But if we want students to learn, and not simply to listen, we must involve them in activities or tasks that they regard as relevant and authentic and get them to think, discuss, investigate, and create.

———

Faculty tend to greatly overestimate their teaching prowess. Nine of ten faculty members believe that their teaching skills are above average, and two-thirds rank themselves in the top quarter—a statistical impossibility. To make matters worse, a faculty member's professional reputation, salary, and receipt of tenure hinge largely on publication, not teaching. Incentive structures, a lack of training, and exaggerated self-regard combine to impede efforts to improve college teaching.[2]

The primary purpose of a college or university is to educate students. But most faculty members receive no formal training in how to teach effectively, and higher education's incentive structures provide few rewards for successful teaching. Almost all teachers teach because they want to awaken a love of learning in their students. But given their lack of training, most teachers mimic the way they were taught, through lectures and discussion. This approach may work well for aural learners with steel-trap memories or for intellectually confident extroverts, but it is less effective for students who aren't as motivated, well-prepared, articulate, or assertive. Success with those students requires fresh approaches to pedagogy that emphasize active learning, an educational approach that involves actively processing the course material through debate, problem-solving, case studies, role-playing activities, and other ways of applying course materials.

A recent study of 12,000 classrooms found that instructors took up 89 percent of class time speaking. Even more striking: instructor-centered classrooms were nearly as common in seminars and discussion classes as they were in lecture courses. This faculty-centric approach persists even though a growing body of scholarship indicates that active learning improves student performance across virtually every dimension, from scores on standardized tests to knowledge retention and the ability to apply skills and content in new situations.[3]

College pedagogy needs to undergo a fundamental transformation from a didactic, teacher-centered approach to a more active, performance-based, student-centered approach. As Robert Barr and John Tagg argued over two decades ago, the chief educational goal of a university should not be to provide instruction but to produce learning. And yet our principal pedagogics—lecture and discussion, instructor-facing classrooms, disconnected courses that are not well aligned with one another, and our predominant assessment tool, the multiple-choice and short response examination, which rewards short-term retention of facts—all reinforce the older model that emphasized knowledge transmission.

The teaching challenge before us is to advance the shift from an institutional paradigm rooted in the industrial age to a new model better suited to the information age, facilitated by new digital technologies that can make higher education more immersive, interactive, inclusive, participatory, collaborative, and personalized. A content transmission model needs to be supplemented by a "constructivist" approach that encourages students to develop their own mental models and understanding. A one-size-fits-all model needs to give way to an education better tailored to the needs of individual students. A time-based model needs to be supplanted by an outcomes- and attainment-focused model. A sink-or-swim mindset needs to be succeeded by a goal of bringing all students to mastery. Assessment for sorting needs to give way to assessment that is developmental and diagnostic.

A variety of factors are prompting this paradigm shift. These include a recognition that students come to our classrooms with radically different levels of preparation and that too many are disengaged and tuned out—or frankly, bored. Then, too, there is a sense that today's students are less willing than past generations to sit passively through lectures and instead want to undertake projects, engage in dialogue, and work independently or in groups.

Equally important contributors to this paradigm shift are findings from the learning sciences—especially those from cognitive and developmental psychology and neuroscience, which have provided fresh insights into memory and information processing and challenged many older assumptions about how people acquire, retain, retrieve, and apply information. A growing body of evidence indicates that the dominant educational paradigm, which emphasizes listening, note-taking, and completing exams, is not nearly as effective in producing "deep" learning than are approaches that stress active engagement, collaboration, peer interaction, mentoring, and reflection.

———

Successful teaching is, at once, an art, a craft, and a science. Teaching, at its best, is a creative act in which a master instructor designs learning experiences that motivate, provoke, stimulate, and inspire. Like with other performing artists, an instructor's effectiveness depends on their ability to improvise, to adjust pedagogy in response to student needs, confusions, and interests. A teacher's passion, imagination, eloquence, humor, flair, and creativity are essential if a class of students is to be engaged. The most successful instructors adjust constantly to classroom realities, to student interests, disengagement, and passions, deviating from a script, outline, or lesson plan.

Partly an art, teaching is also a craft in which an instructor's skills and techniques are continually refined by practice, experience, and iterative improvements. Like any craft, the process of becoming an effective teacher involves the acquisition of certain skills—presentation skills, classroom management skills, and instructional design skills—which can only be acquired through study, preparation, trial and error, intentional practice, and reflection. It also requires close attention to detail: an ability to "read" a classroom and sense when particular students are confused or disengaged or bored or on the verge of participating. The craft of teaching lies precisely in sensing when to shift pedagogies or alter a class's tempo or intervene in a discussion.

Indeed, for all the talk about learning as a science informed by the findings of neurobiology and cognitive psychology, a learner-centered classroom hinges in large measure on such personal qualities as empathy, enthusiasm, awareness, approachability, and adaptability. In other words, teaching cannot be considered a science in the sense that there are certain practices that will automatically enhance learning for a particular student. Still, teaching can and should be scientifically informed. Like scientists, teachers need to frequently evaluate student learning and adjust their pedagogy in response. But learning also has neurobiological, cognitive, affective, and social psychological dimensions that instructors need to attend to.

———

"Learning" is an umbrella term that covers the acquisition of foundational, discipline-specific knowledge, conceptual knowledge, procedural knowledge, and discipline-specific skills. It also entails the development of certain habits of mind, learning strategies, and an assortment of higher order thinking skills, including the ability to synthesize, generalize, reflect, evaluate, and apply knowledge and skills to novel problems and domains. And further, it involves sense making and performance—the ability to demonstrate and apply skills and knowledge.

Learning depends upon a host of factors: motivation, attention, cognitive processing, memory, mindset, prior knowledge, recall, and level of comprehension. Each element is essential in order to master a body of knowledge and skills. Motivation and engagement come first. There is no learning without motivation. If students find a subject boring, frustrating, and irrelevant, they are less likely to learn. Conversely, if students find a subject or activity enjoyable, they are more likely to persist, invest themselves in learning, and pursue their studies intensively.

It is common to distinguish between extrinsic and intrinsic motivations, between behavior that is self-motivated and motivated by reward or punishment. However, neither is sufficient. There are topics that a student must learn whether or not they find the subject interesting. Thus, effective teachers must motivate students to learn these topics and convey their own enthusiasm for a particular topic. Skilled teachers must demonstrate that an activity is meaningful and worthwhile, for example, by explaining the rationale for a particular activity. Faculty members must build on students' existing interests. They must help students develop positive attitudes toward schoolwork and appreciate their progress in mastering a body of material or skills. But motivation is easily discouraged. Failure, or even the fear of failure, can undercut students' motivation to persist. Instructors can reinforce motivation by helping students to discover that learning the material has personal value. When they believe that, their efforts will be effective, and they will view the instructor as someone who cares about them.

Sustained attention is also an essential element in learning. Focus, engagement, alertness, and concentration provide an indispensable foundation for memory and information processing. Attention, however, is limited. Cognitive load theory suggests that individuals are able to process only a limited number of inputs at one time. Attention is also limited in duration. Since a student's cognitive resources are limited, instructors should be attentive to the amount and organization of information that they present. If the information is too complex or if the presentation is poorly organized, students are likely to become confused or disengage. Instructors must attend to other learning challenges as well. Students are easily distracted, and effective instructors must help students develop a capacity to ignore or filter out stimuli that are not salient. Attention is also selective and heavily influenced by students' emotions. Certain emotional states, such as anxiety and stress, can make it harder to pay attention. One of an instructor's primary responsibilities is to maintain students' attention. Successful teachers develop techniques to grab and sustain that attention.

Memorization is yet another key element in learning. Rote memorization and conceptual understanding are often treated as polar opposites. Yet certain kinds of foundational knowledge provide the basis for higher order thinking. Without appropriate factual and procedural underpinnings, advanced thinking isn't possible.

Learning is, in part, about transferring information from working memory to long-term memory. Short-term memory is where we do much of our reasoning and thinking. However, working memory has limited duration and capacity. There are, however, ways to keep information in short-term memory—by rehearsing or visualizing the information or doing what educational psychologists call creating a phonological loop. But working memory is easily overloaded. As we have seen, distractions, stress, and excessive cognitive load can make learning less than optimal.

Memory, it needs to be emphasized, is not a recording. Rather, it is a construction. Unless information is repeatedly processed, it tends to be forgotten or deactivated. So how, then, can instructors help students create lasting durable memories? The answer is that students need to process the information in active ways. They need to connect new information with prior knowledge and memories. Even making mistakes and errors or being confused can be good for learning, if in the process of correcting the mistakes, thinking about the errors, and resolving the confusion, the student actively processes the information.

If learning is to be meaningful, students must be able to retrieve and apply information and skills in a range of contexts. One method for improving retrieval is "cued recall," the use of visual or verbal cues to elicit a memory. Another method is to have students organize information into a map, a diagram, or an outline. This promotes the development of a mental (or conceptual) model that makes it much easier for students to understand a topic on a deep level and apply it to new situations.

Research in cognitive science has identified three strategies that are particularly effective in improving retrieval and transfer. These are retrieval practice, spaced practice, and interleaving. Retrieval practice involves calling information to mind that has been stored previously in long-term memory. Retrieval practice might involve the following: After students read an assignment for the first time and take notes, they put the notes away and try to recall the most important ideas and information they wrote down. Or if they annotated their text, they keep the book closed and try to remember what they annotated and why. Trying to simply recall information is a lot harder than rereading a text or looking at notes, but it is precisely that struggle to recall that embeds and solidifies memories.

Spaced practice offers another proven way to improve retrieval and transfer. Over a century ago, studies demonstrated that spacing out learning sessions in short intervals is a much better way to develop long-term memories than to engage in what's called "massed practice," the repetitive and uninterrupted practice of a skill over a prolonged period of time. The reason that spaced practice works so well for creating durable memories has several explanations. The first is that it takes advantage of the usefulness of retrieval practice. The more often we practice recalling memories from long-term memory, the more easily we are able to access it, and the more resistant it becomes to forgetting. In addition, each new retrieval probably occurs in a different context, unlike massed practice, which usually happens in the same context. These varied contexts of distributed practices also help with retrieval by providing alternative recall pathways. Another important reason is that the act of retrieval is an act of memory modification and reorganization. Each retrieval consolidates new memories and strengthens them. The implications for our students are clear. We need to help our students space their learning when they study.

A third, highly effective learning strategy is a variation of spaced practice called interleaving. This involves not only distributing practice over time but also changing the order of materials studied across different topics. In other words, shifting from one topic to another and then returning to the original topic enhances memory.

----

Teaching is or should be, in part, an applied science, and instructors would do well to think of themselves as learning engineers or architects whose essential task is to design learning experiences that will bring their students to mastery. There is a growing body of core cognitive principles grounded in psychoneurological research and evidence-based instructional practice that can significantly enhance student learning. Here, however, it is important to recognize that the science of learning remains in a nascent state. It has not identified laws of learning, nor does it prescribe specific pedagogical techniques. The impact of various strategies differs with particular individuals.

Indeed, many often recited generalizations lack substantial empirical validation. Is it true, for instance, that students try harder and learn more when classes are smaller or when grading includes rewards, not punishments? Common sense says yes, but the empirical evidence is mixed. Or take the notion that students have disparate learning styles—that some are auditory learners, while others are visual, tactile, or kinesthetic learners (who learn by manipulating objects or engaging in projects) or analytical learners (or prefer information presented in sequential steps) or global learners (who do not like to be bored and prefer various kinds of stimulation). Then there are the other learning styles: competitive, collaborative, independent, dependent, participatory, resistant, and avoidant. It appears that most students learn in multiple ways, so it's best, therefore, to present information in multiple ways rather than place students into rigid categories.

What the science of learning does do is suggest principles and strategies that creative educators can deploy to help students master new knowledge and skills and apply what they have learned to new situations. One such principle is that acquiring long-term knowledge and skill depends largely on practice. The transfer of information from short-term to long-term memory isn't automatic. It requires effort. Practice is key to this transfer process. Effective practice involves attention, rehearsal, and meaningful repetition. As a result, this knowledge can reach automaticity, allowing for focus on more complex knowledge or skills over time.

In addition, a student's mindset can significantly influence learning. In recent years, we have heard a great deal about grit and its contributions to student persistence and learning. The word "grit" combines such traits as determination, self-discipline, perseverance, and passion, which can help students pursue goals despite obstacles or discouragement. Grit may be inborn, but it is also a quality that can be nurtured, encouraged, and reinforced. Students' beliefs or perceptions about intelligence and ability also strongly affect their cognitive functioning and learning. For example, stereotype threat (the fear that one's behavior will confirm an existing stereotype of a group with which one identifies) can have a damaging effect on student performance. Students with a growth mindset, who believe that abilities can be strengthened through hard work, are more willing to take on challenges and rebound more easily than students with a fixed mindset. Teaching students that their intelligence can increase can help them maintain motivation in the face of challenges and promote academic achievement.

Learners also have certain personality characteristics and psychological styles that influence learning. Especially important is regulatory fit. Some students are particularly sensitive to criticism and negative outcomes and are eager to avoid errors. They're highly risk averse. That's called having a prevention focus. Other students, with a promotion focus, look for opportunities. They're risk takers. Learning is enhanced when there is regulatory fit, when the manner in which a student engages in an activity sustains their goal orientation or interests regarding that activity.

Deep, durable learning, we have discovered, requires students to strengthen their metacognitive capacities—the ability to self-monitor, self-regulate, and reflect. Students tend to be poor judges of their command of course material. Many assume that they understand the material better than they actually do. Therefore, instructors need to help students acquire a greater ability to monitor their learning and more accurately gauge their mastery of a particular topic. The answer is simple: frequent quizzing. By exposing areas of confusion or misunderstanding, instructors can show students that even errors can help them consolidate their proficiency with the material.

As students' metacognitive capacities deepen, they become better able to distinguish between familiarity with a topic and achieving genuine conceptual understanding. They can then monitor their mistakes and take steps to correct their errors and attain a stronger grasp of the course material. It's not enough for an instructor to transmit knowledge or build disciplinary-based skills. It's also essential to strengthen students' metacognitive abilities.

———

In addition to its cognitive dimensions, education has affective, social, and developmental dimensions that mustn't be ignored. Learning is shaped by classroom and broader social dynamics. Thus, there is a sociology of the classroom and a psychodynamics of the classroom. To be effective, instructors need to be aware of the influence of psychosocial and developmental factors on learning.

Learning is a process of personal transformation within specific social contexts. Maturation as a learner requires a student to develop a capacity for self-direction, self-monitoring, and self-generation of ideas and shed earlier ways of thinking and earlier forms of self-expression. Because the process of intellectual maturation involves fundamental transformations in a student's self-perception and thinking, it is often emotionally wrenching. Students must also construct a conceptual framework that allows them to integrate and organize new knowledge into a coherent structure. Conceptual learning involves something quite different from the learning of skills or the mastery of content and concepts. It involves the discovery of meaningful patterns, the formulation of generalizations, and constructing arguments that are located in a larger disciplinary conversation.

The psychosocial aspects of learning have been a particular concern among feminist pedagogues, who stress that learning is context sensitive. Proponents of feminist pedagogies view the classroom as a site of power, privilege, and hierarchy and regard teaching as an inherently political act. Yet the politics of the classroom, these scholars maintain, remain obfuscated. Within the traditional classroom, these scholars argue, certain ideas, perspectives, and forms of behavior, discourse, and argumentation are favored. The conceptual design of a course tends to remain hidden and unexamined, while the selection of topics and readings reflects unspoken ideological presumptions. Meanwhile, the approach to teaching in the traditional classroom, whether involving lecture or discussion, takes the significance of a particular text or topic for granted and fails to model the full range of alternative interpretive or analytical approaches. All of these factors lead some, if not many, students to feel marginalized, discouraging deep learning.

What does that mean for pedagogical practice? First of all, instructors need to remain highly attentive to classroom dynamics, always on the lookout for students who are bored, confused, frustrated, or, to use a couple of near expletives, peeved and pissed off. Instructors must also acknowledge and respect students' disparate perspectives, cultural values, and life experiences and become conscious of their own implicit, at times unconscious, biases and frames of reference and the impact of those assumptions and expectations on students. In addition, instructors must recognize how easy it is to make a student feel inadequate or marginal or stupid.

If our goal is to bring 100 percent of our students to mastery, then instructors need to be culturally responsive. In recent years, CRT (critical race theory)—the notion that racism is not merely a product of individual bias or prejudice but is embedded in law, public policy, and social practices—has provoked explosive controversies, even prompting some state legislatures to bar teachers from referring to CRT in public schools. But there is another CRT—culturally responsive teaching—that focuses less on power, privilege, and systems of oppression than on ways to design courses with greater intentionality and responsiveness to students' emotional and learning needs and recognition of their experiences, perspectives, and longer-term goals.

How should you do that? First, make sure that your learning objectives are SMART: specific, measurable, attainable, relevant, and targeted at particular learning goals. Be purposeful in designing activities. Each assignment should have a learning objective as its aim. Next, discuss the purpose and goals of each activity, assignment, and assessment before they are undertaken. Be transparent. Let students know why you have organized the class as you have. Third, frequently gauge and monitor student understanding, for example, by asking them to explain and apply difficult concepts or by having them explain their thought processes when solving problems. Only by monitoring student understanding can an instructor respond to confusions, misunderstandings, or errors in thinking. Also, vary your assessments and be sure to include some that students will consider authentic and meaningful. That's the best way to ensure that students remain engaged and motivated. In addition, construct rubrics, preferably in partnership with your students, and explain how you use these rubrics to evaluate their work and provide timely feedback. Finally, be sure to recognize effort and progress.

When we teach, we need to treat our students as more than recipients of knowledge or learners of skills, but as complex individuals with a wide array of hopes, fears, dreams, interests, and aspirations. Instructors need to recognize that more than a few first-generation students feel like outsiders or impostors and are asking themselves whether college-going will break their connection with their family or community, betray their upbringing, or devalue parts of themselves. Other students may be troubled by conflicts between what they've learned outside college and what they're learning in your class. Don't let such concerns go ignored or unexamined.

Remember: you are not merely a teacher-scholar or subject matter expert. Be prepared to share the challenges and obstacles that you've encountered. Learning hinges on mindset. In many instances, psychology and emotions can be barriers to student success. In today's extraordinarily diverse classrooms, a successful instructor needs to speak to the affective as well as the cognitive.

---

In his 1852 series of lectures titled The Idea of a University, the English theologian John Henry Newman wrote that true learning "consists, not merely in the passive reception into the mind of a number of ideas hitherto unknown to it, but in the mind's energetic and simultaneous action upon and towards and among those new ideas."[4] The notion that true understanding and mastery come from the student, not the instructor, has gathered strength in recent years, fueled in part by a constructivist conception of education that rests on a belief that learning only occurs when students actively construct knowledge and meaning rather than passively receiving information. According to Newman's constructivist view, students do not truly comprehend a subject until they actively construct a framework of understanding.

Recent research in the fields of neurobiology, cognitive science, and social psychology indicates that many common teaching practices are ineffective. Lectures, for example, may help students learn to listen, build, and focus attention, take notes, and model the presentation of an argument that synthesizes a body of complex material. But students do not generally achieve conceptual understanding or build skills by listening passively to lectures. Somewhat similarly, many common study practices are not the best way to master a subject or skill. Cramming for an examination rarely results in lasting memories. Nor is rereading or highlighting a text especially effective. Practicing the same skills for hours on end (an example of mass practice), it turns out, is less effective than spacing practice over a period of time.

What lessons, then, might be drawn from the science of learning? One lesson is that active learning can substantially improve understanding and retention of instructional material and boost student engagement and course satisfaction. Effective instructors engage students in deliberate practice by giving them opportunities to retrieve and apply information in contexts that are authentic. Active learning can take many forms. Students might be asked to organize information in a visual or outline configuration. Or they might be asked to solve a problem or devise a solution to a challenge. Learning is also enhanced when learners take information presented in one format and present it in an alternative format.

For example, consider designing writing assignments that strike students as meaningful and relevant. Instead of a standard term paper, you might ask them to write in a mode that they find more germane to their interests. That might be a policy brief, a case study, a competitive landscape analysis, an environmental impact statement, a feasibility statement, a grant proposal, a job description, a marketing plan, an op-ed essay, a press release, a project work plan, or a newspaper article. Authentic practice is a time-tested way to engage students.

Another major principle that grows out of the science of learning is that deep learning involves deliberate effort. Effortful learning leads to deeper and more durable learning. Difficult challenges, it turns out, are better remembered and more easily recalled. An instructor's challenge is to follow the "Goldilocks principle" and introduce students to material that is neither too easy nor too hard. The educational psychologist Lev Vygotsky described the Zone of Proximal Development as the sweet spot in which a learner is able to master something with the help of scaffolding from an instructor.[5]

Yet another principle is that prior knowledge, beliefs, and attitudes strongly influence learning—for good or bad. Students are not blank slates. The mental models, presuppositions, presumptions, and mindsets that students bring to class are difficult to extinguish, and students often stick to these even in the face of new or contradictory information. Often, students simply graft new information onto the old. In order to bring a student to a more sophisticated level of understanding, an instructor needs to address these embedded assumptions head-on.

Emotions and mindset also influence learning. A student's emotional state has a powerful effect on attention, memory, and retrieval of information. Anxiety and stress can be particularly debilitating. Therefore, it is important for an instructor to create a learning environment that is psychologically safe. Instructors need to avoid using fear, intimidation, or shaming to motivate learning. Also, students' beliefs about intelligence and ability influence their cognitive functioning and capacity to learn. Learning improves when students believe that intelligence is malleable and intellectual growth and skills mastery are possible.

What, then, are some general lessons that instructors might draw from this research? That students learn most when they actively engage and process the course material. That shifting from one topic to another and then returning to the original topic enhances memory. That frequent quizzing of students' command of the material can help consolidate memory and contribute to mastery of essential knowledge and skills. That errors can improve learning by deepening students' engagement with the material if these are treated as learning experiences. That active engagement with instructional material is more effective than passively reviewing the material.

Here are my takeaways. It's important to set and communicate clear learning goals to your students. These objectives need to be specific and moderately challenging. They also need to be accomplishable in the near term (or what psychologists of education call "proximal"). Goals that are distal, overly general, and excessively challenging are not helpful. Also, it's essential to engage and motivate students. Motivated learners pay more attention and expend more effort while learning.

Equally important is helping students develop self-regulation skills. These include the ability to sustain attention, ignore distractions, manage time, shift attention and refocus, and develop strategies needed to carry out cognitive tasks effectively, such as organizing and prioritizing projects. In addition to devising activities and other learning experiences that ensure that students master the knowledge, skills, and habits of mind spelled out in a course's learning objectives, take steps to ensure that your students develop the self-regulatory skills that are essential to academic and career success. Ask students to devise a plan, set goals, and create a timetable. Instructors can assist this process by dividing an assignment into discrete steps, each with its own due date; building in opportunities for debriefing, reflection, discussion, and self-assessment; and providing timely feedback.

If we truly want to bring more undergraduates to a bright future, twenty-first-century teaching needs to differ from its late twentieth-century counterpart. A basic assumption of twentieth-century education was that not all students could "cut it," and it was okay for a significant percentage of students to fail. We blinded ourselves to certain realities: that many students who failed could have succeeded if we taught and assessed learning differently. That 100 percent proficiency in certain subjects may well not be possible, but we have a moral duty to provide the support and supplemental instruction that these students need. After all, once we admit a student to our institution, we have a responsibility to do everything in our power to bring them to success—not by lowering standards or by dumbing down the material, but by adopting engaging active learning strategies.

———

Much teaching advice is common sense. Be transparent about your learning goals. Grab your students' attention with an interesting fact, a provocative quotation, a mystery, a problem, or a paradox. Explain a topic's relevance. Motivate your students to complete the reading. Make your class more interactive by asking questions, soliciting opinions, getting students to give short presentations, encouraging discussions, and using audio, video, and other sources to prompt dialogue and debate.

Also, be clear and well organized. Structure your class logically. Avoid confusing instructions and explanations. Be wary of cognitive overload—making it difficult for students to process information because you provided too much at once or required them to undertake too many tasks simultaneously. Present complex material in multiple ways. Reinforce student understanding if you introduce key concepts or content out loud, but also through relevant readings, visually through charts and graphs, and physically through various activities.

To these pieces of advice, I might add some others. Acknowledge the social and affective dimensions of learning. Learning is often a wrenching process that requires students to confront and question prior assumptions and accept their weaknesses and concede their errors. Therefore, it is essential that instructors be attentive and responsive to the emotions that students feel and help them articulate their thinking, confusions, or anxieties.

In addition, provide regular and substantive constructive feedback. If feedback is to be effective, it must be timely, meaningful, and actionable, and it must be skillfully delivered. Be sensitive; acknowledge the student's effort, strengths, and progress or improvement. Explain what the student is or isn't doing effectively and how performance can be improved. Focus on a specific skill; don't overcomment or nitpick. Above all, avoid using feedback to justify a grade. Instead, be forward-looking, describing specific steps the student should take in future work. The purpose of feedback is to educate, not to critique.

But the most important advice I would offer is to make class time more dynamic. That requires instructors to embrace their inner Socrates and John Dewey. Design learning experiences that are interactive and participatory and that involve active learning strategies: case study analysis, debate, discussion, group projects, inquiry and investigation, peer teaching, problem-solving, role-playing, and more. Active learning requires students to participate in their own learning rather than acquiring information passively. It goes beyond note-taking and memorization by requiring students to actively process information, apply knowledge and skills, construct mental models, and develop their higher order thinking skills, including the ability to apply, analyze, synthesize, generalize, and evaluate. It can be solitary or social and collaborative; it can or cannot be technologically enhanced. It needs to be skills focused and rooted in authentic, real-life tasks and challenge students to do the hard work of presenting and explaining information and solving problems.

One way to make classes more interactive is to deploy the Socratic method: asking probing questions in order to analyze assumptions, clarify concepts, weigh evidence, identify contrasting perspectives, and expose the implications of an argument. The challenge is to go beyond the recall and regurgitation of factual knowledge and ensure that the students engage in higher order thinking by solving problems, evaluating arguments, applying concepts in a fresh context, drawing connections, and advancing generalizations. There are many ways to do this. Give students a case study to analyze. Ask them to interpret and contextualize a text or an image or evaluate an argument. After introducing a body of facts or a scenario or a vignette, have the students make and defend a decision or a prediction and explain their reasoning. Or ask students to apply a concept or identify a theory that might explain a development or series of events. I find it especially powerful to ask students to analyze a subject through contrasting lenses, for example, a feminist, Marxist, or postmodern viewpoint.

Another way to make classes more engaging, immersive, interactive, and participatory is to embrace John Dewey's commitment to learning by doing. Approaches vary by topic and discipline, but here is some general advice. Have students do things: annotate a text or a set of images, individually or collectively. Map concepts or causal relationships. Curate relevant resources. Visualize data. Plot information on a map. Create a word cloud or an infographic or a timeline or a virtual exhibit. Provide peer feedback. Conduct or respond to a survey and analyze the results. Correspond with a virtual pen pal. Mine a text. Contribute to a virtual encyclopedia. Produce a blog, collaborative website, podcast, video story, virtual tour, or wiki. In short, make your students active participants in their own learning.

———

There is no shortage of ways to improve our teaching. We can flip our classrooms, delivering content online outside of class and devoting class time to problem-solving activities. Or we might gamify our classrooms by tapping the motivational power of play: its intensity, its competitiveness, and its subversive elements. Immersive role-playing exercises, for example, can, in John Dewey's words, "shock students out of sheep-like passivity."[6] A striking example is Reacting to the Past. Introduced in 1995, this pedagogical approach has students assume roles informed by classic texts and debate fundamental issues raised during pivotal historical episodes. Now used in over 350 institutions, including liberal arts colleges, honors programs, regional universities, and community colleges, Reacting classes are set in such contexts as the Athenian Assembly after the Peloponnesian War, the Council of Nicaea in 325 CE, the Peel Commission in Mandate Palestine in 1937, and India on the Eve of Independence in 1945.

Yes, we need to improve our pedagogies. Yes, we need to rethink our roles and responsibilities as instructors. Yes, we need to become more thoughtful about how to motivate and assess learning. But we also need to break free from the box that assumes that the most valuable learning takes place within a lecture hall or seminar room. I've increasingly come to believe that the essential teaching and learning problem that we face, dear Brutus, lies not merely in pedagogy but in our failure to embrace other ways to educate students. Let me suggest, very briefly, a number of alternatives to our standard lecture classes and seminars.

We might create communities of inquiry. Create a learning experience that is modeled on a social network, where an interdisciplinary community of scholars and students share information and build knowledge about a topic of intense public interest, such as the pandemic or gender, racial, and class disparities. Or we might form solver communities. These assemble a community of students and scholars to collaboratively devise solutions to a pressing social or scientific problem. Then there's a studio or workshopping approach. Widely deployed in creative writing and the visual and performing arts, workshopping combines individual presentations, brainstorming, group discussion, and engaged criticism to strengthen students' projects. Yet another alternative to business as usual is community service, which integrates community engagement and service activities with instruction and reflection in order to tackle a genuine local need. Practicums and clinicals also give students authentic opportunities to engage in professional practice. Typically, practicums and clinicals are confined to such fields as education, mental health counseling, nursing, or social work, but they can certainly be extended to archaeology, geology, and a host of other disciplines.

Let me suggest some other approaches. How about scaled research? Let undergraduates conduct laboratory, archival, quantitative, qualitative, and other kinds of research under the direction of faculty, postdocs, graduate students, and near-peer mentors. This ought to be a three-phase process involving training in research methods, the supervised research experience itself, and the opportunity for students to present their findings in a public setting. In addition, a growing number of institutions have created makerspaces, or collaborative workspaces within a department or college where students, individually or in a group, can, with faculty support, develop a meaningful project, taking it from an idea to a finished product. Work-based learning is also acquiring traction. Supervised internships, which can be conducted in person or remotely, allow students to acquire genuine career experience while applying academic knowledge and technical skills. Collaborative resource development can also prove to be a valuable learning experience. Teams of students, under the guidance of a faculty member, collaboratively develop resources for a particular class or for a neighboring school, museum, or other cultural and educational institutions. My own students developed a variety of simulations for US history survey courses, including one that allows undergraduates to simulate crossing the Atlantic using current wind and ocean currents, and another that gives students a chance to analyze the information contained in seventeenth- and eighteenth-century graveyards, including naming patterns, life span by gender, and gravestone iconography.

———

Many of the teaching-related issues that trouble us today—grade inflation, student disengagement, boring lecturers—are not new, and many proposed reforms—active learning, project-based learning, even technology-enhanced and personalized learning—are anything but novel. For over a century, every era has witnessed its own batch of proposed teaching reforms. For example, during the 1870s, Henry Adams, the grandson and great-grandson of presidents, introduced the first seminars—those small, intensive courses that emphasized close reading, discussion, and debate—in his medieval history classes at Harvard. After World War I, tutorials, independent study, honors programs, and the first teaching awards debuted. In an effort to raise academic standards and prevent overspecialization, a number of schools, including Antioch, Chicago, and Reed, mandated comprehensive examinations, while Harvard and dozens of other campuses required students to pass department-based comps.

During the 1920s, Rollins College in Florida adopted a "conference plan," which transformed classrooms into intellectual salons where students and faculty collaborated to solve a common problem. Around the same time, the University of Wisconsin established an experimental program that offered a learning and living community with an integrated curriculum, in which students studied ancient Greece during the first year and modern America during the second. The 1930s brought the Harkness table, where the students, rather than an instructor, were expected to lead the discussion.

Many dramatic developments in teaching took place following World War II, of which perhaps the most notable and consequential was the growing reliance on teaching assistants, graduate students who served as graders and sometimes as discussion leaders in breakout sections. The number of teaching assistants tripled—from 11,000 to 31,000—between 1954 and 1964. By 1965, 31 percent of all of Berkeley's undergraduate classes were taught by TAs, while under-classmen at Wisconsin got 76 percent of their instruction from TAs, and upperclassmen 44 percent.[7] Of course, the teaching assistants did this work with little or no supervision or training and for paltry compensation. Other noteworthy, if short-lived, innovations included the first televised college classes, which appeared during the 1950s and 1960s, while computer-assisted "personalized" instruction enjoyed a brief rage during the 1970s and 1980s.

A number of educational experiments were inspired, in part, by the radical approach to teaching and learning described in A. S. Neill's *Summerhill*, which involved dispensing with grades and assignments and treating classrooms like T-Groups or Encounter Groups. Berkeley's Tussman Experimental College, Rutgers's Livingston College, Hampshire College, Pitzer College, University of California Santa Cruz, Evergreen, and State University of New York Westbury tested a variety of innovations. Livingston, for example, sought to provide a setting in which Black, Puerto Rican, and nontraditional white and lower-income students could flourish and interact equitably and democratically. Its curriculum, which had no fixed distribution requirements, emphasized the social sciences and especially the issues involving the United States' urban problems as well as revolution and underdevelopment in postcolonial societies. However, most of those experiments proved transitory, with those institutions gravitating toward a more traditional academic model.

Teaching remains today what it was in the past: an amateur enterprise, without uniform training and ongoing professional development, well-defined, widely shared professional standards, or widely accepted modes of evaluation. Despite the prevalence of teaching awards and the establishment of teaching centers, scholarly research and publication trump teaching in terms of professional visibility and rewards. Institutions base merit increments largely on publication and grant sabbaticals and other leaves to allow faculty to pursue research. Most faculty, even at institutions that claim to be teaching centered, prefer to teach seminars or lecture courses in their area of specialization, rather than introductory, foundational, or service courses. Most, if given their druthers, would teach graduate students rather than undergrads. Then there is an especially disturbing fact. Even though some faculty members devote a great deal of time and care to instruction, some apparently do not. According to one study conducted earlier in the last decade, faculty spent, on average, just eleven hours a week on teaching, class preparation, grading, and advising.[8]

In 1966, William Arrowsmith, a classicist, leveled this widely quoted critique of American higher education: "At present, the universities are as uncongenial to teaching as the Mojave Desert to a clutch of Druid priests. If you want to restore a Druid priesthood, you cannot do it by offering prizes for Druid-of-the-year. If you want Druids, you must grow forests."[9] In other words, it's essential to alter the professional and institutional culture and norms surrounding teaching.

That's easier said than done. Teaching is denigrated in language; after all, we speak of teaching loads, which are often inversely related to faculty salaries. It's also exceedingly difficult to assess teaching quality without well-defined rubrics—and such evaluations are largely a mug's game, given that teaching is an idiosyncratic, deeply human endeavor that depends on the complex interplay between an instructor and individual students. Teaching prizes tend to reward the most charismatic or entertaining or engaging instructors, not pedagogical or curricular innovation or student learning outcomes. The scholarship of teaching is, rightly or wrong, regarded as second-rate, partly because it rarely relies on systematic or stratified sampling or controlled randomized experiments.

My own view is that we need to cease regarding teaching as a matter solely between individual instructors and their conscience. We need to shift, as Robert B. Barr and John Tagg argued in an influential 1995 article, from a teaching to a learning paradigm, with the goal of bringing all our students to a minimal viable level of competency. We must insist on formal instruction in pedagogy and assessment for graduate students and make ongoing professional development in teaching methods much more of a norm. If it's important for faculty to take training in information security, might we not expect some evidence of continuing education in teaching?[10]

Disciplinary associations can certainly help by making professional development in teaching a central component of their annual meetings. Accrediting agencies could demand evidence that institutions are, in fact, taking steps to continually improve teaching quality. Our best-resourced campuses, in particular, need to encourage serious research into teaching and learning. Most important of all, faculty need to think of themselves not just as researchers or lecturers or discussion leaders or graders but as learning architects who are committed to addressing inequities in their classrooms and bringing all their students to mastery. They need to design courses with explicit, measurable learning outcomes and activities and assessments aligned with those objectives.

Notwithstanding the growing body of research into the science of learning and the expansion of graduate training in teaching starting in the 1990s, the adoption of interactive, student-centered pedagogies remains limited. Certainly, many instructors now offer more in-class activities and group projects. But most do not, whether because of worsening student-faculty ratios or increased reliance on overworked and underpaid adjuncts or student teaching evaluations that tend to treat teaching as a popularity contest in which entertainment, theatrics, and charisma matter more than learning, while reinforcing deep cultural biases and contributing to grade inflation and a reduction in rigor, reading, and writing. Faculty, senior campus leadership, accrediting agencies, and major foundations all claim to care seriously about teaching. It's time to live up to that assertion.

# 8

---

# Enhancing Teaching and Learning
# with Technology

PERHAPS YOU REMEMBER INBLOOM, the $100 million initiative, funded largely by the Bill & Melinda Gates Foundation, to aggregate student data and learning tools and allow teachers to individualize instruction. Or how about Purdue's Course Signals or Austin Peay's Degree Compass, which were course recommendation tools intended to inform students which classes they were most likely to pass or fail? And whatever happened to Knewton, math emporiums, Google Glass, Coding for All, or the Year of the MOOC, the massive open online courses that enrolled tens of thousands of students? The history of educational technology is littered with failure. Technology fads have come and gone with remarkable regularity. Mobile learning, personalized adaptive courseware, and clickers all had their vogue. Then their fifteen minutes of fame faded, and new tech fads came and went just like the teaching machines and Skinner boxes of earlier years.

Educational technologies aren't new. In the early nineteenth century, the blackboard was a novel educational technology. But it was the twentieth century that brought a profusion of edtech innovations along with the expectation that they'd upend education. Indeed, the introduction of every new communication technology prompted dreams of revolutionizing education. Radio, the movies, filmstrips, television, and computers all held out the promise of expanding access, reducing costs, and improving the quality of teaching and learning. Yet even though we were told that the technologies were disruptive, transformational, and revolutionary, their impact on pedagogical practice and student performance proved minimal. Far from upending current practices, edtech innovations often reinforced existing instructor-centered, lecture-driven pedagogies and rote memorization.

American society values innovation, and it's not surprising that techno naysayers and skeptics have often been derided as worrywarts and impediments to progress. But often, their doubts and misgivings proved to be right on the mark. I must confess: I am a technophile. I am convinced that higher education would do well to change and that technology has an important role to play in that transformation. I have also been dazzled, often mistakenly, by flimflam, hot air, and hyperbole. So, I write as someone chastened by past disappointments. I know firsthand that technology can be used for good or ill. Still, as the old quip goes, my hopes triumph over my experience.

Which educational technologies hold promise? Only those that help instructors do their jobs better, not displace them. These are technologies that bring a wealth of instructional resources into the classroom; monitor student engagement and performance and prompt timely interventions; provide tools for analysis, annotation, visualization, and project creation; support active, collaborative, and project-based learning; ease grading; and help instructors provide more constructive feedback.

Why hasn't edtech lived up to its promise? The reasons are obvious. Because innovators too often embrace an impoverished conception of teaching and learning. Technology, we were told, would accelerate the transfer of information. Or automate drills and practice. Or provide tutorials. Or personalize and individualize instruction. Or replace instructors altogether. What educational technologies failed to do, however, was to do what a teacher does: motivate students, keep students engaged and on track, scaffold and support student learning, and provide timely constructive feedback.

Why is this the case? Because cost efficiency, rather than learning, tends to drive technological innovation. Despite talk about democratizing quality instruction or individualizing teaching and learning, much of the impetus behind the adoption of teaching technologies is to reduce instructional costs, substituting machines or software for the kind of hands-on support that benefits students most. Because instructors aren't trained to use classroom technologies effectively. In the absence of training or examples of the successful use of classroom technologies, most instructors continue to teach as they have in the past, through lectures, discussion, questions, and demonstrations. Because educational technologies do not align with the way most instructors teach. Most teaching is didactic and instructor focused, involving information transfer and guided discussion. Instructional technologies presuppose very different pedagogical approaches in which students learn individually or work in groups or are expected to engage in an activity in class.

Also, because of a lack of compelling evidence that technology actually improves student learning. Educational technologies are often promoted for nonacademic reasons: because of hype or an exaggerated belief that exposure to them will better prepare graduates for the digital economy. Without empirical evidence of effectiveness, many instructors consider technology a waste of money at best and a distraction and intrusion at worst. Because of the gap between what technology promises and what it delivers. Hypesters consistently overpromise and underdeliver, breeding skepticism and cynicism about technology's value and the motives of its advocates. Despite claims to the contrary, there isn't large unmet student demand for a more technology-enhanced education or evidence that exposure to edtech makes graduates more employable and better prepared for twenty-first-century workplaces. Above all, because creating educationally impactful technologies is difficult. High-impact instructional technologies are, almost always, beyond the ability of a lone innovator. Effective technologies require a raft of specialists: in user experience design, software development, and assessment, to be sure, but also in content creation and imaginative instruction.

All this said, the past need not dictate the future. Just because technology after technology has been swept into history's dustpan, this does not mean that technology can't improve learning. Some technologies have worked. The most obvious is the humble chalkboard, which was first introduced at West Point early in the nineteenth century and underscored the value of visualization, especially when used to illustrate the process of solving a problem or organizing complex material.

Instructors readily adopt technologies that improve student learning or their ability to perform their jobs. It's not an accident that the educational technologies that have been widely embraced—like today's PowerPoint slides or LCD projectors or whiteboards or learning management systems—genuinely contribute to improved student learning and represent indisputable improvements over the tools they replaced: the hornbook, the blackboard, the mimeo, the slide projector, or the paper gradebook. Such technologies were adopted precisely because they made it easier for instructors to prepare classes, engage students, monitor learning, and perform their administrative tasks—because the technologies were regarded as educationally beneficial, not because they were imposed from the top down. Technologies can have a transformational impact, increasing student learning and engagement and improving pedagogical practice. But if technologies are to have a revolutionary impact, we need to think of them as tools that can solve problems instructors actually experience in the classroom.

Let me spell out ways that I find technology useful. Technology can be diagnostic. It can provide the instructor and the student with granular, real-time insights into student engagement and understanding of essential course material and flag areas of confusion and misunderstanding. Technology can prompt midcourse corrections and timely student interventions, as necessary. I am a staunch advocate of dashboards: instructor-facing, student-facing, and both.

Dashboards can reveal time spent on the course website, identify questions that students find difficult or confusing, and chart students' progress. Dashboards can motivate students and prompt instructors to rethink their pedagogy and reach out to students who are off track. Technology can cut the cost of course materials. I'm not just referring to OER, the open educational resources like those offered by OpenStax that can replace costly textbooks, but to instructor- or publisher-developed interactive courseware, which combines the features of a textbook with rich multimedia, a wealth of instructional resources, data banks, tutorials, active learning activities, and embedded assessments. Technology can personalize the learning experience.

Apart from MOOCs, no technology was more overhyped than personalized, adaptive courseware. But just because a technology was oversold doesn't mean that it was a bad idea. Many students do need a more customized, individualized learning experience that identifies gaps in their knowledge, makes recommendations about what to study next, offers tutorials to address confusions, and provides opportunity to practice skills—all at an appropriate pace and with tailored content that the student finds compelling. Computer technologies hold out the prospect of customizing pace, content, activities, assessments, and each student's learning trajectory. By monitoring student engagement and errors and confusions, these technologies can identify students at risk of failure in near real time and provide ready access to tutorials. Such technologies can also connect students to classmates and campus learning centers.

Also, technology can bring previously inaccessible instructional resources into the classroom. Whether these are primary sources, including letters, diaries, and other personal papers; visual resources, such as advertisements, artworks, film clips, maps, photographs, political cartoons, and propaganda posters; unconventional sources like gravestones, fashion hair styles, and naming patterns; or data sources, such as census registers or voting returns, we now have an unparalleled opportunity to let students work with the very sources that professionals do. The pedagogy of scarcity, in which source materials were limited to whatever resources were available in a campus library, no longer limits instructors' options. We need to seize on the possibilities of the pedagogy of abundance, the ready availability of almost limitless source materials that can be accessed through such content repositories as the Library of Congress's American Memory project, my own Digital History website, the Digital Public Library of America, DocsTeach, the Gilder Lehrman Institute of American History, History Matters, and the Stanford History Education Group. Royalty-free images are available at sites like Photos for Class.

In addition, technology can facilitate team-based learning and collaboration. Collaboration and communication tools can connect students with classmates as well as those outside the classroom. Collaborative research projects and presentations can be undertaken remotely and even asynchronously. Connected learning might involve guest lecturers, practicing professionals, alumni, and digital pen pals, among others. These tools can also bring fieldwork or clinicals into a classroom. Then, too, technology can create immersive learning environments. Whether these are virtual worlds, like Second Life, or virtual reconstructions of existing sites, such as ancient Rome, a medieval cathedral, or Chicago's 1893 World's Columbian Exposition, these digital environments provide opportunities for role-playing, collaboration, exploration, problem-solving, and vicariously experiencing life in a radically different context. Nonthreatening environments can also address issues related to performance anxiety and stereotype threat.

There are still other things that technology can do well. It can build skills. Technology can help students master essential skills by providing practice exercises and simulations. Precisely because technology never tires or grows annoyed, it can take care of the more repetitive aspects of teaching and learning. Technology can also make learning a more active process. Education is, of course, not simply a matter of conveying information. Nor is it merely a matter of practice. Deep learning requires students to engage with and process course materials. Technology can help make education more equitable and transform learners into investigators, analysts, and creators of knowledge. It can offer the tools students need to analyze and annotate texts and data; manipulate and visualize data; map concepts, causation, or networks; make dynamic and interactive maps, timelines, and websites; manage bibliographic information; organize and curate research materials; simulate laboratory experiments; and create media-rich narratives and presentations.

Learning should not be a spectator sport. Meaningful learning requires active engagement, critical thinking, and thoughtful reflection. The best way to master a subject is to do what professional academics do—engage in inquiry, problem-solving, analysis, and interpretation. So how can we use technology to make learning more active?

- **Annotation**: You might ask your students to explicate and annotate a written text or document either individually or collectively using apps like hypothes.is or Perusall, or video clips using VideoAnt.
- **Citation**: Show your students how to create a citation from a URL with MyBib citation creator or manage collections of citations with Zotero.
- **Collaboration**: Ask students to collectively create documents and presentations with Google Docs, Slides, and Sheets. Padlet .com lets users create a collaboration space, and Google Jamboard offers a digital whiteboard on which students can collaborate. Slack and Microsoft Teams offer platforms that facilitate team communication and collaboration, while Basecamp, Kanbanchi, and Trello offer project management tools.
- **Concept and network mapping**: Students can map relationships among concepts or networks or causal factors with Coggle, Cliovis, Lucidchart, Popplet, and Sketchboard.
- **Curation**: Students can bookmark websites with symbaloo .com or elink.io and aggregate content with Google Keep, paper.li, livebinders.com, wakelet.com, or webjets.io. Google

Keep offers a simple way for students to curate visual as well as textual resources.

- **Data visualization**: Students might use Google MyMaps to create and annotate maps. The National Archives' docsteach .org offers a simple way to plot primary sources, descriptive text, or boxes for student response on a historic map or an outline map. Wordle makes it easy to create word clouds, while Google Ngrams allows students to analyze changes in word frequency in published books. Students can create visualizations of census data with census.gov/dataviz.
- **Etymology**: The *Oxford English Dictionary* and the *Online Etymology Dictionary* allow students to trace shifts in words' meaning and the introduction of popular terminology, concepts, and slang.
- **Exhibition creation**: Google Slides offers a simple platform on which to create virtual exhibitions.
- **Feedback**: Peer feedback offers a way for students to provide constructive feedback to classmates. One valuable example: ask students to collaboratively construct grading rubrics. Learning management systems like Canvas offer tools that allow students to review and comment on other students' assignment submissions.
- **Geomapping**: Use theclio.com to identify local sites of historical or cultural significance. Historypin is a collaboration tool that allows users to share images from history across time and space and place those memories on maps and timelines.
- **Global learning**: Examples of global learning include paired classrooms and virtual pen pals. Skype in the Classroom offers an easy way to create virtual field trips and virtual, online conversations with content area specialists.
- **Interactive lessons**: Students can respond to a video with edpuzzle.com and enhance a website with insertlearning.com. Instructors can build lessons around TED talks with ed.ted .com.

- **Portfolios and digital galleries**: Students can create portfolios and digital galleries with showcaseedu.com and create and annotate a portfolio with seesaw.me.
- **Project-based learning**: Here are some twenty-first-century alternatives to the classic research paper. You might ask students to create an infographic with Infogram, Piktochart, or Venngage or make an interactive poster with Glogster or Thinklink. They might build a presentation with PowerPoint or Google Slides; a podcast with anchor.fm or Audacity; a digital story with Adobe Spark, iMovie, MS Photo Story 3, or MS Movie Maker; or a virtual museum or exhibition with Google Slides.
- **Student response systems**: Polling and quizzing provide a simple way to monitor student understanding in near real time. Clickers and their equivalent can make listening to lectures a more interactive learning process by inviting students to respond to the instructor's questions or to react and offer their opinions about a particular issue or interpretation.
- **Survey tools**: Consider conducting a survey using Google Forms or SurveyMonkey, and then you can use anonymous survey data in class to explore attitudes, interests, and opinions, or even students' family backgrounds and experiences.
- **Text mining**: A simple tool for mining a text, which can offer insights into word choice, metaphors, and imagery, is voyant -tools.org.
- **Timelines**: TimelineJS and TimeMapper allow students to quickly create a timeline from a spreadsheet.

The future of higher education is likely to be blended, combining the virtual and the face-to-face and melding guided inquiry with active and experiential learning. Technology will play a bigger role in instruction, not simply because of its possible cost efficiencies but because of its potential to address some of the shortcomings in teaching today. These include the need to do a better job of scaffolding learning, tailoring instruction to individual student needs, addressing differences in levels of student preparation, promoting collaboration, monitoring student engagement and learning, and providing more timely, substantive, and constructive feedback.

Technology can help accomplish all these goals, but it will require instructors to rethink their roles and conceive of themselves in a new way: as learning design specialists, learning experience engineers, activity architects, and assessment designers. Why should instructors make the effort to master these educational technologies? Because instructors, especially those in the most challenging, high-demand disciplines, will be under intense pressure to reduce performance and achievement gaps and see that all students in a particular course achieve a minimal viable level of competency; ensure that students acquire discipline-based modes of thinking and can apply discipline-specific skills; expand students' opportunities to engage in inquiry, investigation, and active learning by doing; and make certain that their students remain engaged and on track.

One tool that may help accomplish those goals is interactive courseware, the next iteration of the textbook. Courseware includes multimedia-rich, immersive content, interactives, simulations, and personalized, adaptive learning pathways and virtual tutorials powered by frequently embedded formative assessments. In the ideal world, individual instructors would be able to remix, edit, and modify courseware materials. Courseware holds out the possibility of transforming the online component of a course into a journey in which students will engage in purposeful learning activities intentionally designed to cultivate and build essential skills and command of content. Courseware can also track, scaffold, and proactively support student learning. Embedded assessments will continually monitor and evaluate students' knowledge and skills, including their higher order and critical thinking skills, and provide meaningful, substantive, useful feedback. Courseware can also be gamified, awarding students points as they progress to more advanced levels of understanding and performance. Courseware can do what traditional textbooks cannot: truly bring a subject to life and allow students to interact and engage with the instructional material.

In the final analysis, technology is a tool, not a substitute for a live instructor who can motivate, explain, inspire, guide, support, and respond to student concerns and confusions in real time. If we think of technology as a tool that can enhance learning, then we can begin to appreciate the genuine ways it can support learning beyond drills, quizzes, and the dissemination of instructional material. Technology can give students opportunities to conduct research, evaluate and interpret evidence, analyze texts or data sets, visualize social networks or causal relationships, simulate laboratory experiments, and present information or arguments in compelling ways, through charts and graphs, infographics, podcasts, and video narratives. Developing these kinds of interactive technologies is in most cases beyond the capabilities of individual instructors, which is precisely why we need new kinds of partnerships among disciplinary, learning, assessment, and technology experts. Education's next stage, in short, is less about lone eagles and singular artisans and more focused on teams of collaborators who will create the apps that truly can enhance the learning process.

# 9

## Rethinking Assessment

RIGOROUS ASSESSMENT IS CENTRAL TO EDUCATION. After all, it tells us whether our students are mastering essential skills and knowledge and whether our teaching is effective. But grading also provokes much grousing. Many students complain that grading is arbitrary, inconsistent, and unfair, while many instructors grumble about grade inflation, the excessive amount of time devoted to grading, and the many student complaints that grading prompts. I myself have said that I'd teach for free, but I need to be paid to grade.

Then, there are the more informed criticisms of grading expressed by educational psychologists and psychometricians: that a single, overall grade conflates elements that need to be disentangled; that grades tend to overly reward lower order thinking skills (such as memorization and recall) rather than higher order skills (involving analysis, application, and synthesis); that grades too often fail to accurately reflect student learning or mastery; and that grades are frequently demotivating and discouraging. It is a sad fact that at many institutions we have the worst of all worlds: grades are inconsistent across disciplines; grades offer students little feedback; grades do not reflect engagement and growth; and grades, outside the sciences, cluster around an A-. Too often, grades do not truly recognize students who excel or motivate students to persist and ultimately master the material.

How can we make assessment more meaningful? If we are to improve grading, we must first ask why we grade. Is it to rank students? Is it to measure performance or knowledge or memory or higher order thinking skills? Is it to motivate students to study or to diagnose learning problems or to assess mastery? Grades can serve multiple functions. They can be informational, telling students how they are doing. They can be motivational, encouraging students to study and master essential material. Grades can be diagnostic, identifying weaknesses and strengths. They can be evaluative, measuring mastery of skills and knowledge. Or they can be metacognitive, encouraging self-reflection and helping students develop the ability to assess their own learning. In addition, grades can be formative—prompting students to improve their performance and prompting instructors to address student confusions—or summative, providing an overall assessment of students' success. Grades can serve as a measure of a student's level of understanding, the range of their work, the sophistication of their ideas, their facility with various concepts and skills, the amount of work they have performed, or their growth.

What is it, then, that we want to grade? We can grade process: students' thought processes or their application of skills and knowledge. We can grade effort, which might include time spent or research conducted. We can grade participation and students' active engagement in class activities. Alternatively, we can grade progress—how far students have advanced—or outcomes, students' demonstrated performance.

In addition, our approach to grading can be holistic or targeted (based on discrete assignments); norm-referenced or criterion-referenced (i.e., relative to other classmates or based on predetermined criteria); or based on subjective or objective criteria. We can provide opportunities for extra credit or retakes and revisions—or not.

In recent years, assessment specialists have advocated a variety of innovative approaches to grading that seek to address the concerns voiced by psychometricians. These include the following:

- *Standards-based grading*: Under this approach, students must demonstrate proficiency in well-defined course objectives. Students who meet these objectives get identical grades.
- *Achievement-based grading*: Here, assessment is based on how far students go beyond minimal expectations.
- *Mastery-based grading*: Under this approach, students are given opportunities to retake assignments until an acceptable level of mastery is achieved.
- *Specifications grading*: An instructor creates detailed "specifications" on what it means to adequately do an assignment and then designs activities that give students opportunities to demonstrate that they have met these specifications.

I might add some additional ways to think about grading. A *game-based approach* incentivizes attainment of learning goals by awarding points for completing assignments or badging accomplishments. A *simplified approach* replaces fine-grained assessments with more general categories, such as "Exemplary," "Accomplished," "Promising," and "Developing." A *proficiency-based approach* focuses on progress toward clearly defined learning objectives. Grades, from this perspective, communicate what a student is able to do, but students have extended time to practice and develop their skills.

What advice would I offer? First, make your criteria available ahead of time. There's no reason to surprise students. Discuss the standards you grade by. Next, involve students in defining grading criteria to help them better understand your standards. Have the students draft a rubric and collaboratively evaluate sample answers in class. Then, adopt a multitiered assessment strategy that evaluates student performance in varied ways. These might include checks for understanding, practice sets, project-based assessments, and team-based assessments. In other words, include the application and creation of knowledge within your grading standards.

Also, make grades more meaningful by clarifying their purpose. Let your students know whether you are grading a particular assignment for diagnostic reasons, to assess the quality of their work, or for some other reason. On specific assignments and activities, substitute multiple grades for a single overarching grade. You might offer separate grades for each learning objective, such as depth of research or integration and analysis of evidence. Make grading a more positive experience by making it more forward-looking. That is, place greater emphasis on progress in student learning. Above all, design your grading system so that it encourages and rewards progress toward your learning objectives. Grading improvement shouldn't be confined to elementary school. Just as no single grade should be taken as an assessment of a student's intelligence, no single grade should invalidate a student's later work. Progress over time deserves recognition.

You, perhaps, heard that the San Diego Unified School District in California recently revamped its grading policy. It told teachers not to deduct points from homework that was submitted late. It also required teachers to allow students to retake tests and resubmit graded assignments, to use multiple measures to assess student performance, and to separate nonacademic factors, including behavior, punctuality, or effort, from academic grades. Teachers would not be able to give students a final grade based on the average of their individual grades over the course of a term. Even more controversially, the district proposed to eliminate letter grades, which would be replaced by a four-point scale: "exceeds standards," "meets standards," "approaching standards," and "beginning progress toward standards." Technically, a teacher could still give a grade of Unsatisfactory, signifying little or no progress toward standards, but such grades would, apparently, no longer be factored into a student's grade point average. The district's goal was to eliminate failing grades by giving students additional time to demonstrate that they had met the minimum standards for passing a course.

The district's logic was that former grading practices were biased against students whose life circumstances made it difficult to complete assignments on time; no student should be penalized for getting off to a slow start or for struggling at various points during the term; and the preexisting grading system undercut students' self-confidence while increasing levels of stress and anxiety. Instead, grades should exclusively assess a student's mastery of the instructional material and not conflate mastery with a teacher's subjective evaluation of a student's work habits.

Not surprisingly, these policy revisions outraged critics who regarded the changes as a retreat from academic rigor and a thinly veiled effort to mask the district's failure to successfully reduce achievement and performance gaps. My own view is that both the district and its critics make certain valid points, and the challenge that instructors confront is to create an approach to grading that signals levels of mastery and achievement, rewards progress and effort, incentivizes students to keep on track, and also takes into account that students don't learn at the same pace and some students do encounter serious midsemester challenges that shouldn't automatically lead to failure.

Before those of us in higher education scoff at the grading controversies that have erupted in K–12 education, we should acknowledge the sad fact that today's college grading system, in which a majority of college students receive a grade in the A range, fails to do any of the things that a valid, reliable, and meaningful grading system ought to do. It doesn't do a sufficiently nuanced job of differentiating between levels of student performance, nor does it inform students, in a fine-grained manner, of areas of weakness that require improvement. Worse yet, because most grades depend on a relatively small number of high-stakes assessments, the current system tends to encourage cramming and, yes, academic dishonesty. A better alternative, to my mind, is to assess student work much more frequently with low-stakes quizzes, brief written responses to prompts, and various activities that must be completed but that are graded on a simple three-point scale. By combining these formative and diagnostic evaluations with bigger project-based assessments that students must complete through a sequence of steps, each with its own deadline, we can help ensure that students remain engaged and on track toward genuine mastery of the course material.

―――

One primary purpose of assessment is to ensure rigor—a word that is conspicuously absent in much of the current discourse on educational innovation. Rigor is a concept that goes in and out of fashion, peaking most recently in the 1990s and early 2000s before fading away. The term's absence tells us a great deal about our current priorities, which emphasize access, retention, and completion over and above depth of learning, quality of instruction, and high standards.

Rigor is a loaded term, laden with disparate meanings. It can refer to workload, pacing, degree of instructor support, or level of difficulty and cognitive demand. In common parlance, rigor is often a synonym for a harsh, inflexible approach to education that revels in its difficulty. It is associated with rigid, unyielding academic standards, fixed and rigid requirements, and grueling schoolwork, homework, and examinations that rely heavily on rote memorization. Calls for rigor can be a backhanded way to criticize and combat grade inflation, reduced reading and writing requirements, and trendy, frivolous, or excessively politicized courses of study. Not surprisingly, some respond by claiming that demands for increased rigor represent a form of bias, harming those students with complicated lives whose level of preparation or academic skills are less than the "top" students' or those who learn at a slower pace than their more agile peers.

There's another way to think about rigor that I believe higher education should embrace enthusiastically. A rigorous higher education is one that promotes students' cognitive development, command of a field of study, and relevant skills and knowledge. However, many of our current incentives cut against rigor: nurturing durable skills and broad command of content requires demanding coursework, extensive homework, and lots of scaffolding and feedback from instructors. It can't be done on the cheap, rapidly, or easily.

By now, we're all familiar with studies such as the Social Science Research Council's collaborative partnership with the Pathways to

College Network using data from the Council for Aid to Education's Collegiate Learning Assessment longitudinal study, which found that many classes are anything but rigorous. This study tracked 2,300 students at 24 universities over the course of four years, starting in 2005, and it reported that half of sophomores hadn't taken a single course in the prior semester that required more than 20 pages of writing, and only a third had taken a course requiring more than 40 pages of reading a week. A more recent survey reported that while most students said they're making an effort in their studies, with 64 percent reporting that they put "a lot of effort" into their school work, a third of those students said they spent less than 5 hours a week on studying and homework, and 70 percent said they spent no more than 10 hours a week on schoolwork.[1]

There are certain realistic steps that we can take to raise the level of rigor in our courses, while providing the necessary support to ensure that all students can meet higher standards.

Step 1: **Ensure that students complete required reading through frequent quizzing.** The ability to read a work of literature, a scholarly book or article, or a primary source closely and critically lies at the heart of a college education, and we need to do more to encourage the kind of reading that pays close attention to rhetoric, structure, argumentation, evidence, and conclusions. Frequent low-stakes quizzes can not only ensure that students take their reading assignments seriously, but they can also help students monitor their understanding of the texts and enhance their ability to understand and explicate difficult passages and arguments.

Step 2: **Significantly increase your class's writing requirements.** It's a cliché but true: one learns to write by writing. Instructors need to familiarize their students with the attributes of successful academic writing within their discipline, including how to formulate a research question, craft a sophisticated thesis, situate or contextualize an argument within the existing literature, properly integrate, analyze, and cite evidence, structure an argument, and write an effective conclusion. Peer feedback and a simple four-point proficiency evaluation scale (e.g., advanced, proficient, partially proficient, and insufficient evidence) offer ways to incorporate more writing into your class without significantly increasing your workload.

Step 3: **Require students to complete more skills-building and problem-solving activities inside and outside class.** Design activities that mimic professional practice and that require the use of higher order thinking skills. The possibilities are too many to list in entirety but include researching a particular topic or problem, analyzing a case study, taking part in a debate, evaluating and interpreting data, an object, or a piece of evidence, and engaging in authentic practice—for example, by writing a policy brief or an op-ed essay, creating and administering a survey, or drafting a proposal.

Step 4: **Require students to complete large projects in a series of component parts, each of which must be submitted for inspection and comment**. Thus, a research paper would be broken into smaller requirements: an annotated bibliography, a thesis statement, an outline, and an initial draft, followed by a final draft.

Step 5: **Require faculty members to explain how the proposed course addresses five key dimensions of rigor.** We don't need to use course grades, student evaluations, or a course's syllabus or title to assess a class's rigor. A much more effective alternative is to ask faculty, as part of the institution's course approval or course review process, to explain the following: how the class encourages critical thinking and problem solving; in what specific ways the course is intellectually and academically challenging; which complex materials or skills the course requires students to master; what the outside-of-class time commitment is that students are expected to meet in order to study and complete the course readings and assignments; and what credible, quality work students are expected to produce.

Step 6: **Better align a course's credit hours with the time commitments it demands.** We're all familiar with the rule of thumb that for every course credit hour, a student should expect to spend two to three hours studying outside of class. Might it not make sense to more realistically assess how much study time a particular course actually requires? And might it not make sense to consider awarding credit for the supplemental instruction that many students need to succeed in areas with especially high levels of cognitive complexity?

Rigor is not a four-letter word, nor is it an enemy of equity. In fact, a commitment to rigor rests on the belief that all students are capable of meeting high standards if given sufficient time and support. Rather than equating rigor with harsher grading or more homework or longer reading lists, it's better to think of rigor in terms of the kinds of learning activities that students must undertake and the assessments used to verify and validate their learning. This approach shifts attention to the time spent in inquiry, problem solving, close reading, conducting research, and writing. The six simple steps listed above can raise rigor by helping faculty agree on the appropriate workload for particular classes and the standards of excellence and proficiency that students are expected to achieve.

# 10

Helping Students Become Better Writers

THERE IS NO GREATER GIFT that colleges can give to their students than the ability to write clearly, compellingly, and analytically. Instructors may not be able to help students write with style, grace, elegance, and panache, but they can certainly help undergraduates learn to write with clarity, concision, precision, impact, and coherence. But instructors rarely do that. Writing instruction is largely relegated to first-year rhetoric and composition courses (often taught by creative writers who reject the notion that they work for the department of corrections) or to writing centers.

It's obvious why this is the case. Most faculty members lack any formal training in writing instruction. We lead busy lives, juggling teaching, research, service, and personal responsibilities. We have too many students to pay much attention to more than a few. Anyway, providing feedback that goes beyond substance strikes most of us as too demanding. But failing to engage in writing instruction is anything but a victimless crime. I think it's fair to say that college graduates with weak writing skills will, sooner rather than later, hit a low glass ceiling. Any job above the entry level requires drafting proposals, writing reports, submitting grant or other funding applications, entering employee evaluations, and composing sales pitches and other forms of written expression.

The classic approach to writing advice, exemplified by William Strunk and E. B. White's *The Elements of Style*, lays out a series of Dr. Seuss–like simple, even memorable, rules of grammar, usage, and composition: "Use definite, specific, concrete language." "Avoid starting a sentence with however." "Omit needless words." "Avoid tame, colorless, hesitating, noncommittal language."[1] The text's many well-known injunctions include the following: avoid the passive voice, begin paragraphs with topic sentences, use concrete language, and, at least at first, steer clear of mannerisms, tricks, and adornments. Strunk and White's readers learn how to use parentheses, possessive nouns, commas, colons, cases, and hyphens; how to avoid misspelling or misusing words (such as homonyms); and that they should eschew idiomatic phrases.

All of this is good advice, but it is not especially useful to students who must respond to a prompt or write an essay. Strunk and White's success encouraged a host of competitors to throw their hats into the ring, of which the most widely read include John R. Trimble's *Writing with Style*, Joseph M. Williams's *Style: The Basics of Clarity and Grace*, and William Zinsser's *On Writing Well*. Some of their advice is similar to Strunk and White's: Avoid clutter. Steer clear of trite, wordy, or useless expressions. Value brevity, clarity, and simplicity. Replace fancy language with ordinary words. Focus on nouns and strong, active verbs rather than adjectives and adverbs.

But much of the advice directly challenges Strunk and White's preoccupation with grammatical and stylistic rules. Trimble, Williams, and Zinsser all seek to move beyond Strunk and White's platitudes and show how to translate abstract principles into the construction of coherent, powerful sentences and cohesive paragraphs. Zinsser, for example, emphasizes the importance of voice, flow, and structure by beginning with a lede to engage readers and ending with a kicker, a bang-up conclusion that might consist of a surprising revelation, a poignant or emotional anecdote or quotation, or a powerful summary.

He calls on writers to speak in the first person, talk directly to the reader, and use various tricks to keep readers attentive.

All this advice is very interesting, but it is not appropriate in most academic or occupational settings. The problem with much of the popular advice is that the precepts strike many readers, hungry for useful suggestions, as excessively abstract and rarified. Much more practical is Gerald Graff's *They Say/I Say*, which provides templates that students can deploy. According to Graff, students misunderstand academic writing when they think of it simply as a matter of conveying information. Rather, the key to successful academic writing is to situate an essay in the context of a larger conversation, debate, or controversy. Right on, I say.

More recently, the Harvard cognitive scientist and linguist Steven Pinker offered yet another alternative to Strunk and White. In Pinker's view, language is a living entity that cannot be reduced to a series of rigid rules or precepts. Rather, the measure of success of a work of nonfiction is whether it helps a reader make sense of complicated realities. The art of writing is, therefore, a matter of taking a complex web of ideas and translating these ideas into a narrative or an argument in a linear sequence. Much in the same way that effective teaching benefits from an understanding of certain principles drawn from cognitive science—for example, those involving active engagement, retrieval and transfer, mental modeling, cognitive load, and metacognition—so does writing, too, profit from an understanding of cognitive theory.

Here are a few lessons that I have drawn from my own engagement with cognitive theory that can help us improve student writing at scale. First, make sure your students understand the purpose of a particular writing assignment. Are you certain that your students understand an assignment's aims? Is the goal to describe? Inform? Argue? Assess? Analyze? Persuade? Based on my experience, many students, perhaps most, have no idea what a particular assignment's objectives are—no wonder their written work seems confused. Once students grasp an assignment's aim, they are much better equipped to write appropriately. Students, in short, need to grasp your learning objectives. Only then will they know whether a particular piece of writing should be descriptive, argumentative, analytic, or evaluative.

Then, you should explain how bad writing grows out of flawed thinking. Why do writers rely on the passive voice? Because they are unwilling or unable to explain causality and agency. Why do writers hedge, mix metaphors, rely on jargon and nominalizations, or make use of overly complicated syntax? To mask unexamined assumptions. Why is an essay disorganized? Because the author's argument isn't coherent or logically developed. Sure, we've all encountered bad writing that is largely a byproduct of haste, lack of preparation, or inattention to basic principles of grammar. But more often, such writing represents a failure to clarify and develop one's argument. That ability isn't innate. We, as instructors, need to teach students how to generate and refine a thesis, weigh and evaluate evidence, and organize an argument.

Make sure that your students understand that writing is thinking. Many myths surround the practice of writing: that more words or fancier words are better than brevity or ordinary words; that good writers are born, not made; and that the five-paragraph essay offers a perfect template for any academic assignment. The most destructive misconception, in my view, is that you shouldn't write until you know exactly what you plan to say. In most instances, it's the writing process itself that generates ideas. That's certainly the case for me. As I write, a thesis or an argument emerges and gradually becomes more nuanced as weaknesses or counterarguments appear.

Also, remind your students: An opinion is not an argument. All of us have opinions, intuitions, and prejudgments, many of which reflect implicit personal biases, prejudices, or emotions. An argument, in contrast, must rest on evidence, knowledge, logical reasoning, and critical thinking. Effective writing involves making and developing a nuanced and compelling argument. You must develop the argument in a well-organized manner, marshaling and evaluating evidence and carefully considering alternative viewpoints and interpretations. Instructors need to guide students through that process.

Most important of all, make sure your students understand that writing requires rewriting. Polished prose reads effortlessly. It's witty, engaging, and often conversational. But students need to know that crafting such prose is hard work. It doesn't come effortlessly. Writing is a craft, and like any skill, it requires craftsmanship. It requires practice, professional judgment, attention to detail, taste, and fine-tuning. Let me be clear: writing is not simply yet another marketable skill that will increase a student's value in the job market. It is, in my view, the central skill that lies at the very heart of a college education.

It's only through writing that arguments or ideas take their most sophisticated form. When we teach students to write effectively, what we are really doing is teaching them how to think: how to formulate a compelling thesis or interpretation; how to connect, critically evaluate, and apply ideas; and how to develop generalizations, synthesize contrasting viewpoints, and present an argument logically and persuasively. We've all encountered great talkers. I myself have encountered some of the academy's most impressive conversationalists, and I can say categorically that Dr. Samuel Johnson had nothing that these talkers didn't have. Their humor, cleverness, storytelling ability, passion, and quick wittedness are incredible. But when we review a transcript, their magic typically slips away. The ultimate reality of ideas and arguments lies not in the world of speech but in writing. For without writing, thinking is inevitably unfocused, facile, disorganized, and superficial.

Writing is not merely a mode of communication. It's a process that, if we move beyond simple formulas, forces us to reflect, think, analyze, and reason. The goal of a writing assignment worth its salt is not simply to describe or persuade or summarize: it's to drive students to make sense of difficult material and develop their own distinctive take. Academic writing is not only a method of imparting information or demonstrating understanding, but also the most nuanced and sophisticated way to order, analyze, apply, and synthesize information. That's why assigning writing, irrespective of your discipline, is essential. Writing can enhance your students' ability to think and analyze, evaluate data and evidence, formulate a hypothesis, predict, and generalize.

Journalism as a profession may be in steep decline, but writing for a public audience has never been more popular. Blogging is widespread. More academics than ever write op-eds. A host of platforms have emerged that permit us to share our thoughts—WordPress, Substack, LinkedIn. People, today, write for many reasons: to pontificate, to persuade, to express ourselves, to raise our profile, to establish a brand. But the most important reason to write is to think.

It's during the writing process itself that ideas and arguments emerge. Writing is difficult and demanding not just because crafting artful sentences and paragraphs is challenging or because organizing a piece of writing effectively is a constant struggle, but because formulating an argument is tough. Writing is both a process and a platform: it's where you and I wrestle with other people's ideas, ideate, iterate, and develop a distinctive point of view.

The key to writing, I have found, lies in the process: a process that requires us to think systematically; to enter into a conversation, controversy or debate; to assess and analyze existing points of view; to reconsider the controversy and, in the process, gradually construct a fresh interpretation or thesis; to refine and revise that argument; and to figure out how to convey the argument in an interesting, engaging, and provocative manner, with a catchy lede and a powerful conclusion. What students need to do whenever they write is to take the time to follow the process. First, they must find a topic—a research finding, a news article, a book—that piques their curiosity. Then, they must read widely about the topic. The objective is to uncover the broader conversation or controversy that surrounds that topic. Then, they can gradually come up with their own take.

Academic writing is first and foremost about ideas. As John Warner has argued, "The sentence is not the basic skill or fundamental unit of writing. The idea is." Many weaknesses in students' written expression actually reflect a lack of clarity of thought. Ideas must come first. But ideas do not emerge spontaneously, like Athena popping out of Zeus's head fully grown and wearing a suit of armor. A take or a thesis grows out of engagement with an existing set of arguments. It requires careful reflection and reconsideration and persistence. Ditto for the writing process itself. Writing is a matter of craftsmanship. It entails attention to detail and refinement.[2]

This may make the writing process sound mechanical and formulaic. But, of course, the writing process is anything but effortless or undemanding. It's iterative. At each stage of the process—from research to writing to revision—I must question my argument; I must modify, amend, complicate, and refine my thesis; I must take into account counterarguments; and I must continuously reorganize and reword whatever I am writing.

Done right, I can't imagine a better illustration of Mihaly Csikszentmihalyi's concept of flow. Writing requires you to totally immerse yourself in the thinking and rethinking process. There are no shortcuts. So let's replace the five-paragraph essay with a very different process that consists of the following steps:

Step 1 is the discovery stage. Discover a topic that excites you, incites you, arouses your curiosity, or simply prompts questions.

Step 2 is the preparation stage. Read widely and listen closely and you'll inevitably come across an article, an essay, or a book that you need to come to terms with. At this stage, you may have a visceral reaction or an off-the-cuff opinion—but not a considered or thoughtful response. Do your best to understand the conflicting perspectives on the topic, weighing their strengths, weaknesses, and, above all, insights.

Step 3 is the initial stage of formulating an argument or thesis. Now that you have a general understanding of contrasting points of view, you can begin to formulate your own distinctive stance on the subject. An argument isn't mere description or opinion; it's a carefully considered take, a position grounded in evidence.

How do you formulate a thesis? By asking a series of questions: Do you agree with an existing perspective on the topic? If so, why? If not, why not? Are the existing perspectives too simplistic and need to be more complicated? Is the conventional wisdom on the topic deficient in some respect, and does it need to be modified or revised? Do the existing perspectives omit a key consideration (for example, gender or race or class)? Only after considering such questions can you advance a tentative or provisional argument.

**Step 4 involves refining your argument or thesis.** Crafting a compelling point of view is perhaps the most difficult and demanding part of the writing process. Making your argument more complex, nuanced, and sophisticated isn't easy. It requires you to continuously reevaluate your thesis and qualify, modify, refine, and, in many cases, reject it and start afresh.

**Step 5 is the craftsmanship stage.** Only now are you truly ready to write anything that resembles a polished draft. Successful writing requires patience. It's a matter, first, of organization. Just as the "difference between a mob and a trained army is organization," so, too, does the difference between an effective and an ineffective argument often lie in a piece of writing's structure and sequencing.[3] It not only requires you to advance your argument, but also to take account of counterarguments and alternative interpretations.

Polished writing also requires reader engagement. If you want to convince readers that your argument is correct, you must first grab their attention. There are many ways to do this: with an intriguing anecdote, a controversial quote, a mystery, an anniversary, or something unusual or unfamiliar. A strong conclusion, too, is essential if you want your readers to come away from your piece of writing with a fresh perspective. A summary or recapitulation or restatement of your thesis is not enough. Give the reader a takeaway, an object lesson, a warning, an admonition, or an inspiring vision.

Clarity and word choice are essential. Find ways to be clear even in the face of a knotty, dense, convoluted argument. Make sure you choose the correct words. As Mark Twain put it, "The difference between the almost right word and the right word is really a large matter—it's the difference between the lightning bug and the lightning."[4] Also, be stylish. Play with sentence structure. Inject wit. Pare away nominalizations. Use verbs that are dynamic and nouns that are concrete. Consider using adjectives as verbs. Add a distinctive voice to your writing through your use of tone, syntax, flow, and, most important of all, follow Joe Moran's advice in his *First You Write a Sentence*: make writing conversational.

As the great educational sociologist David Labaree has observed, "Writing is not just how we express our ideas; it's how we develop our ideas." Don't start with a thesis. Only develop your argument as you research the topic and as you engage in the writing process itself.[5]

———

The advent of artificial intelligence–powered text generators has evoked alarm among many faculty members that the new technology will encourage intellectual dishonesty, devalue writing, undermine faculty-student trust, raise doubts about the authenticity and originality of student work, and compromise the college essay. But many of these concerns, I am convinced, are projections or displacements of a more profound concern: that campuses have already downgraded the craft of writing. The sad fact is that faculty in many fields assign very little writing and provide little constructive feedback on the writing projects they do assign.

I actually consider text generators as allies, not adversaries. Think of all the things that these programs can already do. They can generate lists of bibliographical references, tutor students by defining terms and explaining difficult concepts, solve math problems, and debug programs step by step. These tools can also provide first drafts of course syllabi, identify scholarly debates on a particular topic, and explore subjects through differing theoretical lenses. In addition, even in these early stages of their development, text generators can model clearly organized descriptive and argumentative writing on a particular topic, help students learn about different writing genres and forms, and force serious writers to become stylists. In other words, AI text generators will establish a new baseline for student essays.

In my smaller classes, I require students to submit a detailed prompt input into a text generator, the text that the generator "wrote" in response to the prompt, an essay that builds on this foundation, supplemented with additional research that must be cited in a bibliography, and a list of the corrections, revisions, and additions that the student made in producing the reworked essay. In addition, I devote time in class to discussing the strengths and weaknesses of the text that the text generator produced.

I am well aware of the limitations of text generators. They are unhelpful on topics with fewer than 10,000 citations. Their factual references are sometimes false. They are currently unable to cite sources accurately, and the strength of their responses diminishes rapidly after only a couple of paragraphs. Nor can these text generators rank sources for reliability, quality, or trustworthiness. Yet to my mind, the technology, even in its current form, is an asset that faculty would be remiss not to leverage.

I'm no Dr. Pangloss, and I certainly don't want to come across as an uncritical promoter of the new technology, but I do think we shouldn't let our fears outweigh our hopes or let our anxieties overshadow future possibilities. Indeed, I am convinced that generative artificial intelligence will redefine what we mean by expertise.[6] Much as Google devalued memory, electronic calculators sped up complex calculations, Wikipedia displaced the printed encyclopedia, and online databases diminished the importance of a vast physical library, so, too, will the new tools profoundly alter the most prized skills.

It strikes me as likely that the skills most in demand will include, first of all, the ability to know what questions to ask. The quality and value of AI-powered tools hinge on the prompts they are asked. Better prompts elicit richer and more robust responses. A second key skill will be the ability to go beyond crowdsourced knowledge.

Advanced and specialized domain and subject matter expertise will become more valuable, since AI-produced responses will inevitably contain errors or oversimplifications. The capacity to spot inaccuracies, miscalculations, and other mistakes and to correct errors or complicate understanding will be highly valued. Third, we will need individuals who can leverage AI-generated insights into decisions and actions. Information becomes most valuable when it is actually applied in real-world contexts: when we solve problems or translate ideas into tangible products and services. The ability to implement solutions is, of course, well beyond AI's current capabilities. As one commentator put it succinctly, "If we want to retain an edge over machines, it is advisable that we avoid acting like one."[7]

In other words, if a program can do a job as well as a person can, then humans shouldn't duplicate those abilities; they must surpass them. The next task for higher education, then, is to prepare graduates to make the most effective use of the new tools and to rise above and beyond their limitations. That means pedagogies must emphasize active and experiential learning, show students how to take advantage of these new technologies, and produce graduates who can do those things that the tools cannot. It also means producing writers who can communicate even more effectively, less formulaically, and with more style than a text generator can.

It used to be the case that every educated adult knew the story of the Luddites, those early nineteenth-century English textile workers who sought to destroy the mechanized looms and knitting frames that ultimately eliminated their jobs and shattered their way of life. As the great historian of the English working class E. P. Thompson insisted, we mustn't condescend to the Luddites who (like late nineteenth-century southern and western farmers and 1970s- and 1980s-era steel and auto workers) were the tragic victims of "progress." But we must also recognize that their resistance to technology's advance, however valiant, was futile. It was doomed to defeat in the face of industrialization.[8]

As Claudia Goldin and Lawrence F. Katz have pointed out, technology and education are engaged in an ongoing race.[9] Robots and automation did, in fact, displace millions of members of the industrial working class. Computerization eliminated large swathes of middle management jobs. The threat now is to the very knowledge workers who many assumed were invulnerable to technological change. If we fail to instill within our students the advanced skills and expertise that they need in today's rapidly shifting competitive landscape, they, too, will be losers in the unending contest between technological innovation and education.

# 11

---

## Standing Up for Equity

ACROSS THE HIGHER EDUCATION LANDSCAPE, disparities in per student spending on instruction, student services, and academic support are stark. An elite private institution like Yale spends over six times more per student on instruction and student support than Ohio State University, a public flagship, and over twelve times more than Cal State Long Beach. This holds true even though Yale serves a quarter of the number of students as OSU and less than half the number as Long Beach. The actual educational experience could scarcely be less equal. While three-quarters of Yale's classes have fewer than twenty students, less than a third of OSU's classes and less than a quarter of Long Beach's classes can say the same. Furthermore, Yale's student-to-faculty ratio is a third of OSU's and an eighth of Long Beach's. Higher education's inequities could hardly be more glaring or the contradiction with higher education's democratic promise more visible.[1]

Mark Twain once told a story about visiting heaven, where he asked to meet the greatest author who ever lived. He contemplated who he might meet—might it be Dante or Shakespeare?—only to be introduced to a farmer who had never written or published anything.

How could this possibly be? Because in heaven, greatness is defined by what would have been had circumstances been different.

American higher education is a mess of glaring contradictions. Often touted as engines of opportunity and upward social mobility, American colleges and universities are also among the most stratified, reputation-conscious institutions in American society, differing radically in terms of resources, student-faculty ratios, and selectivity in admissions. Despite regular and repeated denunciations of racism and racial disparities from administrators and faculty members, few selective institutions enroll a student body representative of the college-age population's demographics, while Black, Latinx, and students from low-income backgrounds remain concentrated in the least-selective, lowest-resourced institutions. It's no surprise that many selective private colleges focus their recruitment efforts on affluent, predominantly White and often private high schools. But it is astounding that many public flagships visit more out-of-state high schools than in those in-state and also concentrate on affluent, predominantly White high schools, with an emphasis on private schools.

Higher education's faculty ranks among the most politically liberal segments of the US population, yet the professoriate is also extremely status conscious and is highly differentiated by salary, job security, teaching load, research opportunities, and prestige. And even though teaching and mentoring lie at the heart of a professor's responsibilities, most faculty members receive no formal instruction in pedagogy, aren't required to receive any professional development training, and, at many institutions, aren't well rewarded for high-quality instruction or for guiding and motivating students or providing emotional support or serving as role models.

I could go on. Although a majority of undergraduates start at a community college and aspire for a bachelor's degree, and four-year schools would benefit from an influx of new students, barriers to transfer student success, including delays in credit evaluation, transfer credits denied or only accepted as electives, and inequities in financial aid allocations persist, and four-year institutions generally fail to recruit transfer students or provide them with sufficient postenrollment academic or social integration support.

Despite a heightened focus on retention and completion, nearly two-fifths of all students who start at a two- or four-year school fail to attain any degree within six years. While this partly reflects student circumstances, it also reflects institutional policies that conflict with the realities of many students' lives. Meanwhile, many nonprofit institutions behave like for-profits when they offer in-person or online professional master's programs, regarding these programs as profit centers irrespective of student debt loans relative to average postgraduation earnings.

Then there are other kinds of inequities that beset American higher education. Society invests far larger sums of money in a college education than in vocational or technical education. There's the tendency for women and men to gravitate toward different majors, with significantly fewer women in high-demand, high-salary fields like computer science and engineering. But of all of higher education's glaring contradictions, perhaps the most disturbing lies in the gaps in the educational experience that undergraduates receive along class and racial lines and that contribute to marked differences in completion rates and postgraduation employment. Students at broad-access institutions have much less access to advising, counseling, support services, and the high-impact practices that promote student engagement and deep learning. They're also much less likely to interact with a tenured professor who is also a publishing scholar or take part in the cocurricular and extracurricular activities that do so much to provide networking and leadership opportunities, open windows into careers, promote a sense of belonging, and contribute to psychological wellness and cultural enrichment. In other words, it's not just K–12 schools that reflect and reinforce society's inequalities. The higher education sector does too.

Higher education's contradictions stem less from hypocrisy than from the workings of the competitive marketplace, which rewards institutions very unequally and creates incentives at odds with colleges and universities' self-declared democratic mission. Campuses seek prestige, rankings, revenue, and grants, which helps explain why more selective institutions fail to enroll more nontraditional students. Faculty members pursue professional validation. We live in a market society, and it shouldn't surprise us that market considerations drive decision-making at both the institutional and personal levels.

According to the latest statistics I could find, four-year privates spent an average of $25,037 on instruction, student services, and academic support compared to $15,937 at four-year publics and $8,273 at two-year publics.[2] A wealth of statistics underscore the depth of inequity within higher education. A 2012 study by Caroline M. Hoxby and Christopher Avery found that 43 percent of high-achieving low-income students were "undermatched"—enrolling in a college or university less selective than their qualifications would permit. Although less than 2 percent of the nation's students attend private schools, 24 percent of Yale's Class of 2024, 25 percent of Princeton's, and 29 percent of Brown's and Dartmouth's did.[3]

Stratification within higher education is, of course, nothing new, and it's not simply a matter of resources or student selectivity or faculty teaching loads. The gap between a residential education and a commuter experience or between an in-person and online education are only the most obvious divides. But over the course of much of the last century, the long-term trend was toward convergence. Whether students attended a research university, a small liberal arts college, a flagship or land-grant university, a regional comprehensive, or an urban campus, and whether they pursued a liberal arts or a vocational or pre-professional degree, the curriculum, requirements, and pedagogy did not dramatically differ. But now we're seeing the emergence of a new kind of gap. If students go to a selective, well-resourced institution (or take part in an honors program), they are much more likely to encounter a wider range of program offerings, receive a variety of experiential learning opportunities, and participate in rich cocurricular and extracurricular activities. Project-based learning, maker spaces, mentored research, and entrepreneurship activities are far more accessible.

The resounding demands for equity within higher education heard far and wide during the summer of 2020 have, I fear, faded. A 2016 pledge by elite institutions to boost enrollment of low-income students added just 7,713 such students between 2015 and 2021—nowhere near the 50,000 promised by the American Talent Initiative. Regardless of their innate talents or prior educational achievement, students don't start out at the same place. Irrespective of their ability or prior educational achievement, students from lower-income backgrounds are incentivized to attend institutions with fewer resources that, in turn, reduces their chances for graduation and finding a good job. This country's system of postsecondary education relegates the students with the greatest needs to the most under-resourced institutions.

American higher education's inequities and disparities are particularly manifest in access to the fields of study that result in the highest postgraduation incomes. STEM fields, for instance, graduate significantly fewer students from underrepresented backgrounds with similar qualifications as White males. Introductory STEM courses, far too often, serve weed-out functions that, "disproportionately push underrepresented minority students out of the natural and applied sciences."[4] There are gated majors, typically in computer science, engineering, and nursing, and at my institution, business, that require students to earn a minimum grade point average (GPA) in an introductory course in order to declare a major. As Preston Cooper, a senior fellow at the Foundation for Research on Equal Opportunity, explains, "three-quarters of academic departments at the top 25 public universities impose a restriction on declaring the major" in computer science, economics, finance, mechanical engineering, and nursing. The result: to reduce the number of students who earn majors in those fields by 15 percentage points, exacerbating racial and ethnic disparities. Why do departments impose such restrictions? Capacity constraints are a factor but so is a desire to raise a department's rankings. There are also the very large weed-out courses (or simply large lecture classes, like my 400-person sections of the US history survey) without discussion labs or supplemental instruction sessions that have outsized DFW rates.[5]

As a recent report from Georgetown's Center on Education and the Workforce points out, a Black student with above-median 10th-grade-math scores is 22 percent less likely than a White student to earn a college degree and 43 percent less likely than an Asian student. Latino/a students with above-median math scores are 46 percent less likely to earn a degree than a comparable White student and 78 percent less likely than an Asian student. The Georgetown Center describes the implications of these statistics in blunt terms: "Equally talented students don't get the same chance to be all that they can be." I couldn't agree more strongly with the Center's argument: "All children deserve the opportunity to reach their full potential, regardless of their family's socioeconomic status. But many disadvantaged children don't have access to the same community support and enrichment activities as their affluent peers."[6]

So what should the broad-access institutions that serve most of this country's college students do? First, let's state what they shouldn't do. Insofar as possible, they should not retreat from the goal of providing a highly accessible, affordable, quality education, for example, by narrowing their curriculum. Also, while they might supplement course offerings with short-term training and certification programs, faculty and accreditors need to recognize that the outcomes of such programs are mixed, and that an associate's and especially a bachelor's degree offers much more traction in the job market.

What, then, is the answer? Greater equity in resources would surely help, and I certainly favor that. But rather than wait for manna to fall from heaven, I'd urge these campuses to borrow from the best. There are many institutions that punch above their weight. Despite resource constraints, certain colleges and universities bring outsized numbers of Black, Latinx, and Pell Grant–eligible students to success. What do these institutions do that others don't? These pace-setter institutions take onboarding of new students very seriously, offering immersion and bridge programs before classes start to build a sense of belonging, introduce students to campus facilities, services, and academic expectations, and provide every new student with a designated adviser and a degree plan. Some campuses make a special point of reaching out to parents and extended kin and encourage them to participate in orientation programs, recognizing that knowledgeable parents can contribute to success across students' academic journey. These innovative institutions award course credit or certificates to students who participate in a student success or introduction to college program to develop their study skills, learn about campus services, and assist with academic and career planning. They also enroll entering students in thematically focused meta-majors, course clusters, or cohorts to make course registration easier, build a sense of community, and open windows into possible majors and careers. In addition, these industry leaders organize course offerings around time blocks that allow students to consolidate their courses in the morning, afternoon, evening, or on weekends, making it easier to balance academic, work, and caregiving responsibilities. They also use data to track student progress and drive retention, to trigger interventions when students are off track, reduce momentum, or shift majors, to monitor course waiting lists to optimize class scheduling, and identify high DFW (drop, fail, or withdraw) courses to pinpoint curricular bottlenecks.

Other steps that the most successful institutions take include reducing wasted credit hours by coordinating advising and aligning curricula between two- and four-year institutions, replacing remedial courses with corequisite remediation, redesigning math requirements to better meet the needs of particular majors, and using high-impact practices to increase student engagement, enrich the academic experience, build marketable skills, and give students opportunities to apply learning in authentic contexts. Then, too, these institutions embed research and career preparation across the curricula, offer students opportunities to engage in active, experiential, applied, and project-based learning, including through internships and clinical, studio, and field-based courses, and deploy graduation concierges to work with students who are approaching graduation to help them meet all degree requirements.

The competitive marketplace has served some institutions well, bringing them the students deemed most talented and the resources to serve their undergraduates well. But other colleges and universities, those responsible for educating most undergraduates—those with the greatest needs for advising, mentoring, and high-impact practices—are not the market's beneficiaries. If those students are to thrive, our small colleges, regional comprehensives, and urban institutions can't wait for Washington, state legislatures, foundations, or philanthropists to ride to the rescue. And even if a savior does miraculously arrive, those institutions would still need a strategy to help these students realize their God-given potential.

Six decades ago, the Reverend Martin Luther King Jr. spoke about "the fierce urgency of now." "This is no time for apathy or complacency," he declared. "This is a time for vigorous and positive action." Let's take up his banner. For our students, there is "such a thing as being too late."[7] Now is the time to take steps—the steps that will bring many more to academic and postgraduation success.

Equity is many things: an aspiration to pursue, a guiding principle to drive institutional decision-making, and a set of values to steer our conduct as faculty members or administrators. In its simplest terms, equity means fairness, impartiality, and justice—an equal opportunity for all students to participate fully in all the educational and nonacademic opportunities we offer. But these days equity means something more: it entails equality of resources, ideas, respect, and outcomes. In education, equity involves acknowledging differences, then taking steps to bring all students to success. Here are some simple, straightforward steps to advance equity on your campus.

> Step 1: **Conduct an equity audit.** Justice Brandeis was right: "Sunlight is . . . the best disinfectant."[8] Transparency is among the simplest ways to drive improvements in higher education. You can't correct campus problems that remain invisible.

Right now, controversy swirls around predictive analytic tools that treat race as a risk factor. I fully understand the consternation this generates. But this should be an eye-opener and a prod to address gaps in persistence, achievement and completion, variance in grading, and access to high-demand majors and experiential learning opportunities. Remember: transparency is the key to institutional accountability.

Step 2: **Redesign admissions with an eye toward equity.** We must not penalize students because they lacked the privileges or the connections or the enrichment opportunities that others received. While it's certainly the case that some students are more polished and better prepared, the cliché is also true: talent is widespread, and the key attributes of success—creativity, drive, persistence, resilience, leadership potential—aren't correlated with income or social background. A more equitable admissions system needs to diminish the influence of privilege and connections in admissions even as it increases access. It would take into account "distance traveled": the applicant's success in overcoming adversity. It would also place an applicant's record in context: whether the applicant exhibits evidence of leadership and grit and other socio-emotional and noncognitive factors linked to future success, like persistence, determination, and an ability to overcome obstacles. It would look at variety of indicators of talent, achievement, and potential: does the candidate demonstrate proficiency in core competencies, such as the ability to write analytically, and offer other evidence of potential, such as focused achievement in a particular area (such as art, music, or science)? Equity in admissions also entails aggressive outreach and recruitment, including sponsoring after-school and precollege bridge programs and professional development opportunities for high school teachers. But equity in admissions for first-time students isn't enough. It needs to extend to community college students. Nearly half of all students nationwide begin their education at a community college. In Texas, the figure is 80 percent. The failure to bring many more of these students to a bachelor's degree is tragic.

Four-year schools need to work with feeder institutions to align, clarify, and streamline degree pathways; strengthen and coordinate transfer student advising; share data to drive evidence-based improvement; and ensure seamless credit transfer, with credits applying to gen ed and major requirements. Other ways to bring more transfer students to a bachelor's degree are to create tools—like City University of New York's Transfer Explorer—to make it easy for students to see how credits transfer and to offer co-enrollment and admission guarantees to simplify and facilitate the transfer process.

**Step 3: Create a more equitable and inclusive curriculum.** Achieving equity in higher education isn't simply a matter of removing barriers or closing opportunity gaps. It's also about creating a more socially relevant curriculum that acknowledges the exclusion of voices, histories, achievements, traditions, and perspectives from existing curricula. Faculty need to reimagine individual courses not only to make them more inclusive of new topics and texts but to reconsider canonical and noncanonical texts and interpretations in light of the growth of knowledge about colonialism, slavery, the construction of race, gender, disability, class and age classifications, and earlier misuses of the social and natural sciences. Instructors must go beyond revising syllabi to lay bare the implicit and unexamined ideological presumptions and ideas that inform the selection of topics, the choice of readings, and the theoretical and interpretative lenses that their courses have adopted.

One way to do these things is to require students to take courses in diversity, equity, and inclusion. But an attractive alternative is to ensure that every course is culturally responsive. I suspect every academic is now familiar with the phrase "decolonizing the curriculum": questioning master narratives and established canons, decentering dominant voices, interrogating normative hierarchies, and integrating alternative epistemologies and perspectives into our classes. All of us need to reconsider our courses, subject the course design, topics, and readings to critical scrutiny, and see how we can make the class more inclusive and more responsive to student interests and concerns.

A decolonized curriculum need not be confined to courses in art history, English literature, and history, for decolonizing the academy isn't simply about topical coverage. It's also about encouraging and preparing underrepresented students to enter the most important growth areas, like artificial intelligence, computer science, data analytics, machine learning, and neuroscience. And that requires making those fields more attractive and accessible. How? By eliminating weed-out courses and unnecessary requirements; placing a greater emphasis on active and applied learning; linking the emerging fields of study with those that attract a more diverse enrollments, for example, in health care, statistics and business; and establishing certificate programs, boot camps, and data-, AI-, and machine learning-oriented minors and joint majors to reach underserved student population.

Step 4: **Make pedagogy and assessment more equitable.** We often define equity as flexibility in grading, assignments, or due dates and opportunities to demonstrate knowledge in multiple ways. But equity and inclusion require much more: intentionality and an approach that is holistic and multipronged and includes changes in pedagogy, academic support, and assessment. Interviews with underrepresented students in STEM courses underscore the impact of poor pedagogy. "The classes are disorganized," said one, "yet extremely accelerated, graded harshly, and are often taught by professors who are not passionate." Observed another, "Success in classes was determined by those who could best teach themselves."[9]

The solutions aren't a secret. Clearly delineate the course's organization. Explain the material's relevance and the practical application of abstract concepts. Place less emphasis on rote memorization and more on hands-on in-class activities. Pay greater attention to skills-building and problem-solving. View assessment through an equity lens, and make project-based assessments a bigger part of your evaluation strategy. Since high-stakes exams contribute to testing anxiety and stereotype threat, rely more heavily on frequent low-stakes formative quizzes and other kinds of activities that involve active learning. Assess higher-order thinking and skills application rather than memorization. Use authentic project-, inquiry-, challenge-, and problem-based assignments rather than standard exams to assess mastery of essential skills and knowledge. Divide projects into clearly delineated stages that discourages plagiarism and encourages students to remain on track. Have students undertake activities that emphasize skills development. Provide prompt, personalized feedback. Make sure your expectations are crystal clear. Apart from reducing achievement gaps, this approach also has the added advantage of deterring academic dishonesty.

Step 5: **Make the student experience more equitable.** Apart from the obvious step of diversifying the faculty, departments need to foster a sense of belonging and promote faculty and peer interactions through clubs, lunches, potlucks, and other outreach initiatives. They should also cultivate professional identity formation through participation in research, exposure to guest speakers, practicing professionals, and entrepreneurs, and opportunities to attend and present at conferences and serve as a learning assistant. In addition, implement an early warning system to prompt timely interventions and a tiered system of support, including boot camps, bridge programs, clubs, faculty mentoring, learning centers, organized study groups, supplemental instruction, tutors, and tutorials. Tackle unmet financial needs with emergency financial aid. Provide funding for conference travel and research. Hire and award stipends to undergraduate learning assistants.

For all the talk of equity, I fear that too often campus responses involve symbolism and virtue signaling. A genuine commitment to equity goes well beyond letting students take a class pass-fail or allowing them to turn off the camera on their computer—a well-intentioned policy that undercuts an instructor's ability to read the classroom, respond to confusions and misunderstandings, and bring all students into a discussion. True equity entails disrupting and dismantling systemic inequities. It requires instructors to "challenge the normalization of failure"—the expectation, especially in our more challenging classes, that it's OK for a significant proportion of the class to fail or withdraw—by instituting policies to reduce DFW rates.[10] It makes instructors responsible for providing "clear guidance on what it takes to succeed"—sharing the secrets of note taking, efficient reading, and processing, retaining, retrieving, and applying information.[11] It involves implementing evidence-based pedagogical practices that engage and motivate students and promote higher-order thinking and skills development.[12] It means forging a sense of community through breakout groups, team-based projects, and exercises that promote connection, like debates, discussion, peer evaluation of writing, and role-playing activities. Above all, it entails enlarging the canon, considering alternative perspectives, and creating a culture of inquiry and questioning.

It's easy for more senior faculty to feel threatened by the emphatic calls for equity and to view the offensive against privilege as a personal attack. But, of course, those very faculty members once occupied the other side of the barricades. Our society faces several intellectual and moral imperatives: to incorporate the perspectives and contributions of the historically underrepresented into the curriculum, to diversify participation in our disciplines, and to bring many more students to a bright future. No one ever said that this process would be easy, painless, or conflict-free. But it's necessary nonetheless.

# 12

## Supporting Student Success at Scale

HIGHER EDUCATION NOW SERVES as the infrastructure that American society has refused to build. Colleges and universities are not just educational institutions, but providers of health services, psychological services, and disability services. They are expected to take steps to ensure housing affordability and food security. Our institutions also serve as sex education centers and food pantries, and providers of professional development for K–12 teachers and college prep for high schoolers.

Higher education is only as strong as its weakest link; and, at many broad-access campuses, that weak link involves advising and counseling. At every broad-access institution in which I have taught or administered, there has been a severe shortage of advisers and counselors. With an adviser-to-student ratio of 1,000 or even 1,500 to 1, and the number of campus mental health counselors and disability specialists even smaller, students rely heavily on parents or peers for advice and help. But these are notoriously unreliable sources of guidance and support. The results of the lack of advising are everywhere to be seen: in the number of excess credits that students earn, the many who transfer or stop-out after they are closed out of their preferred major, and the number of courses failed because the student is ill prepared to take a particular class. Then there are the mental health consequences: the prevalence of anxiety, depression, substance abuse, extreme loneliness, and mood and behavioral disorders.

No institution is blind to these shortcomings, and institutions have responded in a number of common ways. Many institutions have sought a technological fix. Some have adopted an electronic advising infrastructure to consolidate student profile information, promote workflow efficiencies, and make it easier for students to schedule appointments. Other campuses have adopted a self-service or do-it-yourself model to make it easier for students to access information. They have created and posted degree maps (a road map) for every major. Some have implemented chatbots that respond to frequently asked questions. Still other campuses have responded to the adviser shortage by new forms of outreach, staffing, and internal organization, for example, by relying heavily on peer mentors or by establishing "one-stop-shops" where students can receive assistance with admissions, academic advising, financial aid, course registration, access to records, and housing and transportation. A case management approach, where a designated adviser takes responsibility for all of a student's needs, has also become more common. Simple steps, it turns out, can make a big difference in improving student outcomes. Emergency grants to students who need small amounts of money to pay for car repairs or housing can keep students on track to completion, as can graduation concierges who are empowered to modify degree requirements for students at ninety credit hours or more.

I wholeheartedly support these efforts. Nevertheless, many students still find themselves adrift, without a single reliable point of contact when things go awry. So let me suggest some alternative approaches better suited to the scope and scale of the challenge and acknowledge students' need to interact with a real human being. What unites these approaches is that they are scalable, holistic, and proactive. Given the shortage of professional advisers, a data-driven approach is essential. Used skillfully, such an approach can contribute to student success on the curricular and the individual student levels. Through the careful use of data, campuses can identify curricular bottlenecks, including roadblock courses and classes with significant performance gaps. Data analytics can also help campuses optimize course offerings, ensuring that fewer students are closed out of essential classes and are therefore forced to delay graduation. Data analytics can also identify students at risk, target interventions, and automatically send out behavioral nudges and shoves. Certain red flags should prompt proactive interventions. These include students who perform poorly during their first semester, who enroll in fewer classes during their second year, or who change majors after their fourth semester. Next, create a tiered system of academic support that encompasses tutors, peer-led study groups, small supplemental instruction sections in courses with high DFW rates, and dedicated learning centers in areas in which students need special support: in study and test-taking skills and time management, and in math, science, and writing.

There are other simple steps that campuses can take to promote student success at an institutional level. A first step is to implement a more robust approach to onboarding students. The advice you received as a child is correct: first impressions are lasting impressions. How first-time and transfer students are introduced to a campus has a lasting impact on their subsequent success. Successful institutions introduce students to a dedicated adviser. They inform students about campus services and opportunities. They emphasize the institution's commitment to providing students with the support and services they need to succeed. And they offer preenrollment bridge programs and boot camps to ensure that students succeed in their first-year classes. Every new student should come away from orientation not only with an understanding of the campus's layout and its various services, but with a degree plan and a designated point of contact.

A second step is to offer for-credit student success courses at the lower division level that count toward general education requirements. In addition to a College 101 course to assist students with time management and study, note-taking, and test-taking skills, give undergraduates the opportunity to take classes that deal explicitly with students' social emotional development, ethical behavior, and respect for difference. More than ever, students need courses that address issues such as sexual harassment, consent in sexual relationships, bullying, microaggressions, and coping with loss, disappointment, and criticism. Among the topics that such courses might speak to are students' psychosocial and identity development, transition issues, self-cultivation, and the psychological stresses of emerging adulthood.

A third step is to embed major and career selection in the first-year classes and weave career preparation throughout the undergraduate experience. Most students come to college to enter a fulfilling career. Institutions need to provide students, early in their college experience, with relevant labor-market data, including information on job sectors that are growing, starting salaries, high-demand skills, and educational requirements for particular jobs. Schools also need to inform students about the career opportunities associated with each major and introduce them to alumni who might serve as mentors. In addition, schools might offer workshops to help students develop high-demand skills and provide preprofessional advising and activities to better prepare them for advanced education or the job market. Other strategies that can help students select an appropriate major and initial career path include assignments that require students to reflect on their interests, strengths and aspirations, and opportunities to investigate career options in their area of interest. A class that includes an ethnography of work component, or gives students the opportunity to interact with alumni or employees in a field of interest, can also be helpful.

A fourth step is to encourage the campus's nonfaculty professionals to offer courses in their areas of experience. Much of the growth of employment in higher ed involves nonfaculty experts in disabilities, LGBTQ+ issues, and diversity, inclusion, and identity-conscious strategies for student success. We might encourage these specialists to offer classes that speak to the special challenges faced by today's extraordinarily diverse student population, including low-income students, students of color, international students, students with disabilities, LGBTQ+ students, religious minority students, student athletes, students who are housing insecure, transfer students, commuter and part-time students, adult learners, and military veterans. We should remember: most of these nonfaculty professionals are our own PhD recipients who were unable to find a tenure-track job and who have great expertise to share and are well-prepared to teach.

A fifth step is to expand multicultural cocurricular offerings. I am a strong proponent of classes that combine discussion and analysis with cocurricular activities, such as attending museum exhibitions, concerts, or theatrical, dance, or opera performances. Rather than treating the cocurricular activity as a one-off, like a K–12 field trip, it should itself serve as an integral component of a course. Consider combining visits to exhibitions and performances with a signature seminar where these works can be discussed, interpreted, and evaluated. I can assure you: the programming directors at neighboring venues ensure that the works that the students see are timely and relevant and speak to today's multicultural audience.

A sixth step is to place as many new students as possible in a thematically focused cohort program or a research program with a faculty director and dedicated advising. At most campuses, only two groups of students are members of cohorts: honors students and those in opportunity programs for students from disadvantaged backgrounds. The vast majority of entering students, if they're fortunate, may be in a first-semester seminar or a meta-major or freshman interest group. Otherwise, they're on their own. Transfer students, in particular, rarely get a chance to participate in a cohort. Do place new students in learning communities aligned with their interests, whether these are in business, computer science, health care, international relations, public policy, scientific research, or some other topic. Even research programs, I know firsthand, can be scaled. Not all research must be laboratory based. Groups of students, depending on their interests, might conduct archival research, field research, quantitative research, or survey research. A single faculty member, assisted by postdocs, graduate students, or advanced undergraduates, can oversee teams of undergraduate researchers.

Yet another step is to remove institutional obstacles to success. Excessively complicated and marginally relevant degree requirements, roadblock courses, and unavailable or inconvenient classes can serve as serious hurdles to student success. Majors with steep barriers to entry can demoralize students. So, too, can a refusal to accept credits from feeder institutions. Sometimes these obstacles make sense on pedagogical grounds. But when they don't, change needs to take place. The most successful institutions have expanded course availability, often through online courses. They have simplified degree requirements and taken steps to address curricular roadblocks. They have created a campus culture geared toward success, both academic and career success.

Many campuses have instituted early alerts, behavioral nudges, and automated reminders as well as intrusive advisers and established walk-in math labs; writing, foreign language, and science centers offer and provide peer tutoring. Every instructor offers office hours. But a problem persists: how do we get academically struggling students to take advantage of the supports we offer? It is sad but true: most struggling students do not use their campus's academic support services, even though the evidence for their effectiveness is overwhelming. Which brings to mind the old adage: you can bring horses to water, but you can't force them to drink.

Many students struggle not because they're underprepared or unmotivated, socialize too much, or aren't "smart enough" or "college material," but for other reasons. Sure, some students, especially in the pandemic's wake, are distracted or unfocused and unable to successfully juggle family, work, and academic responsibilities. But for many, the problem is that they don't know how to study effectively or process the material presented in class or take tests or write an effective college-level essay or apply knowledge and methods to new contexts. Our learning centers can help by offering bridge programs, workshops, tutoring sessions, supplemental instruction, and study skills sessions—but only if students attend. And that turns out to be a big "but."

Is it because students are unaware of these supports? No. It's largely because of mindset and attitude: that using such services is a sign of inadequacy. That these services aren't really intended for students like them. That these services won't make a difference. Ironically, attitudes that are sometimes held up as helpful—grit, perseverance, persistence—can compound the problem. Such attitudes can encourage counterproductive behavior by generating a "do-it-yourself" mentality. Many struggling students feel that if they only work harder, success will follow. But without outside help, such efforts too often prove useless. As a result, our support services don't reach these students.

What kinds of academic supports work best with struggling students? Certain approaches are obvious. Spot struggling students early. Be proactive. Alert students to their need for help. Inform students of the support services that are available. But if we are to motivate struggling students to truly take advantage of our support structures, other strategies are essential. Integrate study skills training into the academic experience. Stand-alone, noncredit study skills courses attract few students at commuter institutions. The alternative is to embed study skills into classes or offer study skills courses for some, however small, amount of academic credit.

Work on students' mindset. Let students know that going to a learning center doesn't mean you're dumb. Students fail to take advantage of support services for many reasons, but the main one involves mindset: a pull-yourself-up-by-the-bootstraps mentality that often grows out of a sense of insecurity or inadequacy or disconnection from instructors, classmates, and the institution as a whole. Spread the word: support services work. Encourage your students to take advantage of learning centers. It is essential that faculty convey certain messages: that their students are fully capable of success in your class. One's goal as a teacher should be to bring all students to at least a minimal level of competency. Faculty need to guide students to tutorials and other instructional resources that they can use to remediate weaknesses. Reach out to students personally and motivate them. An increase in student-faculty interaction helps overcome students' sense of disconnection. Demonstrate a personal interest in their academic progress.

Faculty also need to recognize that course design can make a big difference. Incorporating early diagnostics into a course can help students better understand gaps in their knowledge and skills. Integrate collaborative learning into your classroom since students absorb a lot of valuable information from classmates and develop a stronger sense of belonging. Engage students with assignments that address authentic challenges or mimic professional practice. Take preparing students for exams and other high-stakes assignments seriously. Explain what you are looking for. Consider asking students to suggest exam questions. Have your class collaboratively create or evaluate a sample response or draft a grading rubric.

I've long believed that if one student fails, that may well be the student's problem, but if many slip through the cracks, that's my problem. Our institutions invest enormous resources in learning support services. It's our responsibility to ensure that students take advantage of those services.

———

Look at a list of student success strategies and almost certainly one word will be missing: the f-word. Take, for example, the 2021 *Student Success Playbook* created by the educational consulting firm EAB. You'll see the following categories for improvement: eliminate registration and financial barriers; support students with technology-enabled advising; build belonging and academic confidence; reduce the number of nonproductive credits; and enhance the value of the curriculum. What you don't see, except obliquely, is the faculty's critical role in retention and completion. Faculty—through their instructional, policy-making, and mentoring responsibilities—matter more to student success than any other individuals on campus. But you wouldn't know about the importance of faculty from the EAB *Student Success Playbook*. To be sure, the best one can say about faculty as academic advisers and career counselors is that their abilities in those areas are very uneven. Advising isn't a faculty priority and many faculty members have only a vague understanding of departmental or institutional requirements. Few are well versed in the jobs that their department's graduates acquire. But in their role as instructors and through their control over the curriculum, faculty are the key to student success.

The reason that the faculty role in student success is downplayed is, I think, obvious. Administrators have only indirect levers to bring about changes in pedagogy, curriculum, and graduation requirements. What administrators can transform are infrastructure, organizational design, professional advising, information collection, and messaging, and that's what EAB's playbook focuses upon. But there are many ways that faculty can drive student success. They can track student attendance, engagement, and performance; flag students at risk of failure; interact meaningfully with students; counsel and intervene with struggling students; and redesign academic barriers to completion. Faculty members can expedite credit transfer for students moving from a two to a four-year institution. They can also remove pointless prerequisites and major and graduation requirements and simplify degree pathways.

Let's not delude ourselves. Expanding the faculty role in student success won't be easy. If it were unproblematic, this would have already happened. In K–12 schools, it's possible to link teacher salaries to "value-added" measures that purport to quantify an individual teacher's impact on student achievement. That isn't possible in higher education. Shared governance stands in the way, even though it is conceivable, in theory, to measure student persistence within a particular discipline and student performance in subsequent classes (performance measures that some for-profit colleges actually use). Departments could, of course, make teaching potential a bigger factor in hiring or take peer teaching evaluation more seriously. But I feel certain that mandating ongoing professional development in pedagogy is a nonstarter.

If faculty are as important to student success as I believe they are, what can institutions do? Improve faculty access to relevant information. Few department chairs and virtually no faculty members know much about how their withdrawal and failure rates and grade distributions compare or contrast to those of other instructors. Information about grades by gender and ethnicity is also largely invisible, as is the proportion of students in a given course that persist in a major or their performance in more advanced classes. This information is almost certainly already collected; but it isn't shared with individual faculty members. Even less controversial data, for example, involving unmet demand for particular courses, seldom surface. The information exists and should certainly inform departmental decision-making.

Next, strengthen faculty-student connections. A key to student success can be spelled out in a single word: relationships. Among the strongest correlates of student success is a sense of belonging. Students who feel connected to a campus, their instructors, and classmates not only have higher retention rates, but have higher rates of self-efficacy and mental well-being. Contributors to a sense of belonging are participation in extracurricular activities, personal interactions with a faculty member, and active engagement in their courses and in campus life. Most likely to feel disconnected are first-generation college students, commuting students, students from historically underrepresented groups, students with disabilities, international students, veterans, older students, and LBGTQ+ students.

How, then, can campuses nurture a sense of belonging? By ensuring that students have access to a mentor, a staff member, an adviser, a faculty member, or a peer mentor who cares about the student as a person. By creating physical spaces on campus to serve as a resource center and a place to interact with like-minded fellow students. Through membership in an affinity or interest group, a thematic or research cohort, or a learning community. By participating in a research program. By establishing preprofessional centers aligned with specific careers or areas of interest, including the arts, business, health care, information technology, prelaw, public policy, and science.

Simple initiatives can build a sense of connection, like student-faculty lunches, engagement activities (such as a class field trip or a visit to a museum or performance), major-specific receptions, affinity group meet-and-greets, alumni outreach, encouragement to attend high interest guest lectures and performances, individualized invitations to participate in clubs, organizations, intramural athletics, volunteer and service opportunities, and various events, such as sock hops and game or movie nights. In particular, frequent, positive interactions between students and faculty can significantly enhance student persistence, engagement, and performance. To maximize these connections, establish a pool of faculty engagement funds to support cocurricular activities (such as off-campus excursions), underwrite faculty-student lunches, and establish faculty-led cohorts and learning communities. Incentivize behaviors that enhance student success. Financially reward the faculty members who do an outstanding job of mentoring. Also, make mentoring and faculty engagement in other student success initiatives a factor in promotion.

Another way that faculty can advance student success is by providing students with innovative kinds of learning experiences. Make sure students are actively engaged in the learning process and that they feel a strong sense of connection to their classmates and instructors and find personal significance in the college experience. Supplement lecture courses and seminars with learning experiences that are experiential and project-focused. These include scaled research experiences, community engagement and service-learning courses, studio and clinical courses, expanded study abroad opportunities, and participation in maker spaces. Offer financial inducements to those faculty who do create and lead such innovative learning experiences.

Campuses need to create a culture of shared responsibility for equity and student success. Make the promotion of equity and student success a team sport. Technology support services can monitor the students' use of course websites and engagement with other class resources and report to faculty when their students aren't logging in. Deans, department chairs, and other administrators should inform faculty about classes with unusually high DFW rates or with significant performance and achievement gaps and target assistance to help faculty redesign such classes. Learning centers should work with faculty to provide tutoring and supplemental instruction. It might also be worthwhile for department chairs to launch conversations about how to improve rates of equity and student success, for example, by doing more to identify students at risk of failure.

Colleges and universities could do much more to help faculty members grow as educators. Sure, most campuses have a teaching center and instructional technology support. But not enough faculty take advantage of these resources. Therefore, colleges and universities need to be more enterprising. Consider assigning a staff member, a graduate student, or a skilled undergraduate to instructors of key gateway classes who can assist in instructional improvement or in integrating new technologies into the classes. Also, consider awarding stipends to those faculty members who will participate in professional development seminars on or off campus. More than that, offer workshops to help faculty provide the kinds of constructive feedback and support that can enhance student learning. There are other ways to encourage faculty members to take initiatives that might advance engagement, learning, and retention. Provide faculty with the support they need (for example, from instructional designers and educational technologists) to redesign existing courses, create novel learning experiences, or develop online resources to enhance student learning. Empower faculty to create learning communities organized around a theme or a career path.

Let me conclude by adding one additional recommendation. It's at once the easiest and most difficult recommendation to implement. Our campuses need to do a better job of reminding or convincing faculty members that ultimately they—not administrators, nor professional staff—own responsibility for equitable student success. After all, faculty members are in charge of motivating students. Because the faculty designs and delivers instruction, they are the ones best positioned to monitor student engagement and learning and to most readily reach out to struggling students. Faculty must accept a big share of the responsibility for whether their students flourish or flag. Faculty members must recognize that it's not enough to create opportunities for students to learn—though we must certainly do that. Certainly, we can't make students invest the time, attention, and focus that deep learning requires. But faculty can make their classrooms environments that are immersive and inclusive. Instructors can architect learning experiences that involve active engagement, inquiry, and problem-solving. As learning engineers, they can insert formative assessments throughout their courses to monitor student engagement and progress and adapt their teaching accordingly, and can create tutorials and supplements that can address confusions. Above all, faculty can provide students with more of the kinds of substantive, constructive feedback that hold out the prospect of improving student performance.

Please don't misread my argument. Faculty members aren't the only ones responsible for student success. They can't tackle the bundle of factors, including the financial impediments and life circumstances, that hinder success. Equity and success, after all, are a shared responsibility. But if I had to identify a single variable that is most critical to student motivation, persistence, performance, and success, I wouldn't hesitate for a second. I'd say it's the faculty.

# 13

---

## Campus Flash Points

THERE ARE A HOST OF INCENDIARY POLITICAL, legal, and social issues facing today's college campuses that can easily erupt into intense
public controversies, resulting in expensive litigation, inviting public scrutiny, and severely damaging an institution's reputation. Some
of the most explosive involve affirmative action in admissions, free
speech on campus, sexual misconduct by students or faculty, and hazing, sexual assault, and substance abuse at fraternities. Here, I want
to examine a series of campus flash points involving the doctrine of
*in loco parentis*, an institution's responsibility for monitoring and reg-
ulating student behavior and academic freedom, including whether
colleges can restrict the free speech rights of students and faculty in
the interests of a creating a civil and supportive academic environment. Other flash points include college rankings, recent costly and
disturbing college scandals, campuses' increasing reliance on adjunct
faculty, and civics education.

# Reimagining *In Loco Parentis*

Among the most contentious legal issues facing colleges and universities is how to balance students' rights—including students' rights to privacy, free speech, freedom of expression, and a learning environment free of harassment and bias—with an institution's responsibility to protect students from harm. The legal questions that campus leadership confront would test the wisdom of Solomon. For example, do colleges and universities have an obligation to actively monitor students' social media posts and take action when such posts raise alarm bells? Should campuses be able to use photos or text posted online in investigations of misbehavior, including posts that show violations of a school's code of conduct, such as high-risk drinking or drug use, racist or homophobic slurs, or threats to other students' safety? Or should social media accounts be treated as a private matter?

The list of questions goes on and on. Do colleges have an affirmative duty to protect students from self-inflicted harm? Should colleges require a student who attempts suicide, or exhibits suicidal thoughts, to withdraw? Do colleges have a duty to warn parents or others—including classmates and dormmates—about a student's mental health problems, behavior, or criminal record that might conceivably threaten their safety? Are there circumstances in which a college or university can regulate, restrain, or punish student speech—for example, when such statements are regarded as offensive or biased? Or is hostile speech on political and social issues protected, whether inside or outside the classroom, under the First Amendment? These are only a few of the legal issues that campuses must contend with.[1]

For the first six decades of the twentieth century, the courts treated colleges and universities with great deference. The courts did not interfere in college-student affairs and administrators did not have to worry about possible litigation. Colleges were largely free to regulate student lives as they saw fit, whether by imposing curfews or dress codes or by restricting free speech, assembly, or the press.[2] We often speak of this as the era of *in loco parentis*, with colleges acting in the role of parents. The most obvious example involved parietals: the rules that imposed curfews on coeds (the word once used to describe female students) and that governed visits from members of the opposite sex to a college or university dormitory. Dormitory room doors were supposed to be open, and at least three feet had to stay on the floor whenever a male visited a woman's dorm room. Still, it is important to recognize that the courts did not impose on colleges a legal duty to protect or supervise students. Administrators were not deemed responsible for student injuries nor were they required to provide students with due process in disciplinary cases.

During the Civil Rights era, the courts began to recognize college students' constitutional rights to free speech, freedom of assembly, and due process, and to provide for judicial review over disciplinary proceedings. At the same time, colleges' legal immunity for injuries eroded. The result was a welter of contradictions. In certain respects, students were to be treated as fully functioning adults, with the same rights as any adult. Colleges largely ended their efforts to control students' morals and behavior. But at the same time, the standards of care that colleges were expected to provide rose. Courts and legislatures took the position that colleges had a legal obligation to provide a safe learning environment for their students and to protect them against foreseeable threats to their safety and hostile and offensive behavior that interfered with their education. If, on the one hand, the courts tended to regard colleges as incapable of monitoring or restricting certain forms of student behavior, such as underage alcohol consumption or illicit drug use—concerned that such policing would "produce a repressive and inhospitable environment, largely inconsistent with the objectives of modern education"—colleges also had an affirmative duty to address other forms of misbehavior, including hazing, sexual harassment, and sexual assault. Then, there were issues related to student privacy and mental health—for example, whether colleges could or should inform parents about disciplinary, academic, and mental health issues, or what responsibility institutions have to address issues involving anxiety, depression, binge drinking, substance abuse, self-mutilation, eating disorders, and suicidal ideation or attempts.[3]

Further complicating these legal issues was a profound change in the way that parents regarded their children. Beginning in the 1980s, parenting practices and family dynamics underwent a profound shift, as the permissive parenting associated with Dr. Benjamin Spock increasingly gave way to more hands-on approaches that were intended to protect children from risks to their physical health or mental well-being, build up their self-esteem, enrich them academically, and insulate them from disappointment and even boredom. This "new protectionism" resulted in an upbringing, for a growing proportion of children, that micromanaged, sheltered, "structured, supervised, and stuffed with enrichment."[4] Meanwhile, many more parents than before became actively involved in their children's college experiences, and many claimed a right to be informed about their children's lives and felt free to intervene in matters relating to discipline or academic performance. At the same time, developmental psychologists, sociologists of emerging adulthood, and neuroscientists viewed late adolescence and early adulthood as a transitional stage in terms of brain development and social and emotional maturation, when youth receive new freedoms in an environment that is less structured and supervised than most had ever experienced.[5]

Given the somewhat contradictory demands that colleges should not police students' behavior or infringe upon their rights but should protect their privacy and physical and psychological well-being, what should these institutions do? Some steps are easy. There is widespread agreement that colleges and universities should strictly enforce prohibitions on hazing, close down campus-affiliated spaces and organizations that facilitate improper behavior, and punish those involved. Other issues, especially involving students' mental health, have proven to be more complicated.

My personal view is that colleges should, first of all, recognize that traditional-aged undergraduates occupy a transitional stage that requires structure, guidance, and mentoring. A laissez-faire, hands-off approach does not serve these students well. Office hours are not enough. Faculty need to reach out to students and recognize that advising, coaching, and mentoring are essential elements of the professorial role. Second, institutions need to take a more active role in their students' development, academic and nonacademic. The academic side is the easiest to address. Institutions need to identify students at risk of failure and take proactive steps to help them and keep them on track through tutoring, study groups, supplemental instruction, peer mentoring, and outreach. But institutions should not shy away from facilitating students' ethical development, not by preaching or moralizing or merely distributing information (for example, that not all students engage in binge drinking), but rather by promoting active, academically informed campus conversations and debates about timely issues. These might include race and class on campus, free speech, and sexual harassment and sexual assault, with faculty experts on these topics involved in the conversations. Institutions should expose all students, regardless of their major, to the latest scholarly findings about issues relating to safety, psychological well-being, and abuse.[6]

Over the past generation, the role of a parent has shifted profoundly. So, too, must the role of a college. In the age of the helicopter parent, a college should not be a babysitter or bystander, but a facilitator, partner, and mentor.

## Reaffirming Academic Freedom in a Hyperpolarized and Partisan Era

Among the principles that the nineteenth-century Prussian educational reformer Wilhelm von Humboldt championed was *Lehrfreiheit*, or what is now known as academic freedom. Humboldt, a pioneer in the development of the modern research university, wanted to ensure the faculty's intellectual independence and protect their right to choose what to teach and how to teach from government interference.

Today, academic freedom is often in the news. Controversies erupt with some frequency whenever a speaker is shouted down or a faculty member refuses to call a transgender student by the student's preferred pronoun. After the 9/11 terrorist attacks, a professor at the University of Colorado was dismissed for saying, in effect, that the chickens had come home to roost. Perhaps most striking is an increase in the number of college students who question or even reject freedom of speech. In a nationwide survey in 2015 and 2016, 71 percent of incoming freshmen agreed that "colleges should prohibit racist/sexist speech on campus." And 43 percent said that colleges should have the right to ban "extreme speakers," nearly double the proportion who agreed with that statement in 1971. According to a 2017 survey of 800 undergraduates around the country, 81 percent think that words can be violent. The notion that speech can inflict harm and make people feel unsafe has gained traction, as have the ideas that speech is a matter of power used to oppress groups of people and that tolerating offensive speech can make one complicit with those ideas. Some 30 percent of those surveyed—that is, almost one out of three—think that physical violence can be justified to prevent someone from using hateful words.[7]

Teaching in today's highly diverse, hyperpolarized, and partisan classrooms can pose serious challenges. In 2021, University of Michigan Professor Bright Sheng, a MacArthur Fellow and two-time Pulitzer Prize finalist, was accused of committing a racist act when he screened a 1965 film version of *Othello* featuring Laurence Olivier in blackface. A brouhaha erupted. Were undergraduate and graduate students right to publicly denounce Sheng, or were they being oversensitive and overzealous? Did university administrators succumb to campus wokeness by publicly declaring that Sheng's actions "do not align with our school's commitment to anti-racist action, diversity, equity and inclusion" and referring the incident to the university's Office of Equity, Civil Rights and Title IX?[8]

Call Sheng naïve or obtuse, if you wish. Call the student response utterly predictable. But the incident raises issues that all instructors need to ponder. Much of the current controversy centers on a rather narrow issue: whether Sheng's decision to show the Olivier version of *Othello* was justified. Arguments have been made pro and con. It is certainly the case that Olivier's use of blackface and exaggerated gestures was controversial at the time (*New York Times* critic Bosley Crowther likened his performance to *Amos 'n' Andy*, the radio and television sitcom that perpetuated racial stereotypes that predated the American Civil War). Other critics, including Pauline Kael, praised the film, noting that this version represented a self-conscious challenge to earlier adaptations that had downplayed the racial conflict and prejudice at the heart of Shakespeare's tragedy.

But there are bigger issues at stake than whether a professor made a self-acknowledged mistake. These include academic freedom, professorial prerogatives, and, above all, whether campuses, in their effort to create safe spaces and positive and inclusive learning environments, are in fact creating a toxic atmosphere that undercuts the ability of faculty to teach and conduct research without risk of official interference or professional disadvantage. In the not-so-distant past, it was an almost unquestioned article of faith among academics that a major purpose of a college education was to make students uncomfortable and to challenge the received wisdom. Times have changed, and a significant number of students now believe that out-of-touch faculty members are propagating and perpetuating harmful ideologies, and that the professors and the ideas they propound need to be called out.

The incident at the University of Michigan epitomizes two of the big pedagogical challenges of our time: 1) how to balance a respect for students' sensitivities and sensibilities with our professional obligation to question, challenge, and provoke, and 2) how much freedom academics should have in designing the learning experiences that they think their students need. I don't know about you, but I live in fear that a single misstep or misspoken phrase, a misunderstanding, or a misplaced attempt at humor or political commentary could result in an uproar or worse. As a professor of American history, I believe it is essential not to sanitize or censor the past. To this end, I regularly show clips from feature films that contain offensive content; display images, including photographs of lynching, that are profoundly disturbing; and require students to analyze primary source documents, some of which contain slurs. I suspect every student is offended by some source that I include in the class. I, of course, try to contextualize these pieces of evidence and explain my pedagogical purpose in including these resources in my courses. But I wouldn't be surprised if one or more of the hundreds of students I regularly teach consider my approach merely a way to offend and distress students under the bogus guise of enlightenment.

In my 40-plus years in college classrooms, I can fairly say that teaching has never been more fraught or potentially volatile. As instructors, we are judged not simply on whether or not we are engaging or entertaining or easy graders, but on students' perceptions of our political or ideological perspective. Our opinions and our language are subject to close scrutiny. I, perhaps like you, have discovered how inflammatory terminology can be. In US history, words like "slave," "slave owner," "Indian," and "tribe" have become potential land mines.

Irrespective of your discipline, booby traps lie in waiting. Given today's highly politicized environment, don't be naïve or ingenuous. In today's classrooms, faculty should not expect deference. That's not necessarily a bad thing. In humanities classrooms, deference and obsequiousness have no place. We should expect, even welcome, students who question our interpretation—though we hope that this is done respectfully, civilly, and with evidence. Also, don't expect an apology to be sufficient. One takeaway from the Sheng incident is that a regretful admission of error is often not enough to put a controversy to rest. Almost any apology can be (and often is) dismissed as inadequate, insufficient, hollow, and unsatisfactory. Don't assume that your training, expertise, reputation, and high-mindedness give you the last word. The classroom is and ought to be an arena of contention; and, in the marketplace of ideas, no one, no matter how esteemed, should receive a free pass. Should controversy erupt, don't expect unequivocal support from administrators or colleagues. What you should expect is that your pedagogical decisions are likely to be questioned and second-guessed and criticized. We may think of academic freedom as higher education's bedrock principle, but in fact it's only one of many competing values and priorities.

All that said, don't allow fear of igniting a controversy lead you to self-censor in ways that inhibit serious discussion. Remember Sigmund Freud's warning: in discussing infantile sexuality, the father of psychoanalysis said that when we bowdlerize our language, we inevitably censor our thought. Expurgating language renders us incapable of seeing the world as it is. So what advice might I offer? First, be sensitive to students' sensibilities. Anticipate potentially explosive issues. That doesn't imply evading or ignoring hot topics, but it does mean addressing these issues thoughtfully and transparently. Also, build rapport with your students. If you develop a good rapport with your students, many problems evaporate. But if your classroom climate is adversarial and hostile, even small issues are likely to blow up in your face. Building rapport requires instructors to get to know their students and draw out their interests and concerns. Listen, but also be responsive. Next, openly discuss your educational philosophy, terminology, and pedagogical approach. Let your students know why you've chosen to teach the class as you have and why you've included potentially contentious or incendiary material. Do encourage your students to question and criticize your approach.

I'd also urge you to engage the controversies. Gerald Graff is right: higher education should be an intellectual battleground, where ideas are debated and contested.[9] Don't shy away from difficult conversations and hot-button issues. But treat these difficult topics as controversies that need to be confronted, deconstructed, and addressed. But do warn students before introducing any potentially controversial content. A warning, however, might not be sufficient if it doesn't also include properly preparing students in advance by framing and contextualizing the content and acknowledging its disturbing elements. Here, you'd do well to discuss the politics of knowledge. In my US history courses, some students, believe it or not, want a more patriotic, upbeat, comforting, and nationalistic version of the past, while others, not surprisingly, expect a much more critical—indeed, negative—perspective. The best I can do is present multiple and conflicting points of view on past events; place US history in a comparative perspective, which helps students better understand the options and range of possibilities available at the time; show how present-day partisans use the past to advance their agendas; and help students formulate more sophisticated and nuanced judgments about, for example, how people no less intelligent than we are could perpetrate horrors that we find inexcusable, how history's worst villains could believe that they were doing good, and how ideas that we find retrograde and repellent could have been widely embraced.[10]

Public discussions about teaching in today's contentious classrooms are too often reduced to simplistic dichotomies: professors are said to coddle or pander or else offend, bully, abuse, traumatize, and (metaphorically) inflict violence. We can do better. Current parenting advice might provide some suggestions. If you want to raise independent, self-reliant, socially adept, well-behaved, and academically successful children, we are told, then adopt an authoritative parenting style. Authoritative parents have high expectations for their children and set clear guidelines and boundaries, but they are also flexible, are highly responsive to their offspring's emotional needs, and emphasize frequent, open communication.

College students certainly aren't children, and professors mustn't confuse their roles as instructors and mentors with those of mommy or daddy, let alone best friend. Still, we need to be authoritative, too. That requires listening, engaging, explaining, discussing, and reasoning; being responsive to students' views and needs; and, above all, recognizing their independence and giving them opportunities for self-expression and creativity. There is an Oedipal dimension to teaching that we'd be remiss to ignore. We shouldn't be surprised that students at times agitate and defy, overdramatize and overreact. That's part of youth and the process of growing up.

Our job is to be nurturing, responsive, supportive, and authoritative. Our goal is not to expect gratitude in return (however nice that might be), but rather to produce independent, self-directed, self-regulated learners.

# What's Really Wrong with the College Rankings

College rankings have become sources of much controversy. Critics charge that the rankings that emphasize such measures as selectivity and reputation (as opposed to affordability and access and value added) serve primarily to reinforce the existing structure of institutional wealth and prestige. Indeed, it wouldn't surprise me to learn that the *U.S. News* rankings are reverse engineered to ensure that the "right" schools appear at the top.

College ratings take various forms. *Washington Monthly* famously measures economic mobility. Georgetown's Center on Education and the Workforce has released invaluable information on the return on investment of individual colleges and programs. As for *U.S. News*, it tries to measure quality largely in terms of inputs: resources, average class size, faculty qualifications, standardized test scores, and reputation. Each approach has its limitations. Mobility and ROI measures tend to privilege schools located in high-income or fast-growing cities or regions. Even licensure passing rates in engineering and nursing (or bar passage rates for law schools) can be misleading because schools can game the system by restricting admissions into those programs. Indirectly, the *U.S. News* rankings measure students' qualifications. It's my view that the biggest effect of its rankings has been to nationalize the higher ed marketplace by encouraging the most academically successful students to aspire to attend one of the leading national colleges and universities.

None of the college ratings that I'm familiar with truly tries to measure what I consider the single most important variable: the quality of the academic experience. That's not easy to do, but I do think it's possible—because we know it when we see it. If I had to measure quality, I'd try to assess the share of the students who have the opportunity to work one-on-one with a faculty mentor. Or who participate in a learning community, an honors program, or a research or opportunity program. Or who partake regularly in small classes or seminars or a studio courses. Or who participate in an experiential learning opportunity—including a supervised internship, mentored research program, study abroad program, or service learning activity—or create a project in a maker space. Or who produce a capstone project that is evaluated by faculty other than the student's mentor. I can think of still other measures of quality: the proportion of students who share a meal or have coffee with a faculty member, visit a professor's house, go on an off-campus excursion with an instructor, or take part in cocurricular and extracurricular activities.

I hear the objections. Won't those indicators discriminate against schools that serve large numbers of part-time and commuter students? Not necessarily. I'm aware of many institutions, including many of the City University of New York's two- and four-year campuses, that make student engagement and enrichment activities defining features of their undergraduate experience. One byproduct of the awful academic job market is that impressive teacher-scholars can be found at every campus. Every student at a four-year brick-and-mortar nonprofit (and many two-year schools) has the opportunity to study with a genuine subject-matter expert and research scholar. Sure, the average academic qualifications of the undergraduates differ, but talented, highly motivated students, too, are omnipresent.

The big difference among institutions, in my view, lies elsewhere: partly in things that are hard to measure, like the amount and quality of constructive feedback that students get, but mainly in matters that we can quantify, including access to mentoring, the amount of faculty-student interaction, participation in learning and research cohorts and more intimate and interactive learning experiences, and engagement in experiential learning opportunities.

The management guru Peter Drucker once said that "what gets measured gets managed."[11] Conversely, what isn't measured gets ignored. Only if a campus assesses quality will it use that information to drive improvement. Campuses should conduct student satisfaction and exit surveys and compile information about postgraduation employment and earnings. Accreditors, too, need to step up to the plate. Accrediting agencies are especially well positioned to collect the information that applicants need that truly can allow prospective college students to gauge academic quality.

# Scandals in the Ivory Tower

Today's ivory tower is beset by scandal. The most visible scandals involve sexual harassment, molestation, and abuse; bribery and favoritism in admissions; fraternity hazing; gross violations of academic integrity; plagiarized speeches and public presentations; outsize donor or trustee influence; and failure by senior administrators to act. Less visible, but no less significant, are the everyday scandals that include the exploitation of adjunct faculty, teaching and lab assistants, student athletes, international students, and nonteaching professional staff, and commercial partnerships with sports gambling firms and soft drink and alcoholic beverage companies. Then there are issues typically avoided in discussions of scandal involving alcohol and drug abuse, disorderly conduct, and vandalism.

The financial costs of scandal can be extraordinary—at least $237 million at Penn State, $490 million at the University of Michigan, $500 million at Michigan State, $700 million at UCLA, $852 million at USC. But at least as damaging are the invisible costs in terms of campus morale, reputation, bad press, and lives harmed. Nor do the scandals' repercussions quickly end. Colleges and universities must respond by implementing new prevention programs, training procedures, and systems of bureaucratic oversight, reporting, and enforcement at great expense. These responses, in turn, tend to make campus cultures more adversarial, inquisitorial, and administratively top-heavy.

Should we consider these scandals aberrations, an anomalous series of isolated, if deeply regrettable and horrific, incidents? Are scandals, in other words, an inevitable, if deplorable, product of a system of higher education as large and decentralized as this nation's? Or is something deeper going on that will require colleges and universities to radically rethink their mission, priorities, campus cultures, and governance structures? In my view, corruption, fraud, and academic misconduct aren't isolated occurrences in colleges and universities. They're products of misdirected academic structures, incentives, and campus cultures. Instead of viewing scandals as anomalies in an otherwise well-functioning higher education ecosystem, these should be seen as the predictable outgrowth of a highly decentralized system that emphasizes hierarchy, status, exclusivity, prestige, competition, and revenue generation. Rather than viewing scandals as the product of individual bad actors, improprieties are systemic. In some instances, misconduct takes place because of a lack of oversight, lack of clear rules and reporting channels, lack of accountability, or a sense of disempowerment among witnesses or victims or their supporters. In other instances, however, bad behavior is incentivized; indeed, it's built into the existing system.[12]

When I state that misbehavior is incentivized, I mean that deans, department chairs, lab directors, and others are under intense pressure to cut costs, generate student credit hours, maximize margins, and increase contract research. These pressures, in turn, make it more likely that these actors will take steps that can lead to scandal or abuse, for example, by instituting professional master's programs that lack a clear return on investment. In addition, the academy's extreme status hierarchies make it difficult to hold abusive faculty members, especially those with success as grant-getters, to account. Meanwhile, the typical conditions of graduate student mentoring, where a doctoral student is wholly dependent on a single professor's advocacy, can encourage ill treatment or exploitation.

So, what needs to be done? Some responses strike me as straightforward. Ensure that graduate students have access to more than one mentor or adviser. Put into place readily accessible due process procedures for adjunct faculty to protect their academic freedom and prevent improper termination. But other challenges require a more systemic response.

Conduct campus conversations about misconduct. This should include all kinds of misconduct, whether it involves administrators, faculty, staff, or students. Topics should include academic dishonesty, bias, discrimination, fairness in assessment and grading, free speech and academic freedom, *in loco parentis* responsibilities, information privacy, interpersonal relations, plagiarism, and other forms of unethical behavior. These issues are far too important to be left to the general counsel's office. Also, ensure that administrators recognize and respond to red flags of discrimination, abuse, or exploitation. This will require administrators at all levels to closely monitor hiring practices, salary increments, and promotion and tenure decisions. Everyone, not just a Diversity, Equity, and Inclusion office, needs to be accountable.

It's also essential to formulate and enforce policies in areas where discrimination and abuse are common. To take some examples, adjunct faculty need contractual guarantees of academic freedom, limited only by libel and slander statutes. There must also be clearly defined rights for non-tenurable faculty regarding their hiring term, teaching load, rehiring, and benefits, including access to research support. Student athletes need to be informed in writing of their rights involving scholarships, coach-athlete relations, training, health care, time commitments, compensation, complaint procedures, the consequences of dismissal from a team, and other matters. International students need to be protected from bias and wage and work abuses, ensuring that they receive the services that they need to thrive within the university that admits them. Campuses need to regularly review salaries and make adjustments whenever inequities are identified, take steps to prevent the abuse of grievance processes that can undercut academic freedom, and set a high bar for investigations into claims that research or teaching is harmful.

However, the single most important change is to reaffirm and reassert the principle of shared governance in oversight and decision-making. Faculty have a particular stake in ensuring a scandal-free campus. Unlike administrators, most tenured faculty members remain at a single institution for most of their professional life and are therefore invested in the reputation of their campus. Professors should oversee any charges of professorial or administrative misconduct and should be represented on the Board of Trustees. It also seems to me that student representatives should have a role in matters involving student wrongdoing (unless stipulated otherwise by law or government regulations).

Thus far, training sessions, Title IX offices, honor codes, academic integrity committees, student integrity boards, and mandatory reporting requirements haven't proven sufficient to ensure institutional accountability. Self-regulation has proven no more effective on college campuses than in churches, youth organizations, or corporations. At the same time, in some widely publicized incidents, existing grievance procedures have been abused in ways that infringe upon academic freedom and free speech and that subject faculty members to investigations that appear to have had a chilling effect upon research and teaching.

Academics are quite rightly anxious about the ways that a neoliberal emphasis on marketing, commercialization, enrollment management, vocationalism, contract research, and revenue generation have eroded the idea of a college or university as a bastion of disinterested scholarship and liberal education. Many also worry, with good reason, that an increasingly litigious, adversarial, accusatorial campus culture with a high degree of surveillance is at odds with the academic ideals of collegiality and community.

All of us should be concerned that scandals are all too frequent at our institutions and that, without carefully designed reforms, our institutions will face ruinous harm to campus finances and reputation, while undermining public support for higher education as an enterprise—much as the child abuse scandals have severely damaged the Catholic Church. Guarding against scandal is truly a collective responsibility, but one that demands individual and, especially, faculty oversight to ensure accountability.

## The Future of the Professoriate

The news came as a shock: Yale now not only has more managerial and professional employees than faculty, but the university also has about as many nonteaching professionals as it has undergraduates. The institution between 2003 and 2019 added 600 undergraduates, but it nearly doubled its number of professionals. Yale attributed the increase partly to the growing size of its School of Medicine's clinical staff, but the trend toward increasing administration and professional staff while faculty size stagnates is widespread.[13]

To term this trend "administrative bloat" is highly simplistic. After all, the growth has occurred in response to concrete challenges, government mandates, and pressure from students and parents. Institutions have staffed up to address issues involving compliance, contracting, fundraising, and information technology, and in order to manage research, recruit students, and better meet student needs through expanded advising, disabilities, psychological, tutoring, and other services. But the shifting balance between the number of full-time, tenured, or tenure-track faculty and everyone else quite naturally raises questions about institutional priorities.

If colleges and universities are truly serious about the quality of the education that they offer, especially at the lower-division level, why do they delegate responsibility largely to instructors outside the tenure system: to adjunct, part-time, and contingent faculty, as well as to lecturers, professors of the practice, visiting scholars, postdocs, and graduate students? To many people outside the academy it seems perfectly sensible to ask why colleges and universities don't expect full-time faculty to shoulder many of the tasks now entrusted to nonfaculty staff, why these institutions don't increase faculty teaching loads or expand class sizes, and why campuses that claim to value equity and social justice have embraced a two-tiered system of instructional staffing, with many introductory level, foundational, and service courses taught by adjunct instructors, who suffer, among other indignities, low pay, little job security, limited time for research, and a lack of protections against "just-in-time" hiring and at-will non-reappointment. Is this, critics ask, simply a matter of administrators and tenured faculty feathering their own nest?

The simple answer to this question is that institutions are struggling to balance competing pressures and conflicting priorities. Colleges and universities are striving, all at once, to curb costs, expand research, meet government mandates, tap new revenue sources, deal with threats involving cybersecurity, provide faculty with instructional technology support, and, perhaps most important of all, meet ever-rising standards of care for disability services, mental health counseling, and learning support services. These tasks, which lie well outside faculty's expertise, require trained professionals. That's true, yet the conversation shouldn't end there. It is also the case that institutions have chosen to let their instructional budgets stagnate even as expenditures balloon in areas that some would consider optional, like athletics or recreation facilities, or peripheral to their core mission, such as new research centers. To take a Texas example, Sam Houston State University, Texas Christian University, the University of Houston, and the University of Texas at Austin, Rio Grande Valley, and Tyler all recently opened new schools of medicine.

Meanwhile, acting without a conscious plan or intentional design, departments discovered that they could staff many of their lower-division classes at a fraction of the cost of a full-time tenured professor, allowing tenured faculty to avoid this service obligation. It's noteworthy that in establishing this separate teaching track, departments largely eschewed the established mechanisms their institutions use to ensure instructional quality: a rigorous and competitive hiring process, provision of ongoing professional development, regular peer feedback and evaluation, and valid and reliable measures of student learning.

At the same time, some institutions began to view online teaching and continuing education as potential cash cows. There's an ongoing debate over whether online education is cheaper than its face-to-face counterpart. There's no doubt that it can be. In fact, it's as easy as one-two-three. All you have to do is uncap course enrollment, automate grading, and substitute lower-paid graders, teaching assistants, coaches, course mentors, and adjuncts for tenure-stream faculty. If cost cutting is the sole goal, institutions can also create standardized master classes to be "taught" by whoever is cheapest or adopt a self-paced, self-directed educational model to further reduce the need for instructors and support staff. Yes, Virginia, it's possible to radically cut the cost of an education. But the effect is to strip college teaching of precisely the attributes that make it special: above all, the interaction with and regular, substantive feedback from a content expert, an active researcher, or a practicing professional—the artists, performers, authors, health-care providers, judges, lawyers, and technologists who bring real-world expertise and experience into the classroom.

The mega-online providers, nonprofit as well as for-profit, have gone to extreme lengths to reduce instructional costs. These institutions disaggregate the faculty role, separating content experts, who (in theory) design classes, from those who grade, mentor, and even deliver the course content, with no expectation that these course assistants engage in scholarly research or even possess a terminal degree in the relevant discipline. It's possible to do something similar with face-to-face instruction, as all too many community colleges have done: substituting master's degree holders and bachelor's degree-holding teachers for PhDs. Many four-year institutions now use more senior undergraduates as discussion leaders or even as graders. My view, however, is that all college students should be taught by a scholar, a practitioner, or a professional equivalent.

One of the most striking developments in recent years is the increasing democratization of the professoriate, not only in terms of gender, ethnic, and racial diversity but also in terms of scholarly productivity. One side effect of the awful academic job market is that publishing scholars can be found at institutions across the country. There is not a campus that I've visited that isn't full of productive scholars with impressive lists of learned publications. Many of these faculty members feel, with justification, terribly underplaced, overworked, underappreciated, and underpaid. But their students certainly benefit from their professors' expertise. At every reputable institution, students encounter faculty members who are contributing to the scholarly enterprise and are able to bring the fruits of their original research and the latest scholarship into the classroom.

The increasing reliance of colleges and universities on non-tenure-track instructors is no longer a dirty secret. Thanks to scholars like Joe Berry, Herb Childress, Adrianna Kezar, and Kim Tolley, and thanks to union organizers and activists like the New Faculty Majority and the Coalition of Contingent Academic Labor, we have a better understanding of the consequences of adjunctification: the deprofessionalization of large segments of the professoriate, a diminishment in the quality of lower-division education, and weakened protections for academic freedom. The problem is not a new one. We now know that reliance on adjuncts surged beginning in the 1970s and began to arouse a response in the 1980s, with the American Association of University Professors issuing its first statement on contingent faculty in 1980, calling attention to the grim realities of adjunct life.

Higher education's increasing reliance on adjuncts should not be understood simply in terms of administrative greed and tenured faculty members' indifference. The issue is far more complex and reflects broader shifts in the economy, or what business professor David Weil calls "the fissured workplace": the increasing reliance on contingency, outsourcing, subcontracting, partnering, and franchising as ways to increase administrative flexibility, cut costs, and, in many instances, produce a more tractable labor force.[14] Certain broader shifts in the higher education ecosystem have made contingency a fact of academic life. The most obvious contributor is an oversupply of prospective faculty members. The large supply of PhDs and MAs has created a reserve army of potential adjuncts that can be easily drawn upon. Then, there is a reality of fluctuating enrollments and budgets that make staffing flexibility very attractive. As institutional enrollment ebbs and flows, and as demand for particular majors shifts, a contingent labor force makes it easier for institutions to adapt. There is also the transformation of lower-division classes into commodities. As more students acquire gen ed credits in high school and community college, introductory-level courses become increasingly uniform in content, encouraging a belief that these classes need not be taught by tenured faculty.[15]

A heightened emphasis on cost cutting, a search for new sources of revenue, and a desire to increase programmatic flexibility have combined to encourage a reliance on contingent faculty. It's ironic that significantly improving the lot of adjuncts—which should certainly be a priority—would inevitably involve disagreeable trade-offs. Colleges and universities face significant financial constraints in giving adjuncts a better deal, and shifting part-time instructors to full-time status would necessarily reduce the total number of adjuncts, while likely limiting the resources that could be expended elsewhere, for example, on financial aid. This shift might also potentially limit campuses' ability to draw upon practicing professionals who can bring real-world experience into the classroom. In addition, modest improvements in adjunct well-being might well have the ironic effect of further institutionalizing a two-tiered faculty.[16]

Certain remedies strike me as likely to improve the situation, resulting in wage increases, better benefits, greater participation in governance and curriculum decisions, strengthened language on academic freedom, and an adjunct-to-full-time process. These include, first of all, moral and political pressure. The mistreatment and exploitation of adjuncts is increasingly viewed as intolerably inconsistent with the tenured faculties' conception of the professoriate: as individuals who combine teaching with research and who receive a stable income and possess academic freedom. Labor organizing is also making a difference. At many campuses, unions and unionization drives have resulted in noticeable improvements in wages, benefits, working conditions, employment guarantees, participation in campus governance, and access to travel and research funds and professional development opportunities. Publicity is also contributing to change. The higher education press and initiatives like the Delphi Award, presented by the University of Southern California's Pullias Center, increasingly recognize innovative programs to support non-tenure-track faculty, helping to raise the bar at all institutions.

However, I don't understand why the accreditation process hasn't adequately addressed the issues surrounding the status of contingent faculty. Accrediting agencies need to hold institutions accountable for ensuring that their classes are taught by well-qualified professionals who have access to appropriate working conditions and support. Accreditors should push back on efforts to disaggregate the faculty role and reaffirm requirements for "regular and substantive interaction" between faculty and students, the provision of individualized, constructive feedback, and instructors who demonstrate expertise in the discipline being taught.

Let me add that concern for adjuncts should extend even more broadly to encompass other nontenured professionals—including directors of disabilities, learning, preprofessional, and teaching centers, instructional designers, educational technologists, academic advisers, student affairs specialists, and many others—who not only constitute the most rapidly growing number of campus employees, but who also are increasingly made up of PhDs. Let's hire and treat professional staff as the skilled professionals they are. Let's expand these professionals' opportunities to teach, conduct research, and enhance their access to professional development and research support.

The moral challenge we face is not a Manichean contest pitting villainous administrators and trustees against an exploited workforce or a privileged professoriate versus an academic proletariat, but a much more profound conflict involving competing institutional priorities, market forces, vested interests, and professional ideals. I would hope that we would all agree that teaching and learning should be higher education's primary responsibility, and that means holding all instructors, including tenured faculty, to a higher standard of teaching competence coupled with ongoing evidence of continuing professional development and teaching effectiveness.

## Handling Hot Topics in the Classroom

Inside the classroom, students tend to assume a number of rather predictable roles. There's the know-it-all, for example, the class clown or jokester, the slacker, and, please excuse the pejorative term, the suck-up or teacher's pet wannabe. Don't be surprised if you encounter a student who challenges your authority or tries to trip you up. The sniper or sharpshooter, who disagrees with much of what you say and who sometimes attacks you personally, is, unfortunately, a not uncommon classroom type. Then, there are the bomb throwers, who ask a question, at times with racist or sexist undertones, that is designed to arouse their classmates. One example I personally encountered took the following form: "Isn't it true that most sub-Saharan Africans were enslaved by other Africans?"—a question that is deeply misleading. Such a question not only fails to recognize that sub-Saharan Africans didn't think of themselves as a single people, but it also doesn't acknowledge how the European demand for slaves and access to European arms encouraged the slave trade.

How, then, should instructors handle hot topics? First of all, be prepared for tough or fraught moments. These might include shocking or alarming personal disclosures, flashes of anger, or tears. Plan in advance for how best to handle these moments. Consider the following steps. Co-create classroom ground rules. Together with your students try to forge some common norms. For example, advise students to listen to their classmates without interrupting them. Encourage them to avoid personalizing arguments; they should criticize one another's ideas, not their characters. Avoid inflammatory language and personal insults. Respect one another.

Also, clarify your role. You might describe yourself as the emcee, referee, or umpire for the class, or as an information resource or devil's advocate. But also do your best to divide a difficult issue into its component parts. Disaggregate a tough issue into specific areas of contention and disagreement. You might also consider breaking the class into small groups. In a more intimate context like a breakout group, students might be more willing to ask questions, share information, and voice their own opinions. In addition, make it clear that students can remain silent. Don't put students on the spot. There's nothing wrong with allowing students to observe the classroom discussion and, in the process, develop their own point of view.

Most important of all, strive to elevate the conversation. Among an instructor's most significant responsibilities is to help students rise above mere opinion and develop reasoned, evidence-based, logical, theoretically informed arguments. To that end, be the facilitator you ought to be. Provide your students, directly or through classroom readings, with essential historical background and contemporary context, and familiarize them with contrasting perspectives and relevant scholarship. Channel the conversation in a positive direction. Your goal is not to eliminate disagreements over values, but, rather, to help students understand the complexities of an issue, comprehend their detractors' points of view, and make their case as convincingly and compellingly as possible.

We sometimes think of politics as a rough-and-tumble process for achieving consensus. But there is an opposing point of view—called agonism—that I think deserves far more recognition and respect from those outside political science than it generally receives, and it might help us better manage classroom conflict. Derived from the ancient Greek word *agōn*, which refers to various kinds of contests and competitions held at public festivals involving athletics, drama, music, poetry, or painting, agonism views conflict over fundamental values as an essential feature of politics. To deny this basic fact, agonism's proponents argue, is a grave mistake. A critique of the concept that political pluralism leads to consensus, agonism is associated with the German jurist Carl Schmitt and, in very different forms, with the American and Belgian political theorists William E. Connolly and Chantal Mouffe. In Mouffe's view, the opposite of conflict isn't consensus; it's hegemony, as one side in a debate overpowers its opponents.

Our goal as instructors is not to produce an artificial consensus and certainly not to browbeat, intimidate, or badger students into accepting our personal point of view. The best we can do is to help students reflect on their opinions, clarify and critique their own thinking and that of others, and make their arguments with precision, logic, and evidence. Those are plausible goals. What isn't reasonable to expect is achieving a consensus over values where none exists. So, embrace your inner John Stuart Mill and understand that the only consensus that is possible within our classrooms is the agreement to disagree.

## A Civics Education Appropriate for the Twenty-First Century

Civics education is all the rage. If there's any issue that the nation's political leaders agree upon, it's this: that the teaching of civics and knowledgeable, responsible citizenship has never been more important or necessary. A recent *Newsweek* headline sums up the widespread view: "When We Fail to Teach Our Kids the Basics about Civics, We Risk Losing Our Democracy." Support for civics education cuts across the political spectrum. Advocates include Randi Weingarten, the president of the American Federation of Teachers; Stephen Breyer, former Supreme Court justice; district courts that offer teachers' institutes in seven states; Texas's Republican-dominated legislature; and Doug Ducey, Arizona's former Republican governor.[17]

What does civics education entail? There are a lot of disagreements, but certain goals are widely shared: That we should teach students about the history and the workings of the political, judicial, and civil institutions upon which democratic self-government rests. That we should familiarize students with this nation's foundational documents and the controversies surrounding constitutional rights. That we should introduce students to the rights and responsibilities of citizenship. That we should teach students how to speak across differences in background and political views and resolve conflicts. That we should give students opportunities to take part in reasoned, responsible discussions about the many challenges that contemporary society faces (for example, those involving inequality, the environment, the proper size of government, the role of the courts, and how best to balance democratic ideals against concerns for electoral integrity).[18]

All these goals make sense. But at the college level, we need to move up a notch. After all, we already offer introductory courses in American and state government. I wholeheartedly agree with the Civic Learning and Democracy Engagement Coalition, which recently declared in a widely endorsed statement of shared commitments that campuses need to make civic learning for an engaged democracy an expected part of a college education.

Fueling the recent interest in civics education is a widespread consensus among the country's political elites that knowledge about the United States' framework of government and its history has eroded, that tribalism of media sources is exacerbating our differences, and that the stalemates and scorched-earth strategies emanating from Congress are contributing to a deepening cynicism and a mistrust in government. Worse yet, our democracy has not yet lived up to its promises of full participation and equal opportunity for large swaths of US society. All this has contributed to an intense political polarization and a reduced participation in the civic and community organizations that have been at the historic heart of this country's public life. Soberingly, as many as two-thirds of Americans now think US democracy is in crisis.

If American democracy is to thrive, we need a citizenry with a common civic knowledge base as well as the civic skills and dispositions that are essential to informed, respectful debate. Indeed, among the reasons that this society established one of the world's first systems of public education was to prepare a citizenry capable of democratic self-government. But today, per-pupil federal spending on K–12 history and civics education averages $0.05 a year, in contrast to $50 annually on science, technology, engineering, and mathematics education.[19]

Civics education has three broad goals: to ensure that students grasp the nature and principles of the American system of government and how and why these have evolved over time; to cultivate skills essential to responsible citizenship, such as the ability to weigh evidence, grasp conflicting perspectives, and make and defend arguments in a logical, reasoned, evidence-based way; and to help students develop the dispositions essential for the functioning of a diverse, democratic society, including the values of tolerance, empathy, open-mindedness, and respect for differing perspectives.

But the problem isn't simply that students lack civic knowledge or civic skills or the appropriate disposition. It's that we've lost sight of the idea that college's primary purpose isn't career preparation or even economic mobility. Colleges exist to serve society. That's the Wisconsin idea that arose during the early twentieth-century Progressive era and an idea that our institutions need to reaffirm.

So, how might we best infuse an education that emphasizes civic and public purpose into the college curriculum? Let me suggest some possible strategies. One strategy is an inquiry approach that rests on the close reading of primary source documents, especially those that lay out this society's foundational values and the political, constitutional, and legal debates and controversies that have ensued. Close reading reveals a complex text's ambiguities, complexities, contradictions, and conflicting meanings. To read closely is not only to extract a text's surface meaning, but also to parse its implications and deeper significance and to understand its words in context, not only the context in which they were written, but also how they were interpreted and understood at later points in time.

A second strategy is a comparative approach that analyzes how the United States resembles and differs from other nations. The idea of American exceptionalism is profoundly controversial, but as Peter H. Schuck, the Simeon E. Baldwin professor emeritus of law at Yale, has pointed out, there are many ways in which the United States is distinctive. Take, for example, this country's two-party system, the brevity of its constitution and how infrequently it's been amended, the judiciary's power, and the number, length, and cost of elections. All are unusual in comparative perspective. Or, in terms of law, the US Constitution's emphasis on negative as opposed to positive rights (that is, restrictions on governmental powers rather than entitlements to certain government-guaranteed services or benefits), its protections for speech, expression, and commercial advertising, and the country's litigious, adversarial legal culture are all also relatively unusual. Institutionally, the United States is unique in the power and discretion of federal agencies, the distinctive nature of American federalism, with its decentralized educational, criminal justice, transportation and occupational licensing systems, the highly stratified system of higher education, the weakness of labor unions, and the unusually large number of big corporations that possess significant political as well as economic power.[20]

Ideologically, the United States is also distinctive in the absence of a strong socialist party, the acceptance of relatively high levels of economic inequality, the delayed and limited development of government welfare and health programs, and the big role of private think tanks, philanthropies, and religious and nongovernmental organizations in policy formulation and the delivery of social services. Socially, too, the United States is unusual in its ethnic, religious, and racial diversity; its powerful evangelical and moralizing movements; its large numbers of children in single-parent families; its high rates of ethnic intermarriage; and its unusually high incidence of violence. Then, too, the United States is an outlier economically, with its relatively lower tax rates, its diverse, decentralized financial markets, its emphasis on entrepreneurship, and its smaller number of workplace and business regulations. Culturally, it's unusual in its stress on individualism, consumerism, and market competition.

A third strategy for bringing civics education into higher education is experiential: colleges could require undergraduates to participate in a civic engagement activity or community service. Examples might include operating a food pantry or a recycling program, launching neighborhood cleanup campaigns or blood drives, starting community gardens or informational websites, serving in tutoring programs or volunteering at local schools or a youth crisis center or an afterschool reading program, assisting with youth sports programs, organizing Special Olympics events, putting on community musical or theatrical performances, or helping senior citizens.

How, you might well ask, can we scale an experiential approach to civics education? Here are a few suggestions. One way forward is to institute a civic engagement requirement that can be met by taking a course that requires students to participate in a civic-minded activity: tutoring neighborhood students, taking part in a local cleanup drive, registering voters, writing lawmakers, or volunteering at a food bank. Far from being regarded as condescending, paternalistic acts of noblesse oblige, these initiatives can be viewed as energizing and empowering partnerships.

Another approach is to encourage faculty-led projects that have a public service component. In one instance, a psychology professor and a team of students developed a game-like app that medical centers use to draw out information from the notoriously reticent adolescents experiencing chronic pain. In my discipline, which is history, socially purposeful projects might include creating a virtual campus history museum that helps a college or university engage with its complicated past (in the case of my campus, topics might include the appropriation of predominantly Black neighborhoods on which much of the university was built; gay purges during the 1940s that led to the dismissal of the university's president; the troubled and incredibly slow path toward racial integration; the controversies that have surrounded women's athletics; and much more). Another history example would involve the creation of a resource repository for K–12 teachers that would include collections of primary sources on the Black, Latinx, and Asian American experiences and other topics.

Then there is service learning, which, at its best, tackles a genuine local problem and then, through research, identifies a range of policy responses and, in some cases, works in collaboration with local community groups or government to implement a solution. Here, of course, we must recognize that the primary purpose of service learning is to benefit a client. The payback to the students grows out of addressing the client's challenges.

Civics education need not be divisive, nor must it disregard the ideological and partisan divisions or contentious debates over fundamental civic issues that have divided the republic since its founding. As a society, our students do need to develop the knowledge, skills, and dispositions that are essential for a diverse, democratic society to function in a tolerant, broad-minded, and respectful manner.

But our aim should go well beyond duplicating what's already taught in introductory courses on American and state government. Our ultimate goal should be to infuse civic and public purpose into a college education for all college learners, including those in career and technical programs. That's not beyond our ability, and it's certainly not inconsistent with our other goals: to provide career preparation and a well-rounded liberal education, and to equip graduates to meet the complex array of personal and societal challenges they will face as adults.

Colleges and universities, more than any other social institution, apart from the military, are the environments in which the

American ideals of diversity, inclusion, and equity are best, if only partially, realized. But let's not treat our campuses as walled gardens or ivory towers. Let's bridge the town-gown divide, reach out beyond our campuses, and truly embrace John Dewey's vision of an education that emphasizes civic engagement, experiential learning, and courses and programming on themes in the public sphere. Above all, let's reaffirm the Wisconsin idea: that higher education has a responsibility to serve the public.

# 14

---

## The Future of the Humanities

THE HUMANITIES ARE IN DEEP TROUBLE. It's not simply that the number of majors in English, history, and other core humanities fields has fallen by half over the past decade, but faculty jobs, too, are disappearing. According to one scholar's calculation, of the 1,799 graduate students in history who received PhDs from 2019 to 2020, only 175 of them were full-time faculty members three years later. At colleges and universities large and small over broad swaths of the country, the number of tenured or tenure-track historians has declined by a third—or even half—over the course of the past decade. Enrollment hasn't fallen as dramatically because humanists remain responsible for offering much of the general education requirements. But even on that front, threats loom as more and more students acquire college credits in high school and meet college graduation requirements through programs for early college/dual enrollment or in Advanced Placement and International Baccalaureate classes.[1]

Equally worrisome is the share of humanities degree holders who are unhappy about their choice of major. In a recent poll, only about 40 percent would major in the same field, a much higher proportion than those who majored in science, math, or engineering. A similar percentage said that their education failed to prepare them for life. After all, just 28 percent of humanities graduates without an advanced degree found work in a field closely related to their training. Where, then, do humanities graduates wind up? Dispersed widely across the job spectrum, as schoolteachers, specialists in human resources and public relations, technical writers, copywriters and editors, higher ed advisers, and working in media, marketing and sales, academic advising, and much more.[2]

Worse still, a slew of fields that traditionally employed humanities graduates have dried up. There is a lawyer glut. There's a sharp decline in employment in newsrooms, books, magazines, many nonprofits, and, of course, the academy. Trends like these fuel fears that the United States is headed down the same road as Italy or Spain, where overproduction of humanities graduates has sparked unrest, radicalization, and protest—an argument made by Peter Turchin, the Russian-born codeveloper of Cliodynamics, which mathematically models historical dynamics.[3]

The humanities' decline represents a tragedy. What makes the humanities the humanities is the value that their fields place on the life of the mind—the value of intellectual contemplation and the importance of cultivating a rich psychological, emotional, and intellectual interior. The humanities also stress the importance of grappling with life's biggest questions involving aesthetics, determinism and free will, divinity, equity, justice, progress, and the nature of the good life. They embrace honing a familiarity with the contours of the past and the myriad forms of human creativity and customs along with the ability to make informed judgments that reflect an appreciation of context and complexity and a recognition that opposing perspectives, interpretations, explanations, and narratives can all be true. At their best, the humanities engage students in centuries-old, yet ongoing, conversations and debates. The aim is to take part in dialogues with the dead but also with the thinkers and creators and innovators of the present. As the humanities increasingly shed their Eurocentric and patriarchal roots, these conversations should be growing ever richer and fuller. But alas, I fear that isn't the case.

Let's not kid ourselves. Assigned reading, even in the most selective institutions' humanities departments, has declined. Lower-division classes have, in too many instances, become overspecialized, reflecting their instructors' narrow interests rather than considered, collective judgments of what students ought to know and be able to do. Sweeping humanities themes and concerns that cut across department lines are too often neglected. Worse yet, the skills that the humanities nurture—close reading, critical thinking, argumentative writing—can't be taught in the kinds of performative, instructor-focused lecture classes that predominate. This is how the humanities end.

The decline in students' interest in the humanities has, for good reason, stirred distress and despair. Many fear that students' preference for a more vocational, technical, preprofessional, or career-oriented education threatens higher education's very soul and undercuts one of higher education's loftiest purposes: to ensure that graduates receive a truly well-rounded education, acquire essential cultural literacies, and get the skills—in written and oral communication, close reading, and critical, analytical, and interpretive thinking—that distinguish college graduates. A quotation from the physicist Robert R. Wilson, who was a sculptor and an architect as well as one of the nation's leading physicists, said in another context strikes me as apropos. When asked how a particular federal expenditure would contribute to national security, he replied: "It has only to do with the respect with which we regard one another, the dignity of man, our love of culture. It has to do with: Are we good painters, good sculptors, great poets? I mean all the things we really venerate in our country and are patriotic about. It has nothing to do directly with defending our country except to make it worth defending."[4]

The humanities feel besieged from both the left and the right. From one side of the ideological spectrum, there are grossly exaggerated accusations that the humanities disciplines remain Eurocentric; that privileged white male writers, thinkers, political figures, composers, and artists are insufficiently attentive to issues involving gender relations, sexual preference, inequality, exploitation, slavery, race, and imperialism; and that the humanities are an archaic and elitist relic of patriarchy and a thinly veiled defense of colonialism. On the other side is a hyperbolic insistence that jargon-ridden humanists are promoting a "woke" ideology that is overly focused on racial, ethnic, gender, and sexual identities and on racism, sexism, and other forms of injustice.

Increasingly, defenses of the humanities rest on the transferable skills that students acquire, including the ability to reason logically and bring ethical and historical perspectives to bear on hot topics. But the underlying value of the humanities lies not in their utility, applicability, skills conferred, or practical outcomes, but rather in the cultivation of a rich inner life. This is a life dedicated to thought, wonder, aesthetic appreciation, and curiosity infused with a passion for reading, the arts, learning, and reflection. But unfortunately, American society no longer places much weight on those humanistic values.

In 2006, the Andrew W. Mellon Foundation gave the American Academy of Arts and Sciences funds to develop a set of indicators to provide a comprehensive portrait of the state of the humanities in the United States. In recent years, the picture that Humanities Indicators has painted is profoundly disheartening, charting dwindling engagement with books, a downturn in per capita library visits and circulation, and a stark educational divide in visits to historic sites—along with a significant decline in the number of degrees granted in art history, English, history, and philosophy. To be sure, the news isn't all negative. The number of minors in humanities fields has remained stable, and course enrollments have remained high at around six million, largely because the cost of these programs is relatively low, and gen ed and language requirements sustain lower-division enrollments. Also, humanities departments have quite wisely engaged in strategic hiring, helping institutions to meet their diversity objectives. In addition, humanities faculty have been very active in trying to defend their turf, making sure that humanities courses fulfill graduation requirements, instituting new major and minor requirements to increase demand for upper level courses, and offering foreign language courses taught in English, literature courses focusing on cinema and television, and history courses on sports and other popular topics. Because humanities faculty tend to be among the most vocal and actively involved in faculty governance, leading administrators display little interest in incurring the humanists' wrath.

Still, there are grounds for serious concern. The areas of enrollment growth in the humanities lie outside the core disciplines. Communication, linguistics, and ethnic, gender, and sexuality studies are the humanistically related departments, programs, and schools that are exhibiting growth. So, too, are honors colleges. Several of these fields, however, consider themselves social sciences and not part of the humanities at all. Some, in fact, refuse to participate in humanities surveys. Also, claims that the number of adjuncts and part-timers in the humanities has not increased must be regarded with some skepticism. Tenure and tenure-track employment in the humanities appears to have peaked in 2017, but this was at a relatively low level. Current employment figures are likely a statistical artifact, with very large departments at highly selective institutions skewing the results. Also, it is likely that part-time lecturers, non-tenurable professors of practice, and retired faculty are improperly counted. Whatever growth has occurred is taking place outside the traditional humanities departments.

Furthermore, the humanities scholarly infrastructure is in disarray. The life blood of humanities scholarship—peer review, scholarly publishing, journal editorship, and professional meetings—is struggling. This doesn't bode well for the humanities' future. Editors are desperate to find humanities scholars willing to review articles, prospectuses, and book manuscripts. Department chairs are at wit's end as they struggle to get scholars to review tenure and promotion files. Leading humanities journals find it increasingly hard to attract qualified, experienced candidates to serve as editors. Equally disturbing is the disarray within the scholarly book trade. With an average print run of 200 (or fewer) copies, the publication of scholarly monographs is in deep trouble. In fact, many leading scholarly presses are only interested in books with at least a modicum of trade potential.

Otherwise, even a subvention is insufficient to ensure publication. At the same time, interest in publishing anthologies—including those with wholly original essays—has tanked.

There are no easy solutions to these problems. Professional organizations and departments must, of course, reaffirm the idea that humanities faculty have a professional responsibility to review article and book manuscripts and applications for tenure and promotion, and incentivize service as journal editors. But what else can humanities departments do? They must seize the low-hanging fruit. In addition to offering especially appealing courses dealing with popular culture, humanities departments need to offer more courses aligned with the most popular preprofessional programs in business, computer science, engineering, health care, law, and technology. For example, an integrated liberal arts curriculum might examine the global, social, and cultural dimensions of engineering, technology, science, medicine, business, and public policy through the lens of the humanities and social sciences. Humanities departments might also embrace higher ed's most rapidly growing sector: professional master's and certificate programs. Especially promising are programs in museum studies; professional, technical, and nonfiction writing; the medical humanities; and joint programs offered in conjunction with business and engineering.

They must also recognize that business humanities, digital humanities, environmental humanities, legal humanities, and the public and applied humanities offer exciting areas of promise. Not only can such fields contribute to professional identity formation, to ensuring that attorneys, businesspeople, physicians, and technologists internalize their field's core values and develop the perspectives, sensitivities, and interpersonal skills expected of a practicing professional, but they can also awaken graduates to a host of issues ignored in technical courses. Thus, the medical humanities hold out the prospect of educating health care professionals in the experience of pain and illness, care of the dying, health policy, religion and health, medical privacy, and other key topics.

Then, there's what's called the innovation humanities, which combine the humanities with the arts and emerging technologies in areas that include game design, human-computer interaction, simulation and interactive development, media production, and new and immersive modes of communication. The rapidly growing fields of artificial intelligence and machine learning need humanists as well as technologists as they strive to develop algorithms that can mimic human intelligence and creativity and avoid bias and stereotyping. In addition, humanities departments should do much more to help their students acquire the skills most highly valued in the contemporary economy. There is no reason why humanities graduates shouldn't receive training in computational thinking, data mining, data visualization, demographic and geospatial analysis, econometrics, narrative analysis, time series network analysis, provenance, data privacy, 3D digital reconstructions, and simulation modeling. Yet it's extremely rare, at present, for humanities students to get any training in these skills.

As the undergraduate student body grows ever more diverse, it also makes sense to make the humanities more explicitly global, comparative, and cross-cultural. Propelled by demography and economic and technological interconnectedness, the humanities need to forsake Eurocentrism and national insularity and adopt a more international perspective that focuses on differences and similarities within and across cultures and regions. At a time when fundamentalist nationalism is on the rise in many parts of the world, the humanities have a special role to play in combating narrowness and provinciality. Internationalizing the humanities will allow students to gain novel perspectives on how conceptions of race, gender, ethnicity, and cultural hierarchy and difference developed and vary globally. By breaking through the constraints of established canons and national tradition and building on the burgeoning scholarship in comparative literature, comparative religion, ethnomusicology, global art, and world history, the global humanities would explore cross-cultural contacts, influences and exchanges, syncretism and cultural appropriation, colonial and borderland encounters, migrations and diasporas, colonial and postcolonial cultures, and local, regional, and hemispheric linkages. Through rigorous cross-cultural comparisons of aesthetic traditions, philosophical theorizing, and theological frameworks, practices, and intercultural interactions, a truly global humanities curriculum might speak to today's extraordinarily diverse student body in ways that the more traditional humanities courses do not.

Especially promising are efforts to reimagine general education for the twenty-first century. Existing distribution requirements typically consist of a smorgasbord of disconnected courses that might include one or two in rhetoric and composition, literature, and history. There are, however, emerging efforts to transform the box-checking approach to the gen ed curriculum into a more coherent and meaningful experience that treats the humanities more holistically, combining the power and insights of art history, English language and literature, history, and philosophy. We need more courses that can address timeless questions involving aesthetics, citizenship, ethics, evil, justice, and the good life through a multidisciplinary lens and help students appreciate the philosophical, moral, and theological issues that surround business, law, politics, public policy, technology, and an awareness of the power of language. For example, Purdue University's Cornerstone initiative and Austin Community College's Great Questions project are organized around the close reading of transformational texts—books that raise provocative intellectual questions (about citizenship, equity, ethics, identity, justice, power, tragedy, and the nature of the good life, for example) and help undergraduates make sense of their identity, delineate a set of values, and plot a direction in life. Some of these works are classics in the Western canon, but many others are contemporary or international. All contribute to students' intellectual and moral development. For far too long, the American educational system steered the working class toward a practical or vocational or technical education. Working-class students learned, in countless ways, that a liberal education was only for the privileged and the pampered. In contrast, Cornerstone and the Great Questions curriculum have the power to subvert hierarchies of privilege, redeem lost souls, open minds, and transform lives, while helping to instill the writing, reading, and analytical skills essential for academic success.

In recent years, defenses of a humanistic education have grown ever more airy and abstract: that it inculcates twenty-first-century literacies or simply the ability to think critically, for instance. But none of these convey the central features of a humanities education, which entails grappling with issues involving democracy, determinism, equality, economic markets, justice, objectivity, and more. The Cornerstone and Great Questions initiatives demonstrate that the humanities can speak to issues of greater urgency to today's students, such as identity, equity, and power.

Innovations within the humanities are unlikely to come from the top down. The most promising examples have arisen from groups of faculty who have devised their own distinctive approaches to the lower-division curriculum. That's exactly what teams of scholars at Harvard did by creating Humanities 10, a series of Great Books colloquia, and Humanities 11—frameworks courses that introduce students to the art of listening, looking, and close reading. In his 2010 study of the failures of college curriculum reform, *The Marketplace of Ideas*, Harvard's Louis Menand posed three questions that should have spurred (but didn't spur) serious reflection and action. First, he asked, why can't institutions agree on what an educated person ought to know? Second, why aren't most faculty members able or willing to teach outside their disciplines and specialties? And third, why can't colleges offer the kind of robust education in the humanities that will produce well-rounded graduates with the verbal, writing, literacy, and analytic skills we ought to expect?[5] The answer to these questions comes down to professional training, socialization, and reward structures. None show any signs of changing. Still, motivated faculty members are doing their darndest to create opportunities for motivated students to pursue a meaningful, more holistic humanistic education. Our current curriculum model combines excessive requirements without a clearly defined sense of what a graduate should know or do. We can do better. We must do better.

———

The critic and classicist Daniel Mendelsohn offers a simple yet compelling rationale for studying the humanities: "When your father dies, your accounting degree is not going to help you at all to process that experience." Mendelsohn's point is that the humanities examine the most basic questions about human experience. "Great literature," he insists, "will help you think about mortality and losing loved ones."[6] And more than that, an education in the humanities, at its best, cultivates students' aesthetic sensibilities and historical and cross-cultural perspectives, in addition to a richer interior life, an appreciation of moral and psychological complexity, and a capacity for self-reflection. But arguments like these, very unfortunately, have failed to persuade many undergraduates that familiarity with the humanities is worth possessing. What, then, can humanities professors do? Here are some suggestions.

Prior to the Renaissance, when the humanities came to be associated with the study of particular fields—notably, art, history, law, literature, philosophy, and theology—and particular methods—analytic, critical, and speculative rather than empirical—the humanities were thought of as a process. For Cicero, *humanitas* provided the kind of education that was necessary to produce a cultivated human being, one who possessed certain virtues, including empathy, compassion, a capacity for friendship, and an enlightened, mature, skeptical, and critical mindset. The time has come, I am convinced, to reassert this older view of the purpose of the humanities and to embrace the notion that the goals of a humanities education, especially at the lower division, should be to foster critical reflection, cultivate the moral and aesthetic sensibilities, nurture a rich inner life, and teach the arts of living. Humanities students should grapple with life's meaning and purpose, ponder life's deepest questions, and wrestle with the most profound existential issues involving aging, evil, family, friendship, gender, justice, and sacrifice, as well as those of love, loss, memory, and mortality.

Let me suggest some ways that we might do this. This list is certainly not meant to be comprehensive or exhaustive, and, indeed, some of these approaches are already offered by individual faculty members. But these perspectives haven't been embraced on the broader scale that I am convinced is necessary. First, the humanities might look more systematically at the human condition. What does it mean to be human? Some generalizations, however gross or overly simplistic, make sense. These include an ability to communicate through words, sounds, symbols and gestures, movements, and facial expressions; to ponder the past, present, and future; to feel and express deep, powerful emotions; and to make decisions or take actions and experience their consequences. But the true meaning of being human lies in our ability to reflect upon human nature or the relative role of reason, the emotions, and the unconscious on human behavior. And the most powerful and profound insights into those issues are found not in the social and behavioral, brain, or natural sciences, but in the humanities. Anger, envy, fear, gluttony, greed, grief, loss, love, lust, mortality, pain, pride, regret, sloth, and wrath—all are aspects of the human condition that are also best studied through the humanities. It's in works of literature, art, philosophy, theology, and history that we can best learn about human nature: whether people are inherently good or evil, altruistic or selfish, sociable or individualistic. At least thus far, the greatest insights into questions of free will and determinism and the impact of environment and upbringing are found not in the social or natural sciences but through the kinds of documents that humanists examine and produce: novels, dramas, artworks, biographies, and histories.

Secondly, humanities faculty might look at the life course through a humanistic lens. Certainly, social scientists have a great deal to say about the series of stages—infancy, early childhood, middle childhood, late childhood, and so forth—that constitute the life course, as well as the transitions—growing up and growing old—that mark our progression through life. But it's the humanities that reveal the profound transformations that have taken place in the definition and actual experience of the life course and the meanings that human beings have attached to the process of maturation, coming of age, achieving adulthood, and aging. It's a cliché that many of the greatest works of literature and art explore these life changes and pivot points. For students, who are themselves moving across life stages and coming of age, few subjects are more personally relevant than exploring life's passages and the rites and developmental challenges—forging an independent adult identity, finding intimacy, establishing a career, becoming a parent, grappling with grief—that accompany these shifts. Too often, I fear, the study of the life course is left to psychologists or sociologists, but it's through the humanities that we can examine the human meaning of being a child, a girl or boy, an adolescent or youth, or an adult. It's through literature, art, and other humanistic sources that we can help our students navigate their own passage through the life course.

Third, the humanities have a great deal to say about justice: its definition, its complexities and ambiguities, and how it comes about. At this historic moment when controversies over social justice stand at the very center of public debate, many students would benefit greatly from a course that explores the aims of justice and the moral principles that should inform our actions and choices as individuals or members of society. The issues that rack society today—abortion, affirmative action, assisted suicide, capital punishment, free speech, immigration, inequalities of income and wealth, reparations for slavery, the sale of bodily organs, surrogate pregnancy, and a voluntary military, among others—all hinge on people's conceptions of justice. So let our students enter the ongoing conversation about justice and moral reasoning alongside Plato, Aristotle, Locke, Kant, Bentham, Mill, Nietzsche, Rawls, and their contemporary counterparts, and ask themselves what constitutes criminal, distributional, environmental, gender, generational, or racial justice and how these can best be achieved.

Then, there is the problem of evil. Contemporary American culture is obsessed with evil. Political torture, terrorism, suicide bombings, school shootings, and other forms of violence dominate our news coverage, while closer to home, we have grown increasingly aware of the realities of domestic violence, sexual assault, and child abuse. Our popular culture is obsessed with images of evil and violence. Psychopaths, sociopaths, and serial killers pervade our movies and many of our most popular books. Some of the young have self-consciously adopted the Goth style, with its allusions to the forces of darkness.

For more than two millennia, theologians, philosophers, and their modern-day counterparts have pondered the problem of evil. Religious thinkers have asked how an all-powerful and benevolent God can tolerate evil and suffering and whether evil serves some rational purpose or is utterly inexplicable. Philosophers, too, have explored the origins and nature of evil, and they have asked whether people are responsible for evil acts committed as the result of unconscious drives and whether rational explanations of evil reduce human responsibility. In the twentieth century, secular explanations of evil largely replaced religious ones. Psychologists and sociologists have shown how mental disease, past abuse, or dysfunctional upbringing and certain social, demographic, economic, and political circumstances and dislocations have given rise to acts of individual and collective evil.

Humanists might examine how various thinkers, writers, and artists have conceived, explained, and interpreted evil and how we might best understand the sources of human violence and cruelty, the historical factors that make radical evil possible, and the similarities and differences among such examples as mass murder, ethnic cleansing, population displacement, and genocide as the Atlantic slave trade, the destruction of Native Americans, the Armenian genocide, Stalin's great famine, the Holocaust, and the Cultural Revolution in China. Among the questions such a course might investigate are these: Is evil inexplicable, impossible to understand? Or is evil simple to explain? Is it rooted in jealousy, fear, rage, envy, greed, hatred, and the wish to dominate or the sheer joy of killing? Is evil perpetrated by deviants or moral monsters or ordinary individuals? Are men more prone to evil than women, and if so, why? Should we, can we, forgive evildoers?

The humanities also offer numerous insights into how people ought to live. Long before the humanities defined themselves in terms of specialized disciplinary modes of analysis, the humanities offered guides to the well-lived life. The reason to study the humanities was simple and straightforward: to lead a life worth living. The humanities taught individuals how to appreciate the arts and render aesthetic judgments, define a philosophy of life, grieve or cope with life's tragedies and disappointments, make ethical judgments, and understand the course of history.

What constitutes the good life has changed profoundly over time, with honor and reputation, military prowess, or religious observance gradually giving way to work, wealth and possessions, and family and friendship. Some find life's meaning not in private life but in the "religion" of art or science. Others embrace hedonism, thrill seeking and risk-taking. My sense is that there is an intense hunger among many students for opportunities to reflect on how best to live—a yearning that is only partially met by courses in psychology but that might be addressed through courses that draw on humanities texts and tools to tackle life's challenges.

Tragedy, I am convinced, offers yet another broad topic that humanists ought to address frankly and forthrightly, even though this topic might trigger feelings of trauma in students who have suffered horrendous episodes of abuse, violence, assault, pain, and loss. Live long enough, and I suspect that all people undergo tragedy: radical suffering, overwhelming pain, and traumatic loss. Horrific human tragedies surround us, whether these take the form of child abuse, domestic violence, school shootings, or war. We should study tragedy not because it's therapeutic or because it can bring catharsis, but because it will breed empathy and compassion and because no other subject helps us better understand the human condition or human character and how some people have found meaning and inner strength to persist in the face of pain, suffering, and grief. Whether you are a historian, an art or literary critic or theorist, a philosopher, or a scholar of religion, do consider wrestling with human tragedy in your classes and the ways that artists, dramatists, novelists, philosophers, theologians, and others have conceived, depicted, explained, and interpreted it.

It's not an accident that many of the world's greatest works of literature are tragedies. Some retell a version of humankind's fall and expulsion from Eden. Others are tales about tragic heroes, those mighty and often admirable figures whose suffering grows out of an error in judgment, ignorance, or hubris. Then, there are those even more profound tragedies in which misfortune grows out of conflicting conceptions of right, duty, or justice. Reversals of fortune, which grow out of the capriciousness of fate or the gods, are central to many literary tragedies. As the bard of Stratford wrote in *King Lear*, the most tragic of Shakespearean tragedies, "As flies to wanton boys are we to th' gods / They kill us for their sport."[7]

Modern literature tends to focus less on the downfall of elites than on the tragedies of the everyday: of hopes crushed, illusions shattered, dreams denied, love deceived, and bonds of family or friendship betrayed, sometimes out of little more than accident or mundane character flaws like arrogance, avarice, cowardice, gullibility, jealousy, malice, paranoia, or selfishness. These democratic tragedies take place not among the powerful but, rather, ordinary women and men, and they often take as their subtext, as in the tragic 1957 romance *An Affair to Remember*, what might have been had tragedy not intervened. The essence of tragedy, in such works, lies in fantasies unfulfilled, hopes unmet, and potential unrealized. In contrast with the great ancient Greek tragedies, tragedy, suffering, and loss offer no compensation in terms of enlightenment or self-understanding or awareness of one's inner strengths, or, as in the case of Oedipus or Antigone, a kind of immortality. All that's left is a Darwinian or existentialist message about nature's randomness and its lack of inherent meaning or purpose. The result is to leave tragedy's victims only to anguish and despair. Often, as in the naturalist novel, individual suffering is attributed less to personal weakness or flawed character than to some inescapable force—heredity, for example, or nature or the workings of capitalism. A mechanical determinism and an extreme pessimism tend to characterize these works. In the face of such overpowering forces, the only appropriate response is cynicism, resignation, passivity, or fatalism.

Some tragedies are intensely personal; others are collective and grow out of war, displacement, discrimination, or natural disaster, whether fast moving like a tornado, a storm surge, or a forest fire, or slower, like drought, deforestation, or desertification. Even the most privileged experience tragic losses. We all mourn. We all grieve. We all weep. We all wail. But that's not to say that all tragedies are equal. Still, this reminds us that nothing—not our wealth and savings nor our status or virtues—can insulate us from tragedy. Which makes it profoundly ironic that many of the most famous quotations about tragedy are derisive or mordant. There's Oscar Wilde's quip in *Lady Windemere's Fan*: "There are only two tragedies. One is not getting what one wants and the other is getting it." Then there is the oft-repeated phrase almost certainly misattributed to the poet William Butler Yeats: "Being Irish, he had an abiding sense of tragedy, which sustained him through temporary periods of joy." Or a line attributed to F. Scott Fitzgerald: "Show me a hero and I'll write you a tragedy."[8]

Staples of popular psychology are advice about overcoming tragedy. These works typically reaffirm the Stoic belief that adversity breeds strength, often augmented by the Christian notion of the nobility of suffering. Americans, we are sometimes told, are especially allergic to tragedy, finding it, yes, un-American. William Dean Howells is reputed to have said that "What the American public wants in the theater is a tragedy with a happy ending." How, as Henry James observed in his biographical study of Nathaniel Hawthorne, could Americans truly grasp the tragic in a land without "manors, nor old country-houses, nor parsonages, nor thatched cottages nor ivied ruins; no cathedrals, nor abbeys, nor little Norman churches; no great Universities nor public schools—no Oxford, nor Eton, nor Harrow; no literature, no novels, no museums, no pictures, no political society, no sporting class . . ."[9]

Are Americans inimical to the tragic? That's what Hal Brands, a professor of global affairs at Johns Hopkins University's School of Advanced International Studies, and Charles Edel, a senior fellow at the University of Sydney's United States Studies Centre, argue in an important yet neglected essay published in 2017, well before the pandemic, the cultural confrontation over racial inequalities, and the war in Ukraine. Titled "The End of History Is the Birth of History," this essay contains prophetic words: "Americans have forgotten that historic tragedies on a global scale are real. They'll soon get a reminder."[10]

That, of course, was the message conveyed by the Christian realist Reinhold Niebuhr (and, in a different, deeply ironic form, Henry Kissinger's amoral realism). Even as Niebuhr called out the arrogance and hypocrisy of American foreign policy and repudiated any illusions of American innocence and virtue and "every attempt to claim divine sanction for America's goals and struggles," the great ethicist and theologian reaffirmed the nation's historical mission to protect and extend democratic values in a fallen, conflict-riven world. Niebuhr's critics have portrayed him as a Cold War liberal, even a forerunner of later neoconservatives, in his belief that the world's evils could not be attributed primarily to environment or economics and his willingness (in certain circumstances, but not in Vietnam) to use power to promote an American-dominated world. But that view is certainly misleading. After all, Niebuhr was a social activist and fiery proponent for labor rights and civil rights and a staunch enemy of antisemitism.[11]

Brands and Edel argue that American elites, in World War II's wake, understood the realities of tragedy, and recognizing how tragic a breakdown of world order could be, took aggressive steps to construct a new rights-based international system. But, the authors assert, "Americans are serial amnesiacs," and three-quarters of a century after the Second World War, that tragic sensibility had dissipated. "Americans have lost their sense of tragedy," Brands and Edel write. "The U.S.-led international order has been so successful, for so long, that Americans have come to take it for granted." The authors note that "even a casual survey of modern history" exposes the fragility of international order, which breaks down for myriad reasons: "sometimes having to do with relative shifts in the balance of power, sometimes having to do with clashing ideologies, sometimes having to do with simple blunders and other idiosyncrasies of statecraft."[12] Yet these breakdowns and the great power struggles that ensued periodically served as sources of inspiration for efforts to secure a stable international order, from the Peace of Westphalia in 1648 to the Congress of Vienna in 1814 and 1815 to the 1940s, when the United Nations was established and the Bretton Woods international monetary system created.

Brands and Edel maintain that the lessons of the 1940s gradually faded and were increasingly "replaced by a worldview that is equal parts naive, dangerous and ahistorical." Given the many US interventions since the 1983 invasion of Grenada, I think their insistence that the United States has somehow retreated from the preservation of world order is greatly exaggerated. Indeed, one can argue that American action—not inaction—played a central role in undermining the stability of the international system. And yet, I do think that this society has not adequately faced up to the realities of tragedy: tragedies that flow from largely unrestrained gun violence, from poverty and inequitable access to health care and high-quality education, and from the tragedies that have accompanied the American uses of military power. It is in American popular culture that the American failure to face up to the realities of tragedy is most obvious. It was over three decades ago that media studies scholar Mark Crispin Miller described the essence of American popular culture as "deliberate antirealism." That was long before the jukebox musical dominated Broadway, before Marvel superhero films ruled the nation's cineplexes, and before algorithm-driven video streaming governed the small screen. I see scarcely any signs of a tragic sensibility in our mass culture.[13]

Perhaps, however, our recent encounters with so many real-world tragedies will reacquaint Americans with a tragic sensibility that isn't cynical or pessimistic but that nonetheless recognizes that there are crimes and injustices that are tragic and ought not be ignored. I can only hope so. We cannot escape from history nor evade our social responsibilities. But if this society is to truly face up to the tragic in our midst, the humanities must do their part, raising consciousness, opening minds, and leading difficult conversations that are informed by the artistic, literary, philosophical, and theological insights from our forebears combined with the latest thinking today. To teach tragedy is not to succumb to what Susan Sontag called "death porn" or to revel in the sufferings of others.[14] It is, I am convinced, an essential task: to grapple with some of life's deepest mysteries—why pain, suffering, and evil exist and why some, wholly unfairly, suffer much more than others. If the humanities fail to wrestle head-on with these broad philosophical, theological, and ethical issues, then these disciplines truly will accede to irrelevancy.

———

The applied humanities offer still another promising path forward. The idea that the humanities provide practical workplace and life skills is not a new one, and many departments offer courses in the applied humanities, in areas like archival management, museum studies, historic preservation, historical editing, and public policy history. What might be the next iteration of the applied humanities? We might call this the translational humanities—the application of traditional humanities skills in research, interpretation, media literacy, and teaching supplemented with skills in design—to domains beyond the academy. The translational humanities might study emerging media and engage critically with issues raised by artificial intelligence, data analytics, and social media. Program graduates might help inform user interface and user experience design and machine-user interaction and engage in experiments with animation; robotics; virtual and augmented reality; serious gaming; narrative, personalized instructional pathways; and interactive learning. Innovative examples can already be found at Boise State University's College of Innovation and Design, with its programs in games, interactive and mobile media, and human-environment systems, and at the University of Texas at Dallas's School of Arts, Technology and Emerging Communication, with its programs in animation and games, emerging media art, and critical media studies.

Humanists might also do more to open windows into careers. Humanities majors need timely information about labor market trends, the skills that specific jobs require, and the postgraduation career trajectories of students who major in humanities disciplines. In addition to creating more work-related opportunities, including internships, humanities departments should take steps to build undergraduates' social capital by providing networking opportunities with alumni and potential employers. They should also work with other units to develop courses that might strengthen humanities majors' job market qualifications. These might include classes in digital communication; graphic, website, and human interface design; human relations; marketing principles and tools; natural language processing; organizational management and leadership; and project management. None of these initiatives is a panacea, but taken together, such steps can help humanities students chart a direction in life and plot a realistic path toward achieving their career-related goals.

Another avenue for building connections between the humanities and the job market lies in preparing those graduates who will assume leading roles in education, training, advising, counseling, and human services not only within but outside of the academy or K-12 schools. In increasingly multicultural societies, there is a pressing need for intermediaries and trainers and facilitators who can help institutions maximize the effectiveness of exceptionally diverse workforces and address the anxieties that many individuals feel in environments without well-defined norms, expectations, and pathways to advancement.

Then, there's what we might call the critical humanities. A recent anti-humanities diatribe, *Cynical Theories: How Activist Scholarship Made Everything about Race, Gender, and Identity—and Why This Harms Everybody*, a study of postmodern thought since the 1960s, argues that critical theory, which began as a critique of grand theory, subsequently turned into an attack on the intellectual foundations of Western culture: the concept of reason and objective truth, which were now regarded as expressions of power directed against oppressed identity groups. In fact, the ideas associated with postmodern thought—the provisional nature of truth; the cultural construction of knowledge; the ways that narratives, discourse, and language shape understanding; ideology as a mediator between ideas and context; and intersectionality as a way to describe how gender, race, sexuality, and other forms of social hierarchy and discrimination reinforce one another in defining status and power—offer a fresh and exciting vantage point from which to deconstruct concepts, entities, theories, and relationships too often understood far too simply. Instead of reducing the humanities to a rather inconsequential adjunct of the behavioral, physical, psychological, and social sciences, providing historical context, philosophical glosses, or artistic and literary analogues, the critical humanities use postmodern thought to probe, dissect, and critique the assumptions under which those disciplines rest.

One of American higher education's most distinctive features lies in its commitment to ensuring that all students, regardless of their professional ambitions, should receive a rich, robust humanistic education. Until recently, it was taken for granted that the primary purpose of a higher education is not simply to cultivate marketable skills or offer a useful credential but to do what Ignatius meant by *cura personalis* or what Cicero called for when he described a humanistic education as a process and not a body of content or a mess of skills. Transformation and growth—these are the twin goals of a humanistically infused college education. That high ideal, unfortunately, is often compromised in practice. We must not forget why this commitment to the humanities exists: because we want all students—not just the most privileged—to grapple with complex moral issues, develop a mature level of emotional competence and cross-cultural literacy, participate in timeless human conversations, and be able to think critically and analytically and communicate clearly and persuasively whether orally or in writing. In other words, in a democratic society, all students should have access to a liberal education, an education that befits a free person.

If the humanities are to achieve those goals, we need more "big question" classes that don't readily conform to disciplinary norms. Let's not allow narrow specialization to stop us from providing our students with the rich exposure to the intellectual life that college ought to offer and the humanities, properly construed, can furnish. The American theologian Leonard I. Sweet said, "The future is not something we enter. The future is something we create."[15] We can stand back and watch the humanities slowly fade into irrelevance, depending largely for their survival on various service courses. Or we can embrace more inspiring visions that seek to re-energize and revitalize the humanities and ensure that the humanities speak to the issues and needs of our time. We mustn't let inertia or lethargy or a misguided commitment to tradition thwart these efforts to reimagine the humanities. Remember, the humanities' future is in our hands.

# 15

---

## How Innovation Happens

HIGHER EDUCATION, WE OFTEN HEAR, is the social institution most resistant to change. As a wit once quipped, it's easier to move a cemetery than to change a college or university. In fact, American higher education has undergone a series of far-reaching transformations. Over time, it has not only become more accessible, but its curriculum has grown more diverse, relevant, and practical. However, those who argue that colleges and universities remain stuck in the past are right in at least one respect: these institutions need to innovate if they are to better serve today's students and prepare them to function effectively in today's multicultural society and volatile, uncertain, integrated global economy. But as we know all too well, the kind of institutional transformations that are necessary are extraordinarily difficult to implement.

Driving academic innovation is higher education's truly wicked problem. It is wicked because the problem has multiple dimensions. The barriers to change are simultaneously cultural, institutional, structural, and financial. Inflexible academic calendars, rigid course schedules poorly aligned to student needs, incumbent technological infrastructure, curricula built around stand-alone courses, outmoded classroom designs, and rigid faculty teaching-load policies that make it difficult to offer education in unconventional formats all make innovation exceedingly difficult.[1]

There is the motivational challenge: convincing stakeholders that there is a pressing problem or an opportunity that is worth the cost investment in time, money, and energy. Then there is the bystander challenge: whether responsibility for solving a problem or launching an initiative is so diffuse that no one is likely to take charge. There is also the governance challenge. Colleges and universities operate on a principle of shared governance and a wide range of stakeholders—students, faculty, staff, alumni, and others—quite rightly having a vested interest in institutional changes. Any potential threat to perceived quality, integrity, standards, reputation, or jobs is a matter of intense concern. Curricular changes, in particular, are subject to close scrutiny and are exceptionally difficult to institute. All changes require widespread buy-in.

Then, too, there is the implementation challenge: how to institute educational transformations that disrupt entrenched practices, incumbent processes and procedures, established roles, and legacy technologies. Implementation requires leaders and administrators to coax, cajole, entice, and inspire necessary changes. Leadership must be acutely sensitive to the goals and aspirations of key stakeholders. Yet given the right circumstances and incentives, academic innovation is certainly possible. A successful innovation strategy must address issues of motivation, leadership, strategic vision, institutional practice, organizational culture, project management, and sustainability. And it must do so across multiple domains all at once in a context of financial constraints and competition over institutional resources.[2]

The barriers to academic innovation are manifold. Many campuses suffer from initiative fatigue, others from a lack of information about the nature of the institution's problems or the kinds of innovations being launched on other campuses. Complacency and suspicion about the motives behind an innovation initiative tend to be widespread. Past successes, the lack of a visible crisis, distrust, inertia, and well-founded skepticism all discourage a sense of urgency. So does a focus on issues of marginal importance.

The main hurdles to academic innovation fall Into three broad categories. The first and most substantial impediment lies in existing institutional structures, policies, and infrastructure. For example, the information technology infrastructure may be incapable of consolidating student data or supporting such innovations as fractional course credit. A second major hindrance lies in weak incentives to change. There is a profound disconnect, on many campuses, between the purported emphasis on student success and resource commitments. Faculty and staff lack significant inducements or motivations to change and are not provided with the kinds of support and training that they need to innovate, whether in pedagogy, deployment of technology, or advising.

A third major blockage lies in mindsets and governance structures that impede innovation. Risk aversion, skepticism and cynicism, and a narrow sense of self-interest (or what might be termed "zero-sum thinking") all discourage efforts to bring about far-reaching changes. Other factors do as well: tradition, the fear of lowering standards, and objections to efforts to impose change from the outside or the top down. In faculty minds, innovation is often associated with expensive information technology of dubious value, impersonal computer-based instruction, and instructional staffing by non-faculty. There is a sense that innovations are being imposed from outside and that the goal is not to improve learning but merely to achieve cost savings by increasing class size, putting inferior courses online, inflating grades, and granting credit for non-college-level activities. Objections to standardizing education are particularly intense since this appears to threaten faculty autonomy and academic freedom. Some of the most intractable obstructions lie in the widespread beliefs that teaching is a solitary endeavor and that innovations in teaching and assessment are fads, or worse, fetishes that threaten to undercut educational quality.

Perhaps the biggest barrier to innovation is a lack of transparency about institutional resources, spending on instruction and student services, and outcomes. Resistance to releasing detailed outcomes data about persistence and completion rates, performance gaps and grading disparities, and postgraduation employment and earnings outcomes is especially fierce, but nothing is more likely to motivate innovation than rigorous comparisons of the outcomes of peer institutions. Outcomes data can, of course, be easily misused or misunderstood. Such data tells us little about student learning and can also be gamed, for example, by altering admissions practices or reducing standards (or, in the case of law schools, providing campus jobs to recent graduates). One must be especially careful in comparing institutions with very different student profiles located in very different job markets. But data and financial transparency are the most likely vehicles to motivate institutional change.

The colleges and universities that have most dramatically moved the dial on student retention and completion and most effectively promoted students' social mobility are not necessarily those with the highest public profiles or the most charismatic and ambitious presidents or the latest technologies or the most sweeping or flashy programs of innovation. Rather, these are institutions that are honest about the challenges they face, begin by addressing a particular problem and building upon success in that area, empower leaders at all levels of the organization, make extensive use of empirical data, and cultivate a campus culture with a laser-like focus on student success.

Higher education is not averse to change. Institutions have evolved in many significant ways over the past quarter century. Student bodies have become much more diverse. Technology is now infused into research and teaching. Interdisciplinary programs, including those in gender, sexuality, and ethnic studies; brain science; data analytics; and sustainability have proliferated. New pedagogies, especially hybrid approaches to teaching and flipped classrooms, are now widespread. A greater emphasis has been placed on writing across the curriculum, study abroad, and mentored research experiences. Yet despite these developments, many aspects of the academic experience remain largely unchanged.

Innovations typically take one of two forms: sustaining or transformational. Sustaining innovations are incremental, iterative, and evolutionary improvements to an existing process. Transformational innovations, by contrast, disrupt existing practices, targeting new markets, adopting new delivery modalities, or embracing new business models. In higher education, sustaining innovations typically involve enhancements or add-ons. Mandatory freshman or transfer orientations, summer bridge programs, or supplemental instruction are common examples. Without in any way minimizing their value, such initiatives occur at an institution's periphery and tend to have a marginal or minimal impact on retention and completion rates. Such innovations do not fundamentally alter the curriculum, pedagogy, or degree pathways. Nor do they ensure that students receive more constructive feedback or mentoring.

Transformation, that is, dramatically moving the needle on student success, requires the purposeful redesign of the academic experience itself and the integration of evidence-based strategies across the institution. This requires fundamental changes in institutional cultures, breaking down departmental silos, encouraging collaboration rather than competition across college lines, and fostering a culture of experimentation and cooperation. Examples include constructing seamless transfer pathways between community colleges and the military to four-year institutions and forging partnerships between colleges and universities and employers to help identify the skills that students should develop.

———

Many of the changes that have occurred in higher education over the past quarter century are not the ones that futurists predicted. To be sure, some of the dreams of radical disruption have been realized, at least in part. Lower-cost degree options have expanded, mainly due to the efforts of the online nonprofit megaproviders like Southern New Hampshire and Western Governors Universities that have unbundled the traditional college experience and adopted new staffing models. Synchronous and asynchronous online learning has expanded, especially at the master's level. Alternative providers have proliferated, including MOOC distributers like Coursera and edX, tech firms like Amazon and Microsoft, and museums and institutes, sometimes in partnership with degree-granting institutions. Faster, cheaper degree alternatives—certificates and nondegree certifications and apprenticeships—have multiplied.

But the biggest changes have occurred elsewhere. The organizational structure of colleges and universities has grown much more complex. Colleges have become hubs for service provision, including food pantries and greatly expanded mental health service providers. Graduate and professional education has greatly expanded. Research, grants, and contracts loom much larger than in the past. Ancillary income from a host of moneymaking programs (including summer camps and campus rentals) has become much more important to sustaining campuses financially.

So how does innovation occur within higher education? Does innovation flow from the top down or from the bottom up? Is it a by-product of external pressures or from shifts in the zeitgeist? Are administrators the drivers of innovation, or are faculty, students, accreditors, foundations, professional societies, policy advocates, or government agencies? Is the major force driving innovation the quest for revenue and reputation? Fear of litigation or protest? Or are the forces for institutional transformation more idealistic?

In fact, most changes within higher education do not occur as a result of deliberate design but rather through a Darwinian-like process of evolution. This is a process in which institutions adapt, usually incrementally but sometimes more rapidly, to environmental pressures, or as a by-product of experimentation, mimicry, and competition. Here, it's important to distinguish between the actual process of institutional change and the intentional, purposeful efforts by reformers and disruptors to alter fundamental aspects of the educational experience, such as the department structure, the academic calendar, the credit hour, curricula, pedagogy, instructional staffing, student support, or assessment. Many of the most consequential and long-lasting changes in higher education occur not as a result of a novel strategic plan but in other ways.[3]

Many changes in institutions emerge in response to an external development: enactment of a law, rulemaking by a regulatory agency, a court decision or threat of litigation, activist pressure, a highly successful model for emulation, or a wholly unexpected development like the COVID-19 pandemic and reckoning with race and equity and the mental health issues it spawned. Sometimes, change arises in reaction to a perceived threat or opportunity, such as a funding or revenue-generating opportunity. Often, changes are driven by individual faculty members pursuing their own agendas.

Frequently, an innovation's effects are unintended. Take, for example, the introduction of computers. Innovators envisioned computers overturning the status quo by making learning more active, interactive, collaborative, and, above all, more personalized. Computers, early adopters believed, would customize pace, content, activities, assessments, and each student's learning trajectory. That wasn't to be. Computers were quickly assimilated into the existing state of affairs, used to deliver readings and worksheets and facilitate drilling and quizzing. Insofar as computers did ease the research process, these devices, ironically, also made it nearly effortless for students to cut, paste, and plagiarize.

Innovations often fail not only because faculty or administrators are uninterested but due to the sociology of bureaucratic organizations. Misguided incentives, inadequate supports and training, and organizational structures, rules, and procedures that don't easily enable innovation discourage many of the most farsighted, creative, and inventive faculty members from launching educational initiatives that extend outside individual faculty members' classrooms. Also impeding innovation is a conformist bias toward the conventional. Any deviations from standard practice are inherently risky. Just as it used to be said that no one ever got fired for buying from IBM, no one is likely to be criticized for following normal practices, time-honored conventions, and established procedures. Innovations are held to a very high standard, and junior faculty innovate at their own risk.

For anyone interested in innovation within higher education, a Darwinian-informed understanding of how institutions evolve is essential. According to the great British naturalist, the evolution of species is not a product of a guiding hand, nor is it centrally directed, nor does it reflect a preexisting developmental plan. Evolution results from the interplay of such factors as environments that favor certain living forms and disfavor others; random mutations, some of which thrive while others falter; and diversity, which maximizes the possibilities for evolutionary change. A similar process can be found at educational institutions. Sometimes, campus innovations reflect ideas, especially those ideas backed by foundation dollars or encouraged by accreditors or popularized by the higher ed press. Sometimes, these innovations are products of necessity as institutions pursue cost efficiencies or try to tap new student markets. At times, these innovations emerge in response to student pressure. And more often than not, these innovations are championed by associate deans or associate provosts seeking to bolster their reputations or by visionary faculty members whose motives are highly idealistic.[4]

The best-known theories of innovation, like John F. Kotter's eight-step process of organizational change, are top down. Senior leadership not only defines a strategic vision but creates a sense of urgency, builds a guiding coalition, communicates a vision of institutional change, removes barriers, generates short-term wins, cultivates buy-in, and anchors change in the institution's culture. Certainly, there are very few university presidents who succeed in imprinting their vision on an entire institution. Obvious examples are Arizona State University's Michael Crow or Southern New Hampshire University's Paul LeBlanc or Western Governors University's Scott Pulsipher. Then, there are some presidents who make highly strategic use of donor dollars to develop distinctive areas of campus strength and purposely shape a campus's identity.

But in the instances I am most familiar with, many of higher ed's most vaunted innovations started small and were the work of a small number of extraordinarily committed faculty visionaries, like my University of Texas at Austin colleague David Laude, who spearheaded the development of UTeach, a widely duplicated teacher preparation program that prepares STEM teachers; the Freshman Research Initiative, which engages more than 900 first-year students annually in mentored research; and student success initiatives that include the Texas Interdisciplinary Plan and the University Leadership Network, which offer academic support and experiential learning and career readiness opportunities to students from low-income and other underrepresented backgrounds. Or take the example of Michael Steiper of the City University of New York's Hunter College. An evolutionary anthropologist, he created a multidisciplinary program in human biology with tracks in body, mind, and health; human evolution and variation; and human organizations that quickly grew to become the campus's third-largest degree program.

What, then, are some proven ways to drive innovation? First, senior campus leadership should work closely with faculty and staff to identify areas of need and opportunity. Encourage entrepreneurial faculty to tackle existing campus problems or pursue emerging opportunities. Perhaps your campus has a particular problem with sustaining students' academic momentum in year two or advising students who are closed out of their first choice of major or ensuring that transfer students aren't closed out of required courses. Encourage faculty and staff to generate and implement solutions, then recognize and reward them for their efforts. Also, make sure that faculty know about relevant external funding opportunities. In my experience, campuses don't sufficiently embolden faculty members to apply for nationally competitive institutional grants.

Second, let a thousand flowers bloom. Since innovation only rarely comes from the top down, create an environment in which faculty and staff feel encouraged to innovate. Make sure that innovators get the resources, time, and support they need to bring ideas to fruition. Recognize, reward, support, showcase, and scale successful innovations. Don't let inspiring success stories go untold. Also, create islands of innovation where experimentation can flourish. Test beds, innovation hubs, incubators, and accelerators are all the rage in the tech world. These are physical spaces where researchers, innovators, and startups can transform ideas into innovative products and services. Higher education already has something similar in makerspaces—collaborative workspaces where students and faculty can ideate, brainstorm, iterate, and engage in rapid prototyping. Campuses, however, need to create another space where alternatives to standard practice in teaching and learning can be tested, free from many existing institutional constraints. Most large institutions have already created a third space. Usually, however, this takes the form of an honors college that gives high-achieving students access to small interdisciplinary seminars and cocurricular experiences associated with liberal arts colleges. The pedagogy and, indeed, the course content, however, tend to be highly traditional. But one might imagine a true innovation hub, where faculty and staff could experiment with more coherent, thematically unified curricula or experiential learning or embrace a co-op-like "earn to learn" approach.

Third, cultivate a culture of innovation. Organize campus conversations. Stage innovation showcases. Create a system of rewards for innovations that solve campus problems or capitalize on an opportunity. We reward research and teaching, but we also need to do more to acknowledge and value those faculty who dedicate themselves to making the campus a warmer, more welcoming, more vital place.

What is the role of senior leadership in driving innovation? Higher education today talks an awful lot about leadership. The nation's most selective campuses pride themselves on their ability to identify, enroll, and nurture this nation's future leaders—not just its future political leaders but leaders in medicine, science, technology, and other fields as well. More and more campuses offer leadership skills development workshops, where undergraduates learn how to take initiative, delegate responsibilities, handle conflict, and manage and motivate others. In academic environments, a leader's most important skill is not to direct, drive, or spearhead change. Rather, leadership's biggest responsibility is to work with faculty and staff to identify and define campus priorities, increase and appropriately invest campus resources, collect and share data, align incentives with campus goals, and showcase and reward success. Leaders must also motivate, inspire, and empower faculty and staff. That requires senior leadership to listen effectively, share responsibility, and award credit where credit is due. Unfortunately, those leadership skills are, I fear, as rare as a hen's tooth.

Determined leadership at all levels is a prerequisite for institutional change. Academic leaders must clearly define goals, inspire support for a particular vision, instill a sense of urgency, incentivize innovation, align resources and actions to these goals, remove obstacles, and closely monitor results. Leaders are also responsible for ensuring that successful initiatives are scaled and sustained. Successful leaders appeal not only to a sense of fear—that an institution is falling behind its competitors or faces pressing problems that require an immediate solution—but also to a sense of aspiration and opportunity. Inspirational leadership is key to success, fostering a sense of institutional pride and instilling in faculty, in particular, a sense that they are taking a leading role in areas of particular importance.[5]

Successful leaders do not, however, drive change unilaterally. What they can do is streamline procedures, incentivize innovation, empower units, remove obstacles, and celebrate and reward success. Cross-functional collaboration is essential. Successful innovations are not simply the responsibility of deans and department chairs or faculty or support staff, but of all, working together. At many of the most successful institutions, regular meetings bring together a guiding coalition of staff and faculty from all across the campus to discuss enrollment and success data. Any innovation that will have genuine impact must take place across multiple dimensions of transformation. It requires the reengineering of institutional practices, processes, policies, and infrastructure as well as shifts in organizational culture and mindsets. All participating stakeholders must buy into the change agenda and feel confident in their ability to implement the necessary changes in systems, processes, and behavior.

Certain kinds of institutional transformation are especially unlikely to succeed. A top-down approach is more likely to produce resistance than to induce institutional change. Investing in individual innovators or boutique programs is like planting seeds in a swamp. Such approaches are not strategic or sustainable. The process of innovation rarely takes place all at once. Generally, it begins slowly, within a particular office: the registrar's office, the financial aid office, or the provost's or dean's office. Only after demonstrating success within a particular domain does the innovation expand over time.

The biggest problems facing higher education, like stark inequalities in funding and student outcomes, are not going to be solved one institution at a time. Highly competitive institutions engaged in a constant struggle for resources and recognition must begin to act more collaboratively to address shared challenges. Higher education needs to act more like a cohesive enterprise and less like a competitive marketplace with every tub on its own bottom and the devil takes the hindmost. It is not enough for elite private and public institutions to enroll a greater number of low-income students or to admit more sophomore transfers. Certainly, such steps will transform the lives of the handful of students who are admitted. But the number of students affected only represents a drop in the higher education bucket. The best-resourced institutions must recognize a moral responsibility to do more to contribute to the postsecondary ecosystem. These colleges and universities need to give back. And their obligation is not simply moral. These elite institutions benefit disproportionately from federal tax deductions, grants, and contracts.

Answers abound. Bard College, a private liberal arts college with a total undergraduate enrollment under 2,000, has established a network of early college high schools that offer credit-bearing, tuition-free college courses of study in the liberal arts and sciences following the ninth and tenth grades. More than 90 percent of the graduates of these high schools (which target low-income, first-generation students) earn a bachelor's degree within six years of entering college.

Course sharing offers another way for more richly resourced institutions to share their expertise. The Big Ten Academic Alliance uses video technology to offer dozens of the less commonly taught foreign languages to member institutions. Shared resource development, along the lines of Rice University's OpenStax free college textbook initiative, offers yet another way that well-endowed institutions can contribute to higher education as a whole. Somewhat similarly, JSTOR and Artstor, with initial support from the Andrew W. Mellon Foundation, created digital libraries of scholarly journals and visual images to give regional colleges and universities access to resources previously only available at research libraries. Programs like the Mellon-funded Leadership Alliance/Summer Research Program, which gives talented undergraduates from under-resourced tribal colleges, Historically Black Colleges and Universities (HBCUs), and urban and regional institutions the opportunity to receive research training and mentorship at leading research universities, provide another small example of how elite institutions can better contribute to higher education as a whole.

In addition, wealthier institutions might freely license the educational technologies, simulations, and interactives that they develop for their own faculty and students and organize and fund professional development institutes to serve neighboring colleges and universities. MOOC providers could disaggregate their assets—videos, assessments, and other learning tools and resources—and place them in a searchable repository. Carnegie Mellon's Open Learning Initiative, which developed personalized adaptive courseware for high-demand courses, might serve as a model for other institutions.[6]

Given their central role in training the future professoriate, the major research institutions might also give pedagogy and assessment a more central place in their doctoral programs. A horrific academic job market has had the ironic effect of distributing strong junior scholars to institutions of all kinds. But these faculty members need to be better prepared to teach effectively at broad-access institutions.

Change is coming to higher education. For demographic, financial, and political reasons, the status quo is unsustainable except at the most elite institutions. The pressures to ensure that a college education is affordable yet responsive to shifting student needs and a rapidly evolving economy are likely to intensify, even as hopes for a significant increase in public funding remain unrealized. Adding to the challenge is the likelihood that the postsecondary education marketplace will grow even more competitive as more community colleges offer applied bachelor's degrees; more lower-cost online providers deliver self-paced, self-directed education without traditional faculty; more nondegree programs offer short-term certificate programs; and more four-year institutions market online professional master's degrees.

The notion that all students—not just the privileged elite—should have access to a well-rounded liberal arts education and a research faculty wherever they live is among the cornerstones of the American conception of higher education. That vision is currently under threat. Advocates of a cheaper, more convenient, more flexible education promote one kind of education for the mass of students while sending their own children to very different institutions. There are, however, practical, realistic, cost-effective steps that existing colleges and universities can take to ensure that the essence of the education they offer persists, but in ways that are more skills driven, experiential, technology enhanced, data informed, relevant, and learner focused. Failure to take these steps will inevitably lead to a gradual erosion of quality among the institutions that serve the bulk of the population, reinforcing the socioeconomic divisions that are undercutting this country's democratic commitment to opportunity for all.

# EPILOGUE

THERE ARE HARSH TRUTHS THAT INDIVIDUALS and institutions generally don't want to admit. Anyone who cares deeply about American higher education needs to come to grips with a series of hard and unpleasant truths. One such truth is that college teaching today remains largely what it has always been: an amateur enterprise that fails to take into account the insights of the learning sciences. This means that most classes are instructor centered and involve little active or experiential learning apart from instructor-led discussions. Another disturbing truth is that many, and perhaps most, undergraduates exit college pretty much as they enter it: scientifically and culturally illiterate; unable to write well; incompetent in math, data, and statistics; unfamiliar with the methods and theories of the social sciences; and lacking fluency in a foreign language. It's high time to acknowledge and address those disturbing realities.

I can go on. Rich relationships are central to students' academic success and well-being, but fewer than one undergraduate in seven has such relationships. Another inconvenient truth is that the main contributor to rising college costs isn't the price of instruction, which has stagnated; it lies in a growth imperative and ever-rising standards of care—in community colleges' expanding mission (which now includes offering dual-credit or early-college programs, a host of certificate and certification programs, and applied bachelor's degrees) and four-year institutions' expenditures on campus amenities, research and fundraising, as well as mental health, compliance, learning support, and nonteaching professionals.

Perhaps the most disagreeable truths involve the inequities that pervade American higher education. This country's system of postsecondary education relegates the students with the greatest needs to the most under-resourced institutions. It's a system in which high-performing Black and Hispanic students are far less likely to earn a college degree than comparable white or Asian American students. It's also a system that incentivizes departments to severely restrict entry into high-demand, high-salary majors in computer science, economics, finance, engineering, and nursing not because of capacity constraints, but for rankings purposes.

It's not that institutions ignore campus inequities or student learning. The problem is, rather, that other priorities eclipse what campuses claim to value. Today's colleges and universities are pulled in too many directions and need to rededicate themselves to their primary mission. To improve student learning outcomes and increase access to high-demand majors, they need to expand bridge programs and supplemental instruction in especially challenging courses and monitor and redesign courses with high DFW rates, the percentage of students who receive a D, receive an F, or withdraw. Failure to do so is itself evidence of a campus's true priorities.

Today's curricula represent a political compromise designed to maximize faculty autonomy, departmental enrollments, student choice, and completion rates while minimizing instructional costs. If student learning really were the primary concern, then campuses would offer far fewer large lecture classes without breakout or lab sessions and more opportunities for active, interactive, and experiential learning; they would also do more to align coursework with the essential skills and knowledge we want our students to master.

Inadequate system accountability contributes to the failure to provide the learning-centered institutions that students deserve. Accreditors could, for example, require faculty to undergo professional development training in teaching. They don't. Institutions could take steps to increase representation of underrepresented students in high-demand majors. They haven't. Campuses could require more reading and writing. This hasn't happened.

What would it take to change this grim reality? Campuses need to place student learning front and center. That would entail devoting more attention to essential communication and quantitative and statistical skills. To better serve today's diverse, posttraditional students, it would mean rethinking academic calendars, course schedules, and delivery modalities. To increase completion rates and expedite time to degree completion, today's working, commuting, and caregiving students require more block scheduling, varied-length courses, and perhaps more four- or five-credit courses that will allow students to concentrate on a particular class rather than multitask in ways that have proven counterproductive. Campuses also need to think more intentionally and strategically about the knowledge and skills they want students to acquire. If writing and statistical, social scientific, and scientific literacy are truly a priority, we must ask ourselves how we propose to help students acquire those competencies. We must also ask ourselves how students are supposed to gain other skills—study skills, time-management skills, research skills, and leadership and interpersonal skills—that academic and postgraduation success require but that aren't explicitly taught.

Colleges and universities, like individuals, ignore inconvenient and unpleasant truths at their peril. Educational innovation isn't a quick, painless, or friction-free process. So, let's acknowledge the disquieting truths about higher education, face up to them, and do more than claim that our campuses are doing God's work.

Let's take the steps that will make equity and deep learning more than empty promises.

---

No film critic would include the 2006 campus comedy *Accepted* in the pantheon of classic college movies. No one would confuse it with Mike Newell's *Mona Lisa Smile*, Alan J. Pakula's *The Sterile Cuckoo*, John Singleton's *Higher Learning*, Spike Lee's *School Daze*, Curtis Hanson's *Wonder Boys*, or even the Marx Brothers' *Horsefeathers*. It doesn't even rank in humor or sentiment with the adult-enrolls-in-college comedy *Back to School*, the tear-jerker romance *Love Story*, the animated "learning from failure" comedy *Monsters University*, or *Revenge of the Nerds*, in which socially challenged misfits create their own fraternity romp.

Yet *Accepted*, one of many *Animal House* knockoffs, nevertheless points to some of the inadequacies of a conventional college education: how colleges reinforce class divisions, undermine too many young people's self-confidence and self-esteem, and fail to engage students' passions. *Accepted*'s ramshackle plot centers on a group of admissions rejects who create their own college, the South Harmon Institute of Technology, in a former psychiatric hospital. When hundreds of academic rejects enroll in the school—the college website says "acceptance is just a click away"—the friends must create their own curriculum. Combining the philosophies of Jean-Jacques Rousseau and John Dewey, the students—an oddball assortment of rebels, malcontents, loners, cranks, and nonconformists—teach and take whichever courses they want, and, in the process, acquire essential knowledge, obtain valuable skills, and learn significant life lessons.

The film's message is a simple one, but one that bears emphasis: that colleges and universities could do a better job harnessing students' curiosity and intellectual passion and capitalizing on faculty members' creativity and desire to transform students' lives. That, of course, is this book's message. Colleges and universities need to leverage faculty's idealism and students' energies and creativity to invigorate the educational experience.

To thrive in the years ahead, colleges and universities will need to innovate, experiment, adapt, and evolve. However, the history of innovation within higher education is, unfortunately, largely a story of failure: of misplaced hopes, exaggerated promises, and a tendency to gravitate back to the mean. Too often, innovation in higher education goes "the way of all flesh." A recent headline in the *Boston Globe* says it all: "Experimental Colleges Once Were the Future. Now, What Is Their Future?"[1] One after another, the innovators of the 1960s and 1970s are biting the dust, fading, or transforming themselves into pale shadows of their original ambitions. It's not just Hampshire College, but Franconia, Goddard, New College, and perhaps even Evergreen State College. Innovation within higher education is extremely difficult to sustain. Think of North Carolina's Black Mountain College, whose faculty and students included Josef and Anni Albers, Ruth Asawa, Willem and Elaine de Kooning, Buckminster Fuller, Walter Gropius, Robert Motherwell, Robert Rauschenberg, Dorothea Rockburne, Merce Cunningham, and John Cage. Founded in 1933, it didn't make it to its twenty-fifth anniversary.

I, perhaps like you, am a sucker for articles with titles like "14 Spectacularly Wrong Predictions" or "Wrong Again: 50 Years of Failed Predictions" or "Oops! Failed Predictions from History." Predicting the future is easy; anyone can do it. Getting the forecasts right, however, is what's hard. So it is with envisioning the colleges and universities of the future. It's a fool's game, but one that is necessary if we faculty and administrators are to shape that future. Vague forecasts or prophecies aren't enough. We need a detailed vision of the future that we hope to evolve to. Without such a concrete vision, colleges and universities will be wholly at the mercy of outside pressures that have little to do with the quality of the educational experiences they provide. As you might guess, speculations about the future go wrong for several reasons: they convey a false sense of certainty, extrapolate current trends, and fail to anticipate contingencies, those "unknown unknowns" that include unforeseen events and shifting circumstances. After all, who could have anticipated the lasting consequences of the Great Recession or the devastating impact of a global pandemic?

In 2013, I offered a forecast of the future of higher education. In an article in *The Chronicle of Higher Education*, I identified fifteen innovations that I thought were likely to transform the college landscape. A decade later, I looked back to see where I was right and where my crystal ball proved cloudy and distorted. To no one's surprise, my predictions proved to be highly uneven.[2]

In the essay that laid out my predictions, I argued that profound transformations reshaped the higher education landscape at roughly forty- to fifty-year intervals. The first transformation, which took place early in the nineteenth century, involved the initial attempts to democratize higher education. Small colleges founded by religious denominations and civic boosters proliferated and were accompanied by the appearance of the nation's first public universities. This was followed, in the mid-nineteenth century, by the emergence of the earliest alternatives to the classical curriculum, the first federal support for higher education that emerged with the Morrill Act, and a growing number of courses in agriculture, modern history and foreign languages, the natural and social sciences, and technology. The late nineteenth century, in turn, witnessed the rise of the modern research university; of college majors and elective courses; and of "new" professional schools in architecture, business, and engineering. The Progressive Era saw the emergence of the Wisconsin Idea: that public universities should serve the public, along with the development of extension services and junior colleges. Then came the post–World War II transformation of higher education, as normal colleges became regional public universities, community colleges multiplied, and legal segregation of higher education ended in the South. Those same years saw the advent of state and federal financial aid and a sharp increase in federal support for university-based research.

That latter story was filled with ironies and paradoxes. The number of campuses, enrollment, and programs rapidly increased, but the system as a whole may well have overexpanded in ways that the country now finds difficult to support. Similarly, the production of PhDs soared, which ultimately led to an overproduction of instructors relative to the number of available academic positions, especially, but not exclusively, in the humanities and the "soft" or interpretive social sciences. Access to higher education became much more democratic, as colleges and universities embraced first mass higher education and then near universal college education. But as access expanded, so, too, did the stratification of higher education and the depersonalization of the college experience.

A college education increasingly became the primary route to a secure, middle-class income, but this in turn led to soaring student and parental debt. Meanwhile, already selective institutions became even more selective, and the market for students became less local, but students from lower income backgrounds were increasingly concentrated in the colleges with the fewest resources. Contributing to higher education's democratization was the federal government's mounting role, funding university research and subsidizing attendance through federally financed grants and loans. But even as the federal government supported colleges and universities at an unprecedented degree, it also imposed new regulations and compliance burdens and subjected campuses to increasing oversight from Congress, federal agencies, and the courts. More ambiguously, federal support encouraged individual professors and institutions to allow research to trump teaching as the top priority.

Meanwhile, campus divides deepened not only between the arts and humanities and the quantitative social sciences, the behavioral sciences, the brain sciences, the life sciences, and the physical sciences, but also the booming vocational and applied fields of study, from accounting and architecture to business administration, broadcasting and journalism, education, engineering, health care management, marketing, nursing, and technology. In addition, campuses increasingly became political and ideological battlegrounds. Some of the battles were internal, as activist or radical students and faculty strove to alter curricula and campus policies involving diversity, sexual harassment, endowment investments, and other issues. But other battles—for example, over affirmative action in admissions and free speech on campus—were nationwide. The greatest irony, of course, is that even as access increased and standards of care and completion rates rose, disparities rooted in class, race, ethnicity, and gender persisted. These included gaps in access to the more selective, well-resourced institutions, gaps in degree completion rates, and gaps in access to degrees in the highest demand majors.

If the forty- to fifty-year cycle of innovation and makeover persisted, I argued, then the 2010s would witness yet another era of transformation. It certainly did, but not necessarily for the reasons or in the ways that I predicted. My basic argument was that a series of long-term developments—demographic, economic, and technological—would fuel or foment transformation. These included the need to tap new sources of revenue to meet the ever rising costs of new programs, information technology, student life and support services, utilities, facilities maintenance, and more; to better serve the growing number of nontraditional students, whether working adults, family caregivers, part-timers, commuters, first-generation college students, and students with disabilities; to compete with the online for-profit and nonprofit providers who threatened traditional institutions' monopoly over credentialing, including at the master's level; and to exploit the potential of digital technologies to control costs, serve more diverse student markets, raise completion rates, and improve student learning and employment outcomes. I also argued that among the most significant drivers of change was a mounting political challenge: the argument that graduation rates were too low, that levels of student engagement and learning outcomes were unacceptably poor, and that a college education did not provide good value for the money.

All that was true; but, in one respect, I was wrong—or, if not wrong, premature. I was convinced that even then, students, in growing numbers, were embracing or poised to embrace faster and cheaper alternative paths to attainment, including providers such as the massive open online courses (MOOCs) that attracted tens of thousands of students, academic boot camps, and various skills academies. What were the transformations that I thought lay ahead?

1. **E-advising:** At the time, I was thinking largely about predictive analytics and course recommendation tools, like Austin Peay's Degree Compass and Purdue's Course Signals and the Bill & Melinda Gates Foundation's InBloom, a $100 million initiative to aggregate student data. It turned out instead that the future lay in data-driven advising. Georgia State University would serve as the model to emulate: monitoring student engagement, sending out automated warnings, and signaling faculty and academic advisers about impending trouble, thus helping to ensure that students remained on a path to graduation.

2. **Evidence-based pedagogy:** I was convinced that higher education was poised to adopt insights from the learning sciences and would place a greater emphasis on learning objectives, mastery of key competencies, and assessments closely aligned to learning goals. I also thought instructors would adopt more social learning, more active learning, and more real-world assessments. Certainly, many instructors did incorporate more evidence-based practices into their teaching. Nevertheless, the instructor-centered classroom, and the lecture, the seminar, and the cookie-cutter lab, remain instructional mainstays. And yet, I do think that the long-term trend is toward more inquiry-, case-, project-, and team-based learning and more experiential learning, including more applied learning, service learning, field-based learning, maker spaces, and entrepreneurship accelerators.

3. **The decline of the lone-eagle approach to teaching:** I thought, mistakenly, that we'd see much more resource sharing and more course sharing, and a greater embrace of collaboratively developed interactive courseware, simulations, and virtual labs. To be sure, instances of team teaching persist; but resistance to a more collaborative approach to course development remains more intense than I expected.

4. **Optimized class time:** When I wrote in 2013, the flipped classroom was still an emerging idea. Yet despite the efforts

of figures like Harvard's physics professor Eric Mazur, the earlier model, in which the instructor-centered classroom is supplemented by various kinds of homework, remains dominant. In the pandemic's wake, as demand for more flexible, convenient hybrid learning opportunities has intensified, more concentrated use of time on campus strikes me as a genuine possibility.

5. **Seamless credit transfer:** Given the growing attention to the student swirl—the movement of students from one institution to another—and the expansion of access to Advanced Placement courses and the emergence of early-college or dual-enrollment programs, I thought, again in error, that we'd see a much stronger embrace of efforts to make credit transfer automatic—not only for gen ed courses, but also for major requirements. Despite pioneering models, including the Interstate Passport and CUNY's Pathways program, barriers to credit transfer, of course, remain. But political pressure for smoother transfer pathways has certainly increased.

6. **Fewer large lecture classes:** Whew, was I mistaken! I thought colleges and universities would follow the example of medical schools and adopt new ways to offer foundational courses—for example, by developing self-paced, self-directed introductory courses, or competency-based modules, or adopting wholly new online or hybrid formats. This hasn't happened yet. After all, large lecture courses are cost efficient. But these need to be better balanced with other kinds of experiences that involve more active, collaborative, experiential, and project-based learning.

7. **New frontiers for online learning:** Here, I was referring to more collaborative learning (along the lines of the c-MOOCs, which create communities of inquiry surrounding a topic of interest, and solver communities that seek to collectively address a pressing problem), immersive learning environments (modeled on Second Life), hands-on simulations, and serious games. Innovations like these always seem to lie five years in

the future. Faculties and administrators need to see successful examples of these approaches.

I also thought that many more instructors would quickly embrace approaches to assess student learning beyond the traditional research paper, lab report, and exam. Some have. There are a growing number of examples of learning assessments based on digital stories, collaboratively developed class websites, student-written annotated texts and encyclopedias, and multimedia projects like virtual tours or podcasts. But this frontier still remains, to my regret, far too barren.

8. **Personalized adaptive learning:** I was dazzled by the prospect of tailoring education to better meet individual student needs. I thought by now we'd have many examples of interactive courseware that provides personalized learning pathways, customized content, and embedded remediation and that adjusts pace to students' learning needs. It turns out that developing personalized adaptive learning tools is far harder than I thought, and the demand for such tools hasn't grown as rapidly as I expected. This, I suspect, is an area whose time will come.

9. **Competency-based learning and credit for prior learning:** I thought that pressure to accelerate time to degree completion, better measure student learning, and place a greater emphasis on student skills and learning outcomes would lead to an embrace of a competency-based approach that allowed students to advance based on their ability to demonstrate mastery of a particular skill or competency. True, most institutions do offer credit by examination; but that wasn't what I meant. It turns out that despite isolated efforts like the American Historical Association's Tuning Project, US colleges and universities, accreditors, and scholarly societies have not sought to follow the example of Europe's Bologna Process, which has resulted in a series of international agreements to ensure course quality and credit transfer. Credit transfer remains far more difficult than it ought to be, and, as a result,

students still lose too many credits upon moving from one institution to another.

10. **Data-driven instruction:** I thought that by now instructors (and students) would have ready access to data dashboards that would make it easy to track student engagement and areas of student confusion and therefore allow faculty members to focus instruction to better meet student needs and to improve courses over time. I also thought department chairs and executive committees would have the information needed to conduct equity audits, exposing variances in grading and withdrawal rates and performance in subsequent classes to scrutiny. The tools to embrace data-driven instruction already exist; but in the absence of pressure to make use of these tools, practices are unlikely to change.

11. **Aggressive pursuit of new revenue streams:** This has certainly occurred. Departments have become much more entrepreneurial. And yet, I remain struck by lost opportunities. I, for one, don't see sufficient incentives for faculty to pursue external funding to strengthen outreach in admissions or to enrich the curriculum or to offer summer programs for high school, undergraduate, and graduate students from underrepresented groups.

12. **Online and low-residency undergraduate degrees at flagships:** I should have known better than to think that many selective institutions, including public flagship universities, would risk "diluting" or "diminishing" their brand by aggressively expanding access. But maybe, just maybe, these institutions will take alternative steps to increase enrollment. For example, flagship and land-grant universities might greatly expand off-campus learning opportunities, including study abroad, making it possible for these institutions to admit perhaps 25 percent more students.

13. **More certificates and badges:** Alas, in most cases, alternative credentials have not been viewed as a way to broaden undergraduates' education or to build essential, career-aligned

skills, but rather as a way for institutions to make a quick buck by partnering with the big tech companies or with various boot camps and skills academies.

14. **Free and open textbooks:** Pressure to adopt open educational resources is intense, and I am certainly not alone in only assigning readings that are available for free. The range of open textbooks offered by providers like OpenStax is extraordinary. But let's be honest and recognize that this shift has only marginally reduced the cost of a higher education while devastating the market for scholarly monographs. It has, almost certainly, contributed to a reduction in the amount of assigned reading. Worse yet, the pursuit of free textbooks has meant that the kinds of instructional materials that we really need—that are highly immersive and interactive and personalized and make extensive use of advanced simulations—aren't being produced because there is no way for writers or publishers to recoup the development and production costs.

15. **Public-private partnerships:** I originally wrote at a time when many ed tech firms considered themselves disrupters, capable of upending and displacing insufficiently innovative incumbent institutions. In the years since, these firms have touted themselves as educational partners capable of providing a stack of services that existing institutions can't. Among the services they provide are enrollment management, data analytics, technology platforms, online program management, and even experiential learning opportunities.

    Far too often, institutions that are unable to build internal campus capacities become heavily dependent on these partners, entering into long-term contracts that are difficult to break, ceding control over institutional data, and, to my horror, letting online program managers not only define standards for admission into online programs but also design the programs themselves. In short, we've learned a great deal over the past decade about the downsides of public–private collaboration.

In the years since my 2013 predictions appeared, higher education has undergone far-reaching transformations for good and ill. On the positive side of the ledger, access has increased and completion rates have risen, modestly in some cases but more significantly in others. In addition, student bodies have grown increasingly diverse. But, more negatively, the higher education ecosystem has grown more stratified not only in terms of prestige or reputation, but also in resources, facilities, the range of majors, student qualifications, the undergraduate experience, student support services, and even the availability of financial aid.

In a recent *Washington Post* opinion piece, the conservative columnist George Will advances an argument that colleges and universities ignore at their peril. The column questions a series of self-serving assumptions that higher education has propagated but that increasingly draw a skeptical response. The first of these contentions is that ever higher college enrollments are necessary for a healthy economy. Will notes that according to the Federal Reserve, 41 percent of college graduates hold jobs that do not require a college degree. No longer is a college degree a magic wand guaranteeing a middle-class livelihood. A second assertion is that a college degree is necessary for a fulfilling life. As the columnist observes wryly, 62 percent of American adults do not hold degrees, and many are quite contented. All too many college-goers experience disappointment and regret when their college dreams fail to work out or when they flounder in the job market. The third claim is that undergraduate degrees have a high return on investment. Here, Will cites recent reports that 40 percent of college graduates earn no more than the average high school graduate a decade after leaving school. A fourth questionable assumption is that a master's degree will pay off financially. In too many instances, he points out, the pursuit of a master's degree, enabled by excessive student borrowing, is financially dubious. Many of these professional master's programs, Will argues, are motivated not by a demonstrated return on investment but, rather, by greedy institutions eager to siphon off "the ocean of cash available through subsidized student loans."[3]

Before dismissing these assertions out of hand, remember this: those who ignore widely held opinions are like those policymakers and military officers who ignore intelligence assessments. They set themselves up for a fall. Today's colleges and universities, especially those that serve the middle tier of students, need to control costs, dramatically raise completion rates, and ensure their graduates' return on investment. These institutions also need to help more students succeed in the high-demand but especially challenging fields of science, technology, health care, and data analytics—without diluting the liberal arts education that is the hallmark of a well-rounded higher education.

Accomplishing these goals is not a mission impossible. But it will require colleges and universities to question business as usual and become truly learner- and learning-centered institutions. It demands changing onboarding and orientation of students; rethinking curricula, pedagogies, and assessment strategies; altering course schedules and delivery modes; and reimagining the professorial role. The alternatives, I fear, are approaches to education that are cheaper and faster but that transform postsecondary education into training and credentialing, not the robust coming of age, developmental, maturational, and transformative process that should be college's essence. Faculty and administrators alike must resist the pressures to dilute higher education. Alternative routes into the workforce are indeed necessary, and I am not at all opposed to the efforts to expand access to apprenticeships and other forms of skills training and to job-aligned certificates and certifications. But we must fight to ensure that all of those who want something that resembles a traditional college education have the opportunity to experience it.

The vision I advanced in the preceding pages might be characterized as "radically conservative" in its goal. I want to preserve the defining characteristics of a face-to-face college education—regular, substantive interaction with a teacher-scholar, a well-rounded liberal arts education, and a dedication to the preservation, transmission, discovery, and creation of knowledge. I also want to counteract the weaknesses that characterize higher education today: low completion rates, uncertain learning and employment outcomes, and gross inequalities in access to high-quality educational experiences and support service. My goal is to remodel, not to replace; to reinvent and reimagine rather than to disrupt. My aim is evolution, adaptation, and innovation, not revolution.

We have democratized the professoriate. Due to the depressed academic job market, stellar scholars and teachers can be found at every institution of higher learning. Students everywhere have access to content area specialists, skilled researchers, and well-published scholars. The task before us now is to give all undergraduates, not just the most privileged, access to the high-impact practices that unlock minds, open doors, and transform lives.

Rather than differing drastically from the present, the future of higher education will evolve iteratively and incrementally. That will no doubt disappoint those who hope to radically disrupt today's colleges and universities, which they decry as unwieldy dinosaurs: too costly, too elitist, and too resistant to change. Nor will it please those who are entirely happy with higher education as it exists today, with its instructor-centered classrooms, smorgasbord of a curriculum, and heavy reliance on large lectures and seminars. But it will sustain higher education's core commitments to scholarship and to the development of the whole person, not just the provision of short-term skills.

# APPENDIX 1

---

# Insights from the Science of Learning

Every field has its own distinctive vocabulary, and the science of learning is no exception. Cognitive and developmental psychologists and neuroscientists have developed a technical terminology to describe the factors—cognitive, affective, and pedagogical—that can contribute to robust student learning. Here is a list of key terms and concepts used in the scholarship of teaching and learning.

**accountability.** Measures to ensure that students meet predetermined standards and learning objectives.

**active learning.** Students learn material better and remember it longer when they engage in an activity rather than trying to absorb content passively. Pedagogical practices that actively engage students in learning include brainstorming, concept mapping, debate, decision-making, discussion, inquiry, hypothesis generation, problem solving, role-playing, and other activities.

**assessment.** The process of evaluating student learning and teaching effectiveness can take various forms. Diagnostic assessment seeks to understand a student's strengths, weaknesses, knowledge, and skills prior to instruction. Formative assessment allows an instructor to monitor student engagement and learning and identify and address confusions and errors. Summative assessment results in an overall evaluation of student learning. Authentic assessment requires a student to demonstrate the ability to apply essential knowledge and skills to a real-world task.

**asynchronous instruction.** A self-directed, self-paced approach to online teaching that allows students to learn at different times and locations. It is the opposite of synchronous online instruction, in which students learn collectively at the same time.

**attention.** Learning requires focused and sustained attention and the ability to screen out distractions. Multitasking weakens attention and undercuts students' ability to concentrate on a particular subject.

**backward design.** An approach to instructional design that involves identifying learning objectives and then aligning learning activities and assessments with those goals.

**Bloom's taxonomy.** A hierarchy of six levels of cognition—remembering, understanding, applying, analyzing, evaluating, and creating—that moves from recall to synthesis and hypothesis generation.

**cognitive flexibility.** Awareness of multiple viewpoints, perspectives, and points of view can increase a student's ability to think flexibly, shift from one activity to another, and apply knowledge and skills to new domains.

**cognitive load.** Because working memory has limited capacity, excessive or extraneous information makes it difficult for students to process and assimilate information. To avoid overloading working memory, an instructor should divide lessons into smaller units.

**cognitive style.** Relatively stable differences in how individuals obtain and process, structure, and evaluate information.

**constructivist pedagogy.** A theory of learning, associated with such figures as John Dewey, Jean Piaget, Lev Vygotsky, and Jerome Bruner, that treats learning as a developmental and reflective process in which learners build on prior knowledge (the skills, understandings, and misunderstandings students bring to a subject), actively process information, repeatedly practice skills, construct their own frameworks of conceptual understanding, and reflect critically on what they have learned.

**desirable difficulties.** Learning that is effortful and appropriately challenging is more likely to endure in long-term memory than lessons that are too easy or excessively hard.

**dual coding.** Using both verbal and nonverbal information (such as words and pictures) makes learning more durable.

**elaboration.** Asking students to describe, explain, and expand upon what they have learned reinforces and strengthens understanding.

**emotional dimension of learning.** The level of students' emotional well-being influences their educational performance and learning.

**engagement.** Learning depends on attention, focus, and motivation as well as on the extent to which students are actively involved in the learning process.

**expectations.** Teachers' expectations influence their students' motivation and performance.

**feedback.** Clear, explanatory, and timely feedback that is processed by a student helps to improve learning and performance.

**generation effect.** Students more successfully master and remember new material when they self-generate answers to questions and don't simply review correct answers.

**goal setting.** Setting goals that are short-term, specific, and appropriately challenging enhances motivation, persistence, and performance better than setting goals that are long-term, overly general, and excessively challenging.

**growth mindset.** The belief that talents can be developed through study and practice, as opposed to a fixed mindset, which views talents as innate. Motivation is reduced if individuals attribute their failure to a lack of ability rather than a lack of effort.

**higher-order thinking.** Students understand new material better when they move beyond description and recall and undertake analysis, synthesis, and the formulation of generalizations. Questions that ask *why, how,* or *what if* produce deeper understanding than questions that ask *who, what, where,* and *when.*

**interleaving.** Students' mastery of content and skills increases when they switch between different topics rather than when they concentrate exclusively on a single topic.

**learning.** The process through which students acquire knowledge and skills through study, experience, or being taught. Durable learning requires students to actively process information and to practice skills.

**learning outcomes.** The knowledge, skills, competencies, and literacies that a person acquires and that can be measured or assessed.

**mastery and performance goals.** Students are more likely to master a body of knowledge and skills if their goal is to learn rather than to achieve a certain grade.

**memory.** The ability to retain, retrieve, and apply information requires a learner to encode information into long-term memory. This process is most likely to occur when a student considers the information relevant and meaningful and converts the information into a mental construct.

**mental modeling.** Durable understanding requires students to develop a framework for conceptual understanding that gives coherence to disparate material and explains why particular pieces of information are relevant and important.

**metacognition.** To become self-regulated, self-directed learners, students need to develop an ability to monitor, reflect upon, and assess their own understanding and adapt their approach to learning to changing circumstances.

**mindset.** Students' beliefs about the malleability of intelligence and ability affect their learning. Learners who hold a growth mindset and who believe that success is related to effort are more likely to persist than those with a fixed mindset.

**motivation.** Learning is influenced by students' level of motivation and by their motives for learning. Those who are intrinsically motivated, for example, by a desire to master a particular skill or body of knowledge perform better than those who are extrinsically motivated by the desire for a reward or a particular grade.

**multimodal instruction.** Students learn new material better and can remember it longer when they encounter the content at multiple times, in different ways, and at differing levels of abstraction.

**organization effect.** Student learning is enhanced when learners mentally arrange information in meaningful patterns through outlining, visualizing, or synthesizing the material.

**practice.** Mastering knowledge and skills depends on rehearsal and repetition, which increases a learner's ability to retrieve information and deploy a skill automatically. See retrieval practice and spaced practice.

**primacy/recency effect.** Information presented at the beginning or end of class has the greatest impact.

**prior knowledge.** What students already know or believe can advance or hinder their learning. Students learn new material better when it creates impasses in their current mental models—that is, contradictions, conflicts, anomalies, uncertainties, and ambiguities that stimulate curiosity, inquiry, questioning, problem-solving, and deep reasoning to restore "cognitive equilibrium."

**psychosocial dimensions of learning.** The recognition that learning is a social process that is influenced by mindset, the learning environment, and classroom dynamics. A particular concern among feminist pedagogues, who argue that learning is context sensitive, that classrooms are sites of power, privilege, and hierarchy, that teaching is an inherently political act, and that within the traditional classroom, certain ideas, perspectives, interpretive approaches, and forms of behavior, discourse, and argumentation are favored, leading some, if not many, students to feel marginalized.

**regulatory fit.** Learning is enhanced when there is regulatory fit, that is, an instructional approach that matches a student's approach to learning. Students with a prevention focus are especially sensitive to negative outcomes, seek to avoid errors, and are driven by security concerns, while those with a promotion focus are more sensitive to positive outcomes.

**retrieval practice.** Learners' ability to recall key concepts or information is enhanced when they deliberately practice retrieving learning from memory.

**scaffolding.** Learning is enhanced when an instructor supports a student by defining and explaining a difficult concept, modeling a skill, answering students' questions, using visual aids or demonstrations to illustrate a concept, or dividing material into digestible chunks.

**self-regulation.** Students' ability to learn is enhanced if they develop self-regulatory skills, such as the ability to set realistic goals, exercise self-control over their emotions, sustain effort and concentration, and monitor and self-assess their performance. Instructors can help learners develop self-regulatory skills by teaching them how to plan, manage stress and impatience, remain focused, avoid distractions, and self-evaluate their performance.

**social learning.** Learning can be enhanced by observing, imitating, and collaborating with others.

**spaced learning.** Distributing learning and spacing retrieval opportunities over a longer period of time rather than concentrating them all at once (for example, through cramming) strengthens long-term memory and enhances learning.

**stereotype threat.** Fear that one's behavior will confirm an existing stereotype of a group with which one identifies has a negative effect on student performance.

**storytelling.** Students learn better when material is conveyed in the form of a narrative, rather than as a recitation of facts. Storytelling interconnects information, grounds abstractions in specifics, and structures information into a readily digestible format that evokes an emotional response.

**testing effect.** Frequent low-stakes quizzing keeps students engaged and enhances a learner's ability to recall and apply knowledge and skills.

**Tuning Project.** A European Commission project, begun in 2000, to facilitate transfer and create a common vocabulary and standards for higher education across the European Union.

**zone of proximal development.** The learning that a student can achieve with scaffolding from an instructor and peers.

# APPENDIX 2

## The Lexicon of Academic Innovation

Educational innovators have developed a distinctive vocabulary or terminology to identify the issues that they wish to address and the reforms and technologies they seek to promote. Here is a list of the key concepts, pedagogical trends, and emerging educational technologies.

**achievement gap.** Also known as the performance or equity gap, the achievement gap refers to differences in performance on standardized tests on the basis of ethnicity, gender, race, and socioeconomic class.

**active learning.** Pedagogical practices that actively engage students in learning. Examples include brainstorming, concept mapping, debate, decision-making, discussion, hypothesis generation, problem solving, and role playing.

**alignment.** Ensuring that instructional activities reinforce a course's learning objectives and that assessments measure the extent to which students achieve those learning goals.

**alternative assessments.** Alternative ways to assess student knowledge and skills that don't involve high-stakes testing. These include class participation, oral presentations, and individual or group projects.

**alternative credentials.** Alternatives to traditional degrees, the standard ways that knowledge and skills are certified. Examples include badges, certificates, certifications, and licenses.

**articulation.** Agreements that seek to remove barriers to transfer from a two-year to a four-year institution.

**atomic design.** The creation of highly granular instructional units that makes it easy to tailor learning pathways to each learner's strengths, challenges, prior experiences and goals. These atomic units can be used LEGO-like to support a wide range of programs.

**authentic assessment.** Assessment that evaluates students' mastery of knowledge and skills in terms of their ability to solve real-world problems or challenges.

**backward design.** An approach to instructional design that begins by identifying outcomes and then proceeds to devise lessons or activities to help students achieve those goals.

**blended or hybrid teaching.** Instruction that combines in-person and online components.

**block scheduling.** Concentrating all of a student's courses in a particular block of time (e.g., morning, afternoon, evening, or weekends), to help students to better accommodate their work schedules.

**case study.** An approach to instruction organized around the analysis of a realistic situation.

**cohort programs.** Learning communities, research groups, or interest groups in which students traverse the curriculum as members of a cohesive group and which typically couple courses with a faculty mentor, dedicated advising, and an assortment of cocurricular activities, typically including supervised research experiences.

**community of care.** An approach to student support that brings together a network of support, which might consist of faculty, advisers, instructional facilitators, success coaches, and peer mentors, who act in a collaborative, integrated manner.

**community of practice.** A group of people who share expertise and engage in a process of collaborative learning or inquiry.

**competency-based education.** An approach to education that emphasizes demonstrated mastery of essential knowledge and skills rather than seat time. It typically consists of blocks of content that students must master before proceeding to the next block.

**concept map.** A graphical representation of a concept, theory, network, or causal chain.

**constituent relationship management.** The practices and technologies that an institution uses to manage its relationships with its customers or clients. These include methods of communication and of storing and analyzing information about the customers or clients and their interactions with the institution.

**corequisite remediation.** Enrollment of students in regular for-credit courses, combined with supplemental instruction, intensive tutoring, and study groups, rather than in noncredit remedial courses. A proven approach that accelerates academic momentum, it has arisen in response to the unreliability of placement exams and the fact that unevenly prepared students usually have a limited number of discrete areas of confusion or unfamiliarity that can be addressed within the context of for-credit courses.

**courseware.** The next iteration of the textbook, courseware includes multimedia-rich, immersive content, interactives, simulations, and personalized, adaptive learning pathways and virtual tutorials powered by frequent embedded formative assessments.

**curriculum optimization.** Deliberate alignment of course or learning experiences to eliminate redundancies and facilitate learning and time to completion. The resulting curriculum is coherent and consists of synergistic courses.

**design thinking.** A deliberate, structured process for solving problems and fostering innovation that begins with a focus on the end user and that individual's unmet needs, desires, and priorities. Subsequent steps involve brainstorming (or what design thinking calls "ideation"), concepting and blueprinting (combining various ideas into implementable plans), rapid prototyping (quickly designing, developing, testing and evaluating possible solutions), and iterating (a process of continuous improvement through incremental modifications and refinements).

**differentiated instruction.** A pedagogical approach that addresses differences in student preparation, interests, and strengths by offering a variety of learning pathways within the same classroom. These pathways, which might differ in terms of content, focus, activities, or outcome, should not be confused with personalized learning, which involves individualized instruction.

**direct assessment.** Instead of measuring student knowledge and learning in terms of seat time and grades, this approach directly measures student learning through an assessment, such as an examination or project.

**disaggregation.** Breaking down a curriculum, a course, or a class session into its components, which might consist of a module or much smaller instructional units.

**experiential learning.** Forms of learning, including mentored research, supervised internships, apprentices, clinicals, study abroad, and community, field, and service learning, in which students learn by doing and reflect on the experience.

**field of study curriculum.** A set of lower-division courses that can transfer seamlessly and can fulfill degree program requirements.

**flipped classrooms.** A hybrid approach to instruction in which content transmission occurs online, and in-person sessions are devoted to active learning and problem-solving.

**guided or structured pathways.** A clearly defined, structured sequence of courses leading to a credential, intended to keep students on track and optimize the time to a degree.

**hidden curriculum.** The unarticulated lessons and values and unspoken assumptions and cultural messages that are implicit in the curriculum.

**high-impact pedagogy.** Practices associated with high levels of student engagement and learning, including challenge-, inquiry-, problem-, and team-based learning, learning communities, experiential learning opportunities (including internships, service learning, and study abroad), and capstone projects.

**instruction paradigm.** The industrial-era model of teaching that is instructor centered and that emphasizes the transmission of knowledge rather than the active, interactive, and participatory forms of learning.

**island of innovation.** A space for innovation free from the constraints of incumbent processes and technologies.

**knowledge graph.** Faculty, industry, subject matter experts, accreditors, and standard-setters identify critical learning outcomes and evaluation metrics. These graphs serve as the master blueprint that underlies competency-based certificate and degree programs.

**learning analytics.** Fine-grained analysis of data on student engagement, persistence, pace, performance, interactions, and self-efficacy moves that can be linked to student profile information, such as their high school rank, GPA, standardized test scores, and measures of grit, in order to guide advising and prompt timely interventions.

**learning outcomes.** Specific, measurable learning goals.

**learning management system.** A learning management system serves as the interface between students and digital course materials. In addition to providing access to electronic assignments, instructional resources, notifications, a discussion board, and assessments, each in its own compartment or partition, it records enrollment, grades, and learning data. LMSs generally focus on a single course in isolation.

**learning relationship management system.** Unlike a traditional learning management system, an LRM is designed to chart a student's progress along a learning path, support personalized and competency-based learning, and promote a variety of forms of social interactions between students and faculty and among peers, and combines content delivery with advising, coaching, and badging.

**meta-major.** A set of default first-year courses that provide an entryway into a broad area of high student demand, such as the arts, business, education, health care, or public safety. The goal is to maximize first-year student engagement and help students better identify their area of interest and avoid acquiring unnecessary credits.

**microcredentials.** Alternative forms of certification that do not require two or four years to vest. These include badges, certificates, specializations, and MicroMasters.

**MOOC.** A massive open online course. A SPOC is a small private online course. A cMOOC consists of a community of learners who study a common topic or problem, while an xMOOC is a very large online course with a designated instructor.

**numeracy.** The mathematical, data, and statistical skills that have grown increasingly essential in today's big data environment.

**OER.** Open educational resources are instructional content and tools that are available without charge or copyright restrictions.

**persistent progressive profile.** A dynamic record of all of a student's academic and nonacademic accomplishments and proficiencies and which serves as the basis for a universal transcript, a comprehensive catalog of a student's training, education, and experience that can be easily understood by employers and universities.

**personalization or personalized adaptive learning.** An instructional approach that meets students' learning needs, interests, and aspirations by adjusting pace, content, or learning trajectory.

**portfolio.** A collection of examples of a student's work intended to demonstrate their skills.

**rubric.** The criteria by which a work will be evaluated.

**SIS.** A student information system that handles admissions, registers students for courses, tracks student schedules, documents their grades, and maintains their transcripts.

**skills transcript.** A list of the skills that students have demonstrated in the course of their education.

**stackable credentials.** A series of accomplishments that can add up to a degree or another kind of credential.

**student life cycle management.** The services—including financial aid, advising, registration, retention services, and career services—needed to support students from the moment they express interest in an institution, through enrollment and graduation, and beyond.

**student profiles.** The characteristics—which might involve economic, educational, ethnic or familial background, demographic characteristics, work or familial responsibilities, or mindset—that define student subpopulations.

**student swirl.** The tendency of students to attend multiple institutions and to take courses from different providers, sometimes even during the same semester.

**supplemental instruction.** Approaches, including dedicated smaller class sections, breakout and discussion sessions, organized study groups, and individual and group tutoring, that are intended to assist students whose initial performance indicates a likelihood of failure.

**tracking.** Assigning students to groups based on their academic skills.

**transformational teaching.** Rather than expecting students to assimilate information on their own (the defining characteristic of transactional or didactic instruction) or phyletic (in which the teacher serves as a role model), this is a heuristic approach that engages students in inquiry and discovery. It is more self-conscious about its objectives and methods and seeks to help students develop a deep conceptual knowledge of a topic and give them opportunities to engage in discipline-specific methods of research, analysis, and reporting.

**transmedia case application.** An application to support case-based learning that utilizes a variety of media, including text, video, and such next-generation approaches as augmented and virtual reality.

**trauma-informed pedagogy.** Attention, memory, cognition, and a capacity to plan and regulate emotions all suffer when students are under overwhelming stress, hindering their ability to focus, process information, organize their time, or cope with frustrations and disappointments. To better support students: be attentive and responsive to student struggles; prepare students for difficult topics; create a class atmosphere that is respectful, supportive, compassionate, sensitive, and inclusive; be flexible and empathetic; give students a sense of agency; and make sure activities are worth an investment of students' time and energy.

**Universal Design for Learning.** An approach to instructional design that gives all students, including those with learning disabilities, an equal chance to succeed.

**vertical.** A clearly defined curricular pathway that can begin in middle school or high school and extent into graduate, professional, and continuing education.

**wraparound services.** The 360-degree supports for students to meet their academic, financial, mental health, and basic needs for food, housing, and transportation.

**X-factor educators.** Instructors who adapt their pedagogy to meet their students' diverse needs, seek to bring all students to success, and are committed to their social and emotional, as well as their cognitive, development.

# APPENDIX 3

---

# Next-Generation Pedagogies

**case-based learning.** In a case-based approach, students examine and analyze an actual series or sequence of events and their outcome or a realistic scenario or simulation in order to understand its history, context, etiology, and consequences. This approach gives students the opportunity to explore the decision-making process and consider options or alternatives or to mirror the diagnostic process in which information is gathered, assessed, and acted upon.

**collaborative and cooperative learning.** Collaborative learning is a pedagogy that involves groups of students working together to solve a problem, complete a task, understand a concept, or undertake a project. Group learning offers a way to help students develop social skills, problem-solving skills, collective decision-making skills, and presentation skills. Its effectiveness requires individual and group accountability. The difference between collaborative and cooperative learning is that the latter typically involves preassigned roles or responsibilities.

By making learning a social process, this approach to learning holds out the prospect of producing intellectual synergies, building collaboration skills, tapping the energy that comes when groups of students engage in a common project, and transforming teams into communities of inquiry, practice, and support. Examples include collective brainstorming and problem-solving, engaging in debate, and social annotation, in which students mark up a text.

**critical and transformational pedagogy.** The starting point for critical pedagogy is a recognition that classrooms are sites of power, privilege, and hierarchy; that teaching is an inherently political act; and that the politics of the classroom are obfuscated and need to be revealed and critically assessed.

Within traditional classrooms, proponents argue, certain ideas, perspectives, and forms of behavior, discourse, and argumentation are favored. The conceptual design of a course remains hidden and unexamined, while the selection and interpretation of topics and readings reflects unspoken ideological presumptions. Meanwhile, the approach to teaching in the traditional classroom, whether involving lecture or discussion, takes the significance of particular texts or topics for granted and fails to model the range of alternative interpretive or analytical approaches. All of these factors lead some, if not many, students to feel marginalized, discouraging deep learning.

The goals of critical pedagogy are to alter the student-faculty relationship, awaken a student's critical consciousness, encourage them to examine the role of the standard curriculum in reinforcing structures of power, offer multiple perspectives, and interrogate and critically assess conventional assumptions.

**culturally responsive teaching.** This is an instructional approach that makes students' cultural identities an important aspect of teaching and learning. Inclusion is one of this pedagogy's goals: to bring the students' diverse backgrounds and lived experiences into the learning process. This approach seeks to ensure that all of today's students' cultures are acknowledged and validated and that classmates gain awareness about cultural diversity and become knowledgeable about other cultures.

**experiential learning.** This is an umbrella term for forms of learning through experience and reflection. Internships, undergraduate research, clinical experiences, study abroad, and service learning are but a few examples of ways that students can gain practical experience, purposefully apply knowledge and skills in authentic contexts, and reflect on what they have learned.

Effective experiential learning activities must be carefully structured and supervised; involve meaningful relationships; have clearly defined expectations, goals, responsibilities, and activities; and offer opportunities for feedback and reflection. A student must document clear evidence of learning and produce an outcome, typically logs of observations, a reflective essay, or a completed product or project.

**field- and place-based learning.** Learning need not take place in a classroom or laboratory. A hallmark of archaeology, geography, and environmental science courses, field-based learning can take place in almost any discipline and give students the opportunity to apply their research skills. Underlying this approach is a belief that neighboring communities and environments outside the classroom contain assets that can significantly enhance student learning. Examples of field- or community-based learning include collecting interviews and oral histories, investigating historical sites, and undertaking participant observation. To be educationally meaningful, the students need to formulate a research question; undertake background research; collect, process, and interpret data; and draw and present conclusions.

**gamification.** This approach integrates gamelike elements—such as interactivity, competition, playfulness, and immediate feedback—into teaching and learning. The use of rewards, recognition, points, and levels helps motivate students and encourages perseverance.

**global learning.** To enhance students' ability to participate in a globally interconnected world, this approach examines international relations, complex global challenges, cultural differences, and transnational processes (like migration) and gives students the tools to communicate and engage meaningfully and effectively across national and cultural boundaries. Ways to foster global learning include foreign language instruction supplemented with cultural activities, paired classrooms and digital pen pals.

**immersive learning.** This approach places students in a realistic virtual or simulated environment in which they can analyze a setting or context, reenact various scenarios, role-play, or practice and apply a variety of skills and techniques. The most exciting examples place students in virtual reconstructions of historical sites and structures.

**inclusive teaching.** A pedagogical approach that seeks to engage all students and to bring their diverse backgrounds, abilities, and lived experiences into the learning process.

**inquiry-based learning.** Inquiry-based learning is a form of active learning that places students at the center of the learning process. It begins with a question or problem that students must investigate. The students, then, conduct research; identify, analyze, and interpret the evidence they uncover; draw conclusions; and present their findings. The inquiries can be structured or more open, and the outcomes can be known in advance or only discovered in a process of investigation.

An inquiry approach builds on the adage, "Tell me and I forget, show me and I remember, involve me and I understand." It requires students to take responsibility for their own learning.

**learning by making and doing.** Learning by doing helps students link theory to practice and translate academic knowledge and skills into tangible products. The best-known form of learning by doing is project-based learning. It involves more than simply completing a project; rather, it is the primary way that students master skills and knowledge. Ideally, project-based learning requires students to go through a multistage process of design, planning, execution, a public presentation, critique and revision, and formal assessment. The project outcome need not be a physical product. It can consist of a detailed policy proposal, a teaching resource, a briefing paper, or another authentic outcome.

Maker spaces, design studios, visualization and prototyping labs, digital media labs, and innovation hubs and accelerators are physical or virtual spaces where students can receive support (including legal and business expertise and assistance with design, programming, and commercialization) as they take a concept to execution. A growing number have expanded their focus beyond technology projects to encompass the arts, humanities, and social sciences.

**project-based learning.** A pedagogical approach through which students acquire and apply knowledge and skills as they create, individually or collaboratively, a project or presentation.

**public scholarship.** Public scholarship supports the academy's civic mission by speaking to public issues and collaborating with cultural institutions outside higher education, such as archives, historical societies, libraries, museums, newspapers, performance venues, schools, and humanities councils. There is no reason why students can't engage in public scholarship, for example, by partnering with community institutions to develop educational resources or websites; serving as docents, teachers' aides, and leaders of after-school programs; and creating documentary films.

**research-based learning.** Research-based learning gives students hands-on experience in applying the epistemologies, methodologies, and modes of dissemination of a particular discipline.

Opportunities to engage in authentic independent research are scalable. The Freshman Research Initiative at the University of Texas at Austin gives more than 1,000 incoming students a year opportunities to undertake independent research in one of thirty research streams in astronomy, computer science, biology, chemistry, neuroscience, mathematics, and physics. Each stream is directed by a faculty PI and supported by postdocs, graduate students, and undergraduate peer mentors. During the first semester of a three-semester sequence of course work and laboratory research, students are introduced to the scientific process, taught research techniques, helped to formulate a research question, and shown how to maintain a lab notebook. Students, supported and mentored by faculty and others, subsequently conduct research and write up and present their findings.

**service learning.** Service learning allows students to connect skills and knowledge acquired in the classroom to a specific community need or challenge. It is not simply community service. Rather, it combines specific learning goals with an outcome deemed significant by a particular community client. Service learning requires researching the problem or need, devising and implementing an action plan resulting in a meaningful outcome, and engaging in a rigorous process of reflection and assessment.

**technology-enhanced learning.** Technology is a tool, not a pedagogy. Nevertheless, new instructional tools have the power to transform education by facilitating new forms of collaboration and interactive learning, Examples abound and include blogging, concept and network mapping, creating podcasts, data visualization, digital storytelling, etymology, exhibition creation, social annotation, text mining, and timeline construction. Students can create and analyze virtual scenarios.

# APPENDIX 4

_____

# Technology-Enhanced Active
# Learning Tools

Learning should not be a spectator sport. Meaningful learning requires active engagement, critical thinking, and thoughtful reflection. The best way to master a subject is to do what scholars do: engage in inquiry, problem solving, analysis, and interpretation. How can instructors use technology to integrate active learning into their classes? Listed here are some tested strategies.

### Annotation
You might ask your students to explicate and annotate a written text or document, either individually or collectively, using Hypothes.is or Perusall or video clips using VideoAnt.

### Citation
Show your students how to create a citation from a URL with Mybib citation creator or manage collections of citations with Zotero.

### Collaboration
Ask students to collectively create documents and presentations with Google Docs, Slides, and Sheets. Padlet.com lets users create a collaboration space and Google Jamboard offers a digital whiteboard on which students can collaborate. Slack and Microsoft Teams offer platforms that facilitate team communication and collaboration, while Basecamp, Kanbanchi, and Trello offer project management tools.

### Concept and Network Mapping
Students can map relationships among concepts or networks or causal factors with Coggle, Cliovis, Lucidchart, Popplet, and Sketchboard.

### Content Libraries
Leading content repositories in US history include American Memory, Digital History, Digital Public Library of America, DocsTeach, Gilder Lehrman Institute of American History, History Matters, and the Stanford History Education Group. Royalty-free images are available at Photos for Class.

### Conversion Tools
A tool for file conversion is Zamzar, and a tool for video conversion is Media.io.

### Curation
Students can bookmark websites with Symbaloo.com or elink.io and aggregate content with Google Keep, Paper.li, livebinders.com, wakelet.com, or webjets.io. Google Keep offers a simple way for students to curate visual as well as textual resources.

### Data Visualization
Students might use Google MyMaps to create and annotate maps. The National Archive's DocTeach.org offers a simple way to plot primary sources, descriptive text, or boxes for student response on a historic map or an outline map. Wordart and WordClouds make it easy to generate word clouds, while Google Ngrams allows students to analyze changes in word frequency in published books. Students can create visualizations of census data with http://www.census.gov /dataviz/.

### Etymology
The *Oxford English Dictionary* online and the Online Etymology Dictionary allow students to trace shifts in words' meaning and the introduction of popular terminology and concepts.

### Exhibition Creation
Google Slides offers a simple platform on which to create virtual exhibitions.

### Feedback
Peer feedback offers a way for students to provide constructive feedback to classmates. You might consider asking students to participate collaboratively in the construction of rubrics.

### Geomapping
Use theclio.com to identify sites of historical or cultural significance. HistoryPin is a collaboration tool that allows users to share images of history across time and space and place those memories on maps and timelines.

### Global Learning

Examples of global learning include paired classrooms and virtual pen pals. Skype in the Classroom offers an easy way to create virtual field trips and conversations with content-area specialists.

### Interactive Lessons

Students can respond to a video with edpuzzle.com and enhance a website with insertlearning.com. Instructors can build lessons around TED talks with ed.ted .com.

### Portfolios and Digital Galleries

Students can create portfolios and digital galleries with Showcaseedu.com and create and annotate a portfolio with seesaw.me.

### Project-Based Learning

Here are some twenty-first-century alternatives to the classic research paper. You might ask students to create an infographic with Infogram, Picktochart, or Venngage, or make an interactive poster with Glogster or Thinklink. They might make a presentation with PowerPoint or Google Slides, a podcast with Anchor.fm or Audacity, a digital story with Adobe Spark, iMovie, MS Photo Story 3, or MS Movie Maker, and a virtual museum or exhibition with Google Slides.

### Student Response Systems

Polling and quizzing provide a simple way to monitor student understanding in near real time.

### Survey Tools

Consider conducting a survey using Google Forms or Survey Monkey—and then you can use anonymous survey data in class to explore attitudes, interests, and opinions—or even students' family background and experiences.

### Text Mining

A simple tool for mining a text that can offer insights into word choice, metaphors, and imagery is https://voyant-tools.org/.

### Timelines

Timeline.js and Time Mapper allow students to quickly create a timeline from a spreadsheet.

# APPENDIX 5

---

# Strategies for Enhancing Equity and Student Success

Here, in a nutshell, are fifteen evidence-based steps that institutions can take that will strengthen students' sense of connection, optimize the curriculum, enhance engagement, deepen learning, and improve student outcomes.

1. Expedite transfer credit evaluation.
2. Provide a robust orientation for all new students.
3. Guarantee access to essential gateway courses.
4. Make sure every entering student has a degree plan.
5. Place as many students as possible in a cohort program or learning community with a mentor and a dedicated adviser to enhance students' sense of belonging and connection.
6. Make student success training and major and career exploration integral parts of the first-year experience.
7. Adopt block scheduling to allow students to concentrate their time on campus and better balance academic and work and caregiving responsibilities.
8. Implement an integrated data-driven system to identify impediments to student success, inform course scheduling, monitor student progress, and prompt proactive interventions when students are off-track.
9. Institute a tiered system of student advising and support that includes one-stop and online access to services, as well as peer tutors, peer-led study groups, supplemental instruction sections in high DFW courses, and learning centers in math, science, and writing.

10. Create intentionally designed coherent degree pathways, consisting of synergistic courses, for high-demand majors.
11. Offer more lower division courses that address enduring issues and contemporary controversies from an interdisciplinary perspective and build students' cultural, historical social science, statistical and mathematical, and scientific literacies and their digital, research, and writing skills.
12. Replace remedial courses with corequisite remediation that includes supplemental instruction.
13. Embed career exploration and preparation across the undergraduate experience.
14. Supplement existing lecture and discussion classes with other kinds of learning experiences that involve more active and experiential learning opportunities, including mentored research, supervised internships, practicums, clinical experiences, studio courses, field research, making spaces, and community service.
15. To better serve commuter students, integrate cocurricular experiences into existing classes and support engagement activities that connect students with faculty.

# NOTES

## Introduction

1. Michael Feldstein, "If You Were Designing Cal State Today: A Proposal out of MIT," *eLiterate* (blog), https://eliterate.us/if-you-were-designing-cal-state-today-a-proposal-out-of-mit/.

## Chapter 1. Higher Education's Perfect Storm

1. Bruce A. Kimball with Sarah M. Iler, *Wealth, Cost, and Price in American Higher Education: A Brief History* (Baltimore: Johns Hopkins University Press, 2023).

2. Catherine Rampell, "One of America's Most Successful Exports Is in Trouble," *Washington Post*, December 18, 2018, https://www.timesonline.com/story/opinion/columns/2018/12/18/america-s-successful-export-is/6619553007/; Irwin Feller, "This Time It Really May Be Different," in *The University under Pressure*, Research in the Sociology of Organizations 46, ed. Elizabeth Popp Berman and Catherine Paradeise (Bingley, UK: Emerald Group Publishing, 2016), 453–88.

3. Left-wing critiques include Dennis Hayes, *Beyond McDonaldization: Visions of Higher Education* (New York: Routledge, 2017) and Hayes, *The McDonaldization of Higher Education* (New York: Praeger, 2002). Right-wing criticisms include Charles J. Sykes, *Fail U.: The False Promise of Higher Education* (New York: St. Martin's, 2016) and Warren Treadgold, *The University We Need: Reforming American Higher Education* (New York: Encounter Books, 2018).

4. Michael S. McPherson and William G. Bowen, *Lesson Plan: An Agenda for Change in American Higher Education* (Princeton, NJ: Princeton University Press, 2016).

5. Niu Gao and Hans Johnson, *Improving College Pathways in California* (San Francisco: Public Policy Institute of California, 2017), https://www.ppic.org/publication/improving-college-pathways-in-california/; "Student Pipeline—Transition and Completion Rates from 9th Grade to College," NCHEMS Information Center, http://www.higheredinfo.org/dbrowser/?year=2002&level=nation&mode=data&state=0&submeasure=119.

6. George Mehaffy, "The Disruption of Higher Ed (and How to Prepare for It)," *EdTech*, July 26, 2012, https://edtechmagazine.com/higher/article/2012/07/disruption-higher-ed-and-how-prepare-it.

## Chapter 2. The Challenges Ahead

1. The term "wicked problem" was coined by C. West Churchman in an essay titled "Wicked Problems," *Management Science* 14, no. 4, Application Series (December, 1967): B141–B142; Derek Newton, "Please Stop Asking Whether a College Degree Is Worth It," *Forbes*, December 16, 2018, https://www.forbes.com /sites/dereknewton/2018/12/16/please-stop-asking-whether-college-is-worth-it /#4f4068d030d2. Also see Anthony P. Carnevale, Stephen J. Rose, and Ban Cheah, *The College Payoff: Education, Occupations, Lifetime Earnings* (Washington, DC: Georgetown University Center on Education and the Workforce, 2011); Pew Research Center, "The Monetary Value of a College Education," March 7, 2012, http://www.pewresearch.org/fact-tank/2012/03/07/the-monetary-value-of-a -college-education/.

2. Jon Marcus, "Colleges' New Solution to Enrollment Declines: Reducing the Number of Dropouts," *Hechinger Report*, March 6, 2022, https://hechingerreport .org/colleges-new-solution-to-enrollment-declines-reducing-the-number-of -dropouts/; Friedrich Huebler, "International Education Statistics," January 2011, https://huebler.blogspot.com/2011/01/usa.html; Bureau of Labor Statistics, "College Enrollment and Work Activity of 2010 High School Graduates," April 8, 2011, https://www.bls.gov/news.release/archives/hsgec_04082011.pdf.

3. Michael Nietzel, "As Enrollments Decline, Colleges Respond with Technology, New Curricula and Business Partnerships," *Forbes*, October 17, 2022, https://www.forbes.com/sites/michaeltnietzel/2022/10/17/as-enrollments -decline-colleges-respond-with-technology-new-curricula-and-business -partnerships/.

4. Amanda Ripley, "Why Is College in America So Expensive?," *Atlantic*, September 11, 2018, https://www.theatlantic.com/education/archive/2018/09 /why-is-college-so-expensive-in-america/569884/.

5. Jennifer Ma and Matea Pende, *Trends in College Pricing and Student Aid 2022* (Princeton, NJ: College Board, 2022); Jon Marcus, "Some Colleges Are Totally Unaffordable, and This Tool Proves It," PBS NewsHour (November 9, 2018), https://www.pbs.org/newshour/education/some-colleges-are-totally-unaffordable -and-this-tool-proves-it.

6. Jon Marcus, "New Data Show Some Colleges Are Definitively Unaffordable for Many," *Hechinger Report*, October 18, 2018, https://hechingerreport.org/new -data-show-some-colleges-are-definitively-unaffordable-for-many/.

7. College Board, "Average Net Price over Time for Full-Time Students, by Sector, Published and Net Prices in 2018 Dollars by Sector, Full-Time Undergraduate Students, 1990–91 to 2018–19," https://trends.collegeboard.org/college -pricing/figures-tables/average-net-price-over-time-full-time-students-sector; Rick Seltzer, "Net Price Keeps Creeping Up," *Inside Higher Ed*, October 25, 2017, https://www.insidehighered.com/news/2017/10/25/tuition-and-fees-still-rising -faster-aid-college-board-report-shows; Marcus, "New Data Show."

8. College Board, "Trends in College Pricing," 2017, https://trends .collegeboard.org/sites/default/files/2017-trends-in-college-pricing_0.pdf.

9. Kathryn Wilson, "What's behind the Sky-High Cost of a College Educa-tion?," CBS News, November 5, 2022, https://finance.yahoo.com/news/whats-behind-sky-high-cost-110017900.html.

10. National Center for Educational Statistics, "Price of Attending an Under-graduate Institution," May 2022, https://nces.ed.gov/programs/coe/indicator/cua/undergrad-costs; College Board, "Trends in College Pricing," 2022, https://research.collegeboard.org/trends/college-pricing.

11. Katherine Knott, "Fewer Affordable Options for Pell Grant Students," *Inside Higher Ed*, October 31, 2022, https://www.insidehighered.com/news/2022/10/31/college-affordability-trends-moving-wrong-direction.

12. Andrew Kreighbaum, "Rethinking Federal Lending to Parents," *Inside Higher Ed*, April 16, 2019, https://www.insidehighered.com/news/2019/04/16/report-recommends-congress-cap-borrowing-parents-college-students.

13. Emma Kerr and Sarah Wood, "The Cost of Private vs. Public Colleges," *U.S. News*, June 8, 2022, https://www.usnews.com/education/best-colleges/paying-for-college/articles/2019-06-25/the-cost-of-private-vs-public-colleges; Student Loan Hero, "A Look at the Shocking Student Loan Debt Statistics for 2022," July 29, 2022, https://studentloanhero.com/student-loan-debt-statistics/; Adam Looney and Vivien Lee, "Parents Are Borrowing More and More to Send Their Kids to College—and Many Are Struggling to Repay," Brookings Institution, November 27, 2018, https://www.brookings.edu/research/parents-are-borrowing-more-and-more-to-send-their-kids-to-college-and-many-are-struggling-to-repay/.

14. Hannah Bareham, "Why Students Who Need Financial Aid the Most Aren't Getting Enough of It," Bankrate, November 16, 2022, https://www.bankrate.com/loans/student-loans/why-students-dont-get-enough-financial-aid/#pressure.

15. Eric Hoover, "A New Push to Make Financial-Aid Offers More Transpar-ent," *Chronicle of Higher Education*, November 29, 2022, https://www.chronicle.com/article/a-new-push-to-make-financial-aid-offers-more-transparent.

16. Annie Nova, "More Than 1 Million People Default on Their Student Loans Each Year," CNBC, August 13, 2018, https://www.cnbc.com/2018/08/13/twenty-two-percent-of-student-loan-borrowers-fall-into-default.html.

17. Board of Governors of the Federal Reserve System, "Report on the Eco-nomic Well-Being of US Households in 2016," May 2017, https://www.federalreserve.gov/publications/2017-economic-well-being-of-us-households-in-2016-accessible.htm.

18. Richard Fry, "U.S. Still Has a Ways to Go in Meeting Obama's Goal of Producing More College Grads," Pew Research Center, January 18, 2017, http://www.pewresearch.org/fact-tank/2017/01/18/u-s-still-has-a-ways-to-go-in-meeting-obamas-goal-of-producing-more-college-grads/.

19. Judith Scott-Clayton, "The Looming Student Loan Default Crisis Is Worse Than We Thought," *Brookings Institution Evidence Speaks Reports*, 2, no. 34 (January 10, 2018), https://www.brookings.edu/wp-content/uploads/2018/01/scott-clayton-report.pdf.

20. National Student Clearinghouse Research Center, "Completing College—National—2018," https://nscresearchcenter.org/signaturereport16/; Paul Fain, "Broader College Completion Data from the Feds," *Inside Higher Ed*, December 5, 2018, https://www.insidehighered.com/quicktakes/2018/12/05/broader-college-completion-data-feds; Paul Fain, "National College Completion Rate Rises Again," *Inside Higher Ed*, December 15, 2017, https://www.insidehighered.com/quicktakes/2017/12/15/national-college-completion-rate-rises-again.

21. Emily Tate, "Graduation Rates and Race," *Inside Higher Ed*, April 26, 2017, https://www.insidehighered.com/news/2017/04/26/college-completion-rates-vary-race-and-ethnicity-report-finds; Anthony P. Carnevale, Martin Van Der Werf, Michael C. Quinn, Jeff Strohl, and Dmitri Repnikov, *Our Separate & Unequal Public Colleges* (Washington, DC: Georgetown University Center on Education and the Workforce, 2018).

22. Susan Dynarski, "For the Poor, the Graduation Gap Is Even Wider Than the Enrollment Gap," *New York Times*, June 2, 2015, https://www.nytimes.com/2015/06/02/upshot/for-the-poor-the-graduation-gap-is-even-wider-than-the-enrollment-gap.html.

23. Mikhail Zinshteyn, "The Slow Growth of College-Graduation Rates," *Atlantic*, April 12, 2016, https://www.theatlantic.com/education/archive/2016/04/the-slow-growth-of-college-graduation-rates/477798/.

24. Imed Bouchrika, "College Dropout Rates: 2022 Statistics by Race, Gender & Income," Research.Com, September 26, 2022, https://research.com/universities-colleges/college-dropout-rates.

25. Johanna Alonso, "A Holistic Approach to Transferring Credits," *Inside Higher Ed*, November 30, 2022, https://www.insidehighered.com/news/2022/11/30/model-promotes-holistic-credit-transfer-solutions.

26. Interstate Passport, https://interstatepassport.wiche.edu/.

27. Sarah Pingel and Martin Kurzweil, "Earning Credit from Multiple Sources Is the Norm in Higher Ed," *Inside Higher Ed*, December 1, 2022, https://www.insidehighered.com/blogs/beyond-transfer/earning-credit-multiple-sources-norm-higher-ed.

28. Jennifer Glynn, "Persistence: The Success of Students Who Transfer from Community Colleges to Selective Four-Year," Jack Kent Cooke Foundation, 2019, https://mrodriguez01.wpenginepowered.com/wp-content/uploads/2019/01/Persistance-Jack-Kent-Cooke-Foundation.pdf.

29. Delta Cost Project Database, https://www.deltacostproject.org/delta-cost-project-database. On stratification within higher education more generally, see Robert B. Archibald and David H. Feldman, *The Road Ahead for America's Colleges and Universities* (New York: Oxford University Press, 2017).

30. Susan Dynarski, "Breaking Barriers to College for High-Achieving, Low-Income Students," *Econofact*, March 17, 2019, https://econofact.org/breaking-barriers-to-college-for-high-achieving-low-income-students.

31. Caroline M. Hoxby, "The Changing Selectivity of American Colleges," *Journal of Economic Perspectives*, 23 (2009), 95–118; Hoxby, "The Return to Attending a More Selective College: 1960 to the Present" (unpublished

manuscript, 1998), Department of Economics, Harvard University, http://
citeseerx.ist.psu.edu/viewdoc/download?doi=10.1.1.197.6607&rep=rep1&type
=pdf.

32. Anthony Carnevale et al., "Born to Win, Schooled to Lose," Georgetown
University Center on Education and the Workforce, 2019, https://cewgeorgetown
.wpenginepowered.com/wp-content/uploads/FR-Born_to_win-schooled_to_lose
.pdf.

33. Max McConn, "How Much Do College Students Learn? Results of the
Carnegie Foundation Study in Pennsylvania," *North American Review* (1821–1940),
232, no. 5 (November 1931): 446.

34. Richard Arum and Josipa Roksa, *Academically Adrift: Limited Learning on
College Campuses* (Chicago: University of Chicago Press, 2011); Kevin Fosnacht,
Alexander C. McCormick, and Rosemarie Lerma, "Time Use during College: Is It
Study or Party Time?," *NSSE Sightings*, January 5, 2017, https://nssesightings
.indiana.edu/archives/340.

35. Alexander W. Astin, "In 'Academically Adrift,' Data Don't Back Up
Sweeping Claim," *Chronicle of Higher Education*, February 14, 2011, https://www
.chronicle.com/article/in-academically-adrift-data-dont-back-up-sweeping
-claim; David M. Lane and Fred L. Oswald, "Statistically Adrift: Why a Central
Conclusion in *Academically Adrift* Is Faulty," n.d., https://davidmlane.com
/hyperstat/academically_adrift.html; Doug Lederman, "Less Academically
Adrift?" *Inside Higher Ed*, May 20, 2013, https://www.insidehighered.com/news
/2013/05/20/studies-challenge-findings-academically-adrift.

36. Stuart Rojstaczer and Christopher Healy, "Where A Is Ordinary: The
Evolution of American College and University Grading, 1940–2009," *Teacher's
College Record*, 2012, https://www.gradeinflation.com/tcr2012grading.pdf. For a
2016 update, see "Grade Inflation at American Colleges and Universities,"
https://www.gradeinflation.com/. Also see Jeffrey T. Denning, Eric R. Eide,
Kevin Mumford, Richard W. Patterson, and Merrill Warnick, "Why Have College
Completion Rates Increased?" NBER Working Paper 28710, National Bureau of
Economic Research, April 2021, https://www.nber.org/system/files/working
_papers/w28710/w28710.pdf, which argues that grade inflation has contributed
to rising college completion rates.

37. Brandon Busteed, "When GPA No Longer Matters," *Forbes*, November 16,
2022, https://www.forbes.com/sites/brandonbusteed/2022/11/16/when-gpa-no
-longer-matters/.

38. Anthony P. Carnevale, Ban Cheah, Martin Van Der Werf, and Artem
Gulish, "Buyer Beware," Georgetown University Center on Education and the
Workforce, 2020, https://cew.georgetown.edu/cew-reports/collegemajorroi/.

39. Samanda Dorger, "27 Jobs That Pay Over $60,000 a Year with Just an
Associate Degree," *The Street*, October 30, 2022, https://www.thestreet.com
/personal-finance/27-jobs-that-pay-over-60000-year-just-associate-degree.

40. Stig Leschly and Yazmin Guzman, "Degree-Specific Earnings Outcomes of
Graduates from Colleges in Massachusetts," *College 101*, December, 2021, https://
college101.org/ma-report/.

41. Christian Smith, "Higher Ed Is Drowning in BS," *Chronicle of Higher Education*, January 9, 2018, https://www.chronicle.com/article/Higher -Education-Is-Drowning/242195.

42. Roger Meiners, "An Economist's Defense of Tenure," James G. Martin Center for Academic Renewal, August 15, 2010, https://www.jamesgmartin .center/2010/08/an-economists-defense-of-tenure/.

43. Jeffrey J. Selingo, "College Students Say They Want a Degree for a Job. Are They Getting What They Want?," *Washington Post*, September 1, 2018, https:// www.washingtonpost.com/news/grade-point/wp/2018/09/01/college-students -say-they-want-a-degree-for-a-job-are-they-getting-what-they-want/?utm _term=.e5d0a4096130.

44. Holden Thorp and Buck Goldstein, *Our Higher Calling: Rebuilding the Partnership between America and Its Colleges and Universities* (Chapel Hill: Univer- sity of North Carolina, 2018).

45. On the failure of colleges to help students define realistic career objectives and pathways, see Barbara Schneider and David Stevenson, *The Ambitious Generation: America's Teenagers, Motivated but Directionless* (New Haven, CT: Yale University Press, 2000).

46. Julie Halpert, "Late to Launch: The Post-collegiate Struggle," *New York Times*, December 4, 2018, https://www.nytimes.com/2018/12/04/well/family/late -to-launch-the-post-collegiate-struggle.html.

47. Hart Research Associates, "Falling Short? College Learning and Career Success," 2015, https://dgmg81phhvh63.cloudfront.net/content/user-photos /Research/PDFs/2015employerstudentsurvey.pdf.

### Chapter 3. The Shifting Higher Education Landscape

1. Lewis Carroll, *Alice's Adventures in Wonderland* (London, 1865; Open Books Electronic Edition, 2007), 71–72, https://www.open-bks.com/alice-71-72.html.

2. Anthony Carnevale and Nicole Smith, "Training Programs Are Welcome, but Let's Not Overlook the Benefits of a Bachelor's Degree," *Hechinger Report*, December 5, 2022, https://hechingerreport.org/opinion-training-programs-are -welcome-but-lets-not-overlook-the-benefits-of-a-bachelors-degree/.

3. Lindsay Ellis, "How the Great Recession Reshaped American Higher Education," *Chronicle of Higher Education*, September 14, 2018, https://www .chronicle.com/article/How-the-Great-Recession/244527; Jeffrey R. Brown and Caroline M. Hoxby, eds., *How the Financial Crisis and Great Recession Affected Higher Education* (Chicago: University of Chicago Press, 2015).

4. Thomas Friedman, "Come the Revolution," *New York Times*, May 15, 2012, https://www.nytimes.com/2012/05/16/opinion/friedman-come-the-revolution .html.

5. John Warner, "How about We Put Learning at the Center?," *Inside Higher Ed*, January 4, 2023, https://www.insidehighered.com/blogs/just-visiting/how-about -we-put-learning-center.

6. Friedman, "Come the Revolution."

7. "Gainful Employment Information," Federal Financial Aid, https://student
aid.gov/data-center/school/ge.

8. Jill Barshay, "The Number of College Graduates in the Humanities Drops for
the Eighth Consecutive Year," *Hechinger Report*, November 22, 2021, https://www
.amacad.org/news/college-graduates-humanities-drops-eighth-consecutive
-year.

9. Derek Thompson, "Colleges Have a Guy Problem," *Atlantic*, September 14,
2021, https://www.theatlantic.com/ideas/archive/2021/09/young-men-college
-decline-gender-gap-higher-education/620066/; "Undergraduate Graduation
Rates," National Center for Education Statistics, Institute of Education Sciences,
May 31, 2022, https://nces.ed.gov/fastfacts/display.asp?id=40; Justin Wolfers,
"More Women than Men Are Going to College. That May Change the Economy."
*New York Times*, November 23, 2021, https://www.nytimes.com/2021/11/23
/business/dealbook/women-college-economy.html.

10. "Data Snapshot: Contingent Faculty in US Higher Ed," American Association of University Professors, October 11, 2018, https://www.aaup.org/sites
/default/files/10112018%20Data%20Snapshot%20Tenure.pdf.

11. Rita Kirshstein, "Colleges' Reliance on Part-Time Faculty: Who Wins? Who
Loses?," Noodle, October 5, 2015, https://www.noodle.com/articles/the-rise-of
-part-time-faculty-and-its-effect-on-higher-ed131; Bethany Ann Potts, "An
Exploratory Study of Adjunct Faculty Professional Growth Experiences," (EdD
diss., Portland State University, 2021), https://pdxscholar.library.pdx.edu/cgi
/viewcontent.cgi?article=6828&context=open_access_etds.

12. Preston Cooper, "Why Are Colleges Restricting Access to High-Paying
Majors?," *Forbes*, February 15, 2022, https://www.forbes.com/sites/preston
cooper2/2022/02/15/why-are-colleges-restricting-access-to-high-paying-majors
/?sh=5147a138183a.

13. Debra Bragg and Tim Harmon, "Making the Case for Community College
Baccalaureates," New America, December 5, 2022, https://www.newamerica.org
/education-policy/briefs/making-the-case-for-community-college-bacca
laureates-what-supply-and-demand-analysis-reveals-in-two-midwest-states/.

14. Ryan Craig, "The HTD Revolution: Hire-Train-Deploy," *Forbes*, October 1,
2021, https://www.forbes.com/sites/ryancraig/2021/10/01/the-htd-revolution
-hire-train-deploy.

15. "Student Pipeline—Transition and Completion Rates from 9th Grade to
College," 2018, NCHEMS Information Center, National Center for Higher
Education Management Systems, http://www.higheredinfo.org/dbrowser/index
.php?measure=72; "The 8th Grade Cohort Longitudinal Study: 10 Year Anniversary," Texas Higher Education Coordinating Board, October 2017, https://apps
.highered.texas.gov/DocID/PDF/10117.PDF.

16. Delece Smith-Barrow, "Can 'Work Colleges' in Cities Become a Low-Cost,
High-Value Model for the Future?" *Hechinger Report*, July 26, 2018, https://
hechingerreport.org/can-work-colleges-in-cities-become-a-low-cost-high-value
-model-for-the-future/.

17. Adrienne Raphel, "The Work-College Revival," *New Yorker*, April 12, 2015, https://www.newyorker.com/business/currency/the-work-college-revival.

18. Matthew Dembicki, "DataPoints: The Growth of Credentials," *Community College Daily*, December, 7, 2022, https://www.ccdaily.com/2022/12/datapoints -the-growth-of-credentials/.

### Chapter 4. Lessons from the History of American Higher Education

1. Clay Shirky, "The End of Higher Education's Golden Age," blog, April 1, 2014, http://shirky.com/weblog/2014/01/there-isnt-enough-money-to-keep -educating-adults-the-way-were-doing-it/. Also see Bryan Alexander, "Peak Education 2013," *Academia Next*, September 18, 2013, https://bryanalexander .org/uncategorized/peak-education-2013/; Bryan Alexander, "Academia after Peak Higher Education," *Academia Next*, May 29, 2018, https://bryanalexander .org/future-of-education/academia-after-peak-higher-education/; Bryan Alexander, "Has Higher Ed Peaked?," *Inside Higher Ed*, April 7, 2014, https:// www.insidehighered.com/views/2014/04/07/essay-considers-whether-higher -education-us-has-peaked; Bryan Alexander, "Peak Higher Education, 4 Years Later," *Academia Next*, September 12, 2017, https://bryanalexander.org/research -topics/peak-higher-education-4-years-later/; Steven Brint, "Is This Higher Education's Golden Age?," *Chronicle of Higher Education*, January 9, 2019, https:// www.chronicle.com/article/is-this-higher-educations-golden-age/; Brian Rosenberg, "This Is Higher Education's Gilded Age," *Chronicle of Higher Education*, February 3, 2019, https://www.chronicle.com/article/this-is-higher-educations -gilded-age/; Richard Vedder, "Is This Higher Education's Golden Age, Gilded Age, or Beginning of a Gentle Decline?," *Forbes*, February 25, 2019, https://www.forbes .com/sites/richardvedder/2019/02/25/is-this-higher-educations-golden-age -gilded-age-or-beginning-of-a-gentle-decline.

2. John R. Thelin, Jason R. Edwards, and Eric Moyen, "Higher Education in the United States," StateUniversity.com Education Encyclopedia, https://education .stateuniversity.com/pages/2044/Higher-Education-in-United-States.html.

3. National Center for Education Statistics, "120 Years of American Education: A Statistical Portrait," US Department of Education, January 1993, https://nces.ed .gov/pubs93/93442.pdf.

4. National Center for Education Statistics, "Federal Support for Education," U.S. Department of Education, 2001, https://nces.ed.gov/pubs2002/2002129.pdf.

5. Brint, "Is This Higher Education's Golden Age?"

6. Rosenberg, "This Is Higher Education's Gilded Age."

7. Drew DeSilver, "A Majority of U.S. Colleges Admit Most Students Who Apply," Pew Research Center, April 9, 2019, https://www.pewresearch.org/fact -tank/2019/04/09/a-majority-of-u-s-colleges-admit-most-students-who-apply/.

8. Steven Mintz, "Are U.S. Universities Losing Their Pre-eminence?," *Inside Higher Ed*, May 10, 2022, https://www.insidehighered.com/blogs/higher-ed -gamma/are-us-universities-losing-their-pre-eminence.

9. Vedder, "Is This Higher Education's Golden Age."

10. Melanie Hanson, "Average Student Loan Debt by Year," Education Data Initiative, January 19, 2022, https://educationdata.org/average-student-loan-debt -by-year.

11. Shirky, "End of Higher Education's Golden Age."

12. Margaret A. Nash and Jennifer A. R. Silverman, "'An Indelible Mark': Gay Purges in Higher Education in the 1940s," *History of Education Quarterly* 55, no. 4 (November 2015): 441–59, https://www.jstor.org/stable/26356322.

13. David F. Labaree, *A Perfect Mess: The Unlikely Ascendancy of American Higher Education* (Chicago: University of Chicago Press, 2017).

14. Vicki L. Baker, Roger G. Baldwin, and Sumedha Makker, "Where Are They Now? Revisiting Breneman's Study of Liberal Arts Colleges," *Liberal Education* 98, no. 3 (Summer 2012): 4–53.

15. Irwin Feller, "This Time It Really May Be Different," in *The University Under Pressure*, eds. Elizabeth Popp Berman and Catherine Paradeise (Bingley, UK: Emerald Publishing, 2016), 453–88.

### Chapter 5. A Learner- and Learning-Centered Vision for the Future of Higher Education

1. Quoted in Scott Rosenberg, "Virtual Reality Check Digital Daydreams, Cyberspace Nightmares," *San Francisco Examiner*, April 19, 1992, C1.

### Chapter 6. Thinking outside the Box

1. Larry Cuban, "Reforming the Grammar of Schooling Again and Again," *American Journal of Education*, 126 (August 2020): 665–71. https://www.journals .uchicago.edu/doi/abs/10.1086/709959.

2. Sam Roberts, "Henry Rosovsky, 95, Builder of Black and Jewish Studies at Harvard, Dies," *New York Times*, November 16, 2022, https://www.nytimes.com /2022/11/16/education/henry-rosovsky-dead.html.

3. C. P. Snow, "The Two Cultures," *Leonardo*, 23, nos. 2/3 (1990): 169. https:// www.jstor.org/stable/1578601.

4. Alan D. Sokal, "Transgressing the Boundaries: Towards a Transformative Hermeneutics of Quantum Gravity," Social Text, 46/47 (1996): 217–52. https:// physics.nyu.edu/sokal/transgress_v2/transgress_v2_singlefile.html.

5. Stephen Hilgartner, "The Sokal Affair in Context," *Science, Technology, & Human Values* 22, no. 4 (Autumn 1997): 506–22. https://www.jstor.org/stable /689833.

6. Emily Bergerson, "The Historical Roots of Mistrust in Science," American Bar Association, June 14, 2021, https://www.americanbar.org/groups/crsj /publications/human_rights_magazine_home/the-truth-about-science/the -historical-roots-of-mistrust-in-science/.

7. Naomi Oreskes, *Why Trust Science?* (Princeton, NJ: Princeton University Press, 2019); Paul Bloom, "Scientific Faith Is Different from Religious Faith," *Atlantic*, November 24, 2015, https://www.theatlantic.com/science/archive/2015 /11/why-scientific-faith-isnt-the-same-as-religious-faith/417357/; James C.

Zimring, *What Science Is and How It Really Works* (New York: Cambridge University Press, 2019); Phil Plait, "Is Science Faith Based?," *Discover*, February 18, 2008, https://www.discovermagazine.com/the-sciences/is-science-faith-based.

8. Anne Stein, "Math as a Civil Rights Issue," *Haverford College Alumni Magazine*, September 16, 2019, https://www.haverford.edu/college-communications/news/math-civil-rights-issue.

9. John Fensterwald, "Deep Divisions, Further Delay for California's Math Guidelines," *EdSource*, July 26, 2022, https://edsource.org/2022/deep-divisions-further-delay-for-californias-math-guidelines/675881; Christopher Edley Jr., "At Cal State, Algebra Is a Civil Rights Issue," *EdSource*, June 5, 2017, https://edsource.org/2017/at-cal-state-algebra-is-a-civil-rights-issue/582950; Nation's Report Card, "2022 Mathematics and Reading Report Cards at Grades 4 and 8," https://www.nationsreportcard.gov/.

10. Heather C. Hill, "After 30 Years of Reforms to Improve Math Instruction, Reasons for Hope and Dismay," Brookings Institution, February 4, 2021, https://www.brookings.edu/blog/brown-center-chalkboard/2021/02/04/after-30-years-of-reforms-to-improve-math-instruction-reasons-for-hope-and-dismay/; Stein, "Math as a Civil Rights Issue."

11. John Fensterwald, "Deep Divisions, Further Delay for California's Math Guidelines," *EdSource*, July 26, 2022, https://edsource.org/2022/deep-divisions-further-delay-for-californias-math-guidelines/675881.

12. Fensterwald, "Deep Divisions."

13. Robert Q. Berry III, Basil M. Conway IV, Brian R. Lawler, and John W. Staley, *High School Mathematics Lessons to Explore, Understand, and Respond to Social Injustice* (Thousand Oaks: Corwin, 2020).

14. Catherine Gewertz, "Teaching Math through a Social Justice Lens," *EducationWeek*, December 2, 2020, https://www.edweek.org/teaching-learning/teaching-math-through-a-social-justice-lens/2020/12; Diane Ravitch, "Ethnomathematics," *Hoover Institute Digest*, July 30, 2005, https://www.hoover.org/research/ethnomathematics.

15. Jay Caspian Kang, "What Do We Really Know about Teaching Kids Math?," *New Yorker*, November 18, 2022, https://www.newyorker.com%2Fnews%2Four-columnists%2Fwhat-do-we-really-know-about-teaching-kids-math.

16. Wayne D'Orio, "Tackling Math Anxiety," *U.S. News*, May 12, 2022, https://www.usnews.com/education/k12/articles/tackling-math-anxiety.

17. D'Orio, "Tackling Math Anxiety"; Kelly Dickerson, "'I'm Not a Math Person' Is No Longer a Valid Excuse," *Business Insider*, November 19, 2013, https://newsroom.unl.edu/announce/csmce/3781/20372.

18. Wellesley College, "Quantitative Reasoning," https://www.wellesley.edu/QR; Galileo Galilei, *The Assayer*, 1623, https://web.stanford.edu/~jsabol/certainty/readings/Galileo-Assayer.pdf.

19. Wellesley College, "Quantitative Reasoning."

20. Quoted in J. B. Birks, ed., *Jubilee: Rutherford at Manchester* (London: Heywood, 1962).

### Chapter 7. From Teaching to Learning

1. Alfie Kohn, "It's Not What We Teach; It's What They Learn," *Education Week*, September 10, 2018, https://www.alfiekohn.org/article/teach-learn/.

2. Jeffrey R. Young, "Most Professors Think They're Above-Average Teachers. And That's a Problem," *EdSurge*, May 24, 2018, https://www.edsurge.com/news/2018-05-24-most-professors-think-they-re-above-average-teachers-and-that-s-a-problem.

3. Cathy N. Davidson and Christina Katopodis, *The New College Classroom* (Cambridge, MA: Harvard University Press, 2022).

4. John Henry Newman, *The Idea of a University Defined and Illustrated: In Nine Discourses Delivered to the Catholics of Dublin* (Project Gutenberg, 2008), 5, https://www.gutenberg.org/files/24526/24526-pdf.pdf.

5. Seth Chaiklin, "The Zone of Proximal Development in Vygotsky's Analysis of Learning and Instruction," in *Vygotsky's Educational Theory and Practice in Cultural Context*, eds. Alex Kozulin, Boris Gindis, Vladimir S. Ageyev, Suzanne M. Miller (Cambridge: Cambridge University Press, 2003), 39–64.

6. Mark C. Carnes, *Minds on Fire: How Role-Immersion Games Transform College* (Cambridge, MA: Harvard University Press, 2014).

7. Jonathan Zimmerman, *The Amateur Hour: A History of College Teaching in America* (Baltimore: Johns Hopkins University Press, 2020), 165.

8. Jonathan Zimmerman, "In Search of 'College-Level' Teaching," *Journal of the Gilded Age and Progressive Era* 14 (2015), 429–32.

9. William Arrowsmith, "The Future of Teaching," *Arion: A Journal of Humanities and the Classics*, third series 2, nos. 2/3 (Spring 1992–Fall 1993), 177–93.

10. Robert B. Barr and John Tagg, "From Teaching to Learning: A New Paradigm for Undergraduate Education," *Change* 27 (1995), 13–26.

### Chapter 9. Rethinking Assessment

1. Frederick M. Hess, "Are College Classes Too Hard for Today's Students? Alarming Numbers Say 'Yes,'" *USA Today*, November 19, 2022, https://www.aei.org/op-eds/are-college-classes-too-hard-for-todays-students-alarming-numbers-say-yes/.

### Chapter 10. Helping Students Become Better Writers

1. William Strunk Jr. and E. B. White, *The Elements of Style*, 4th ed. (New York: Pearson, 1999).

2. John Warner, *Why They Can't Write: Killing the Five-Paragraph Essay and Other Necessities* (Baltimore: Johns Hopkins University Press, 2018).

3. Edward Elwell Whiting, *Calvin Coolidge: His Ideals of Citizenship* (Boston: W.A. Wilde, 1924), 154.

4. Mark Twain, letter to George Bainton, October 15, 1888, reprinted as "Reply to the Editor" in Bainton, ed., *The Art of Authorship* (New York: D. Appleton, 1890), 88.

5. David Labaree, "Joe Moran: First You Write a Sentence, Pt. 1," *David Labaree on Schooling, History, and Writing* (blog), November 16, 2020, https://davidlabaree .com/2020/11/16/moran-first-you-write-a-sentence/.

6. Tomas Chamorro-Premuzic, "How ChatGPT Is Redefining Human Expertise: Or How to Be Smart When AI Is Smarter than You." *Forbes*, January 12, 2023, https://www.forbes.com/sites/tomaspremuzic/2023/01/12/how-chatgpt-is -redefining-human-expertise-or-how-to-be-smart-when-ai-is-smarter-than -you.

7. Chamorro-Premuzic, "How ChatGPT Is Redefining."

8. E. P. Thompson, *The Making of the English Working Class* (London, Victor Gollancz, 1963).

9. Claudia Goldin and Lawrence F. Katz, *The Race Between Education and Technology* (Cambridge, MA: Belknap Press of Harvard University Press, 2008).

## Chapter 11. Standing Up for Equity

1. Steven Mintz, "Equity and Access," *Inside Higher Ed*, January 7, 2016, https://www.insidehighered.com/blogs/higher-ed-gamma/equity-and-access.

2. *Chronicle of Higher Education*, "Spending per Full-Time-Equivalent Student on Instruction and Other Selected Areas, by Sector, FY 2016," August 19, 2018, https://www.chronicle.com/article/spending-per-full-time-equivalent-student -on-instruction-and-other-selected-areas-by-sector-fy-2016/.

3. Scott Jaschik, "The Missing Students," *Inside Higher Ed*, December 11, 2012, https://www.insidehighered.com/news/2012/12/11/study-says-many-highly -talented-low-income-students-never-apply-top-colleges; Caitlin Flanagan, "Private Schools Have Become Truly Obscene," *Atlantic*, April, 2021, https://www .theatlantic.com/magazine/archive/2021/04/private-schools-are-indefensible /618078/.

4. Colleen Flaherty, "'The System Needs to Be Changed': New Paper Suggests Introductory STEM Courses Disproportionately Push Underrepresented Minority Students Out of the Natural and Applied Sciences," *Inside Higher Ed*, October 4, 2022, https://www.insidehighered.com/news/2022/10/04/study-finds -intro-stem-courses-push-out-urm-students.

5. Preston Cooper, "Why Are Colleges Restricting Access to High-Paying Majors?," *Forbes*, February 15, 2022, https://www.forbes.com/sites/preston cooper2/2022/02/15/why-are-colleges-restricting-access-to-high-paying -majors/.

6. Georgetown Center on Education and the Workforce, "Born to Win, Schooled to Lose: Why Equally Talented Students Don't Get Equal Chances to Be All They Can Be," 2019, https://cew.georgetown.edu/cew-reports/schooled2lose/.

7. Martin Luther King Jr., "Beyond Vietnam: A Time to Break Silence," April 4, 1967, https://inside.sfuhs.org/dept/history/US_History_reader/Chapter14 /MLKriverside.htm.

8. Louis D. Brandeis, *Other People's Money* (New York: Frederick Stokes, 1914), chapter 5, https://louisville.edu/law/library/special-collections/the-louis-d. -brandeis-collection/other-peoples-money-chapter-v.

9. The AIP Task Force to Elevate African American Representation in Undergraduate Physics and Astronomy (Team-Up), *The Time Is Now: Systematic Changes to Increase African Americans with Bachelor's Degrees in Physics and Astronomy* (College Park, MD: American Institute of Physics, 2020), 106, https://www.aip.org/sites/default/files/aipcorp/files/teamup-full-report.pdf.

10. Jennifer Gonzalez, "10 Ways Educators Can Take Action in Pursuit of Equity," Cult of Pedagogy, December 2, 2018, https://www.cultofpedagogy.com/10-equity/.

11. Gonzalez, "10 Ways."

12. Gonzalez, "10 Ways."

### Chapter 13. Campus Flash Points

1. Robert D. Bickel and Peter F. Lake, *The Rights and Responsibilities of the Modern University: Who Assumes the Risks of College Life?* (Durham, NC: Carolina Academic Press, 1999).

2. Philip Lee, "The Curious Life of *In Loco Parentis* at American Universities," *Higher Education in Review*, vol. 8 (2011) 65–90, https://scholar.harvard.edu/files/philip_lee/files/vol8lee.pdf.

3. University of Denver v. Whitlock, Supreme Court of Colorado, 744 P.2d 54 (1987).

4. David Brooks, "The Organization Kid," *Atlantic*, April 2001, https://www.theatlantic.com/magazine/archive/2001/04/the-organization-kid/302164/.

5. David Brooks, "Organization Kid"; Kathleen Elliott Vinson, "Hovering Too Close: The Ramifications of Helicopter Parenting in Higher Education," IHELG Monograph, 11–12, 2011, https://www.law.uh.edu/ihelg/monograph/11-12.pdf.

6. Peter F. Lake, *The Rights and Responsibilities of the Modern University: The Rise of the Facilitator University*, 2nd ed. (Durham, NC: Carolina Academic Press, 2013).

7. Jonathan Zimmerman, "We Must Denounce the Idea of Speech as Violence," *San Francisco Chronicle*, March 1, 2019, https://www.sfchronicle.com/opinion/article/We-must-denounce-the-idea-of-speech-as-violence-13656639.php.

8. John McWhorter, "What I See in the Latest Blackface 'Scandal,'" *New York Times*, October 15, 2021, https://www.nytimes.com/2021/10/15/opinion/blackface-michigan-sheng.html.

9. Gerald Graff, *Beyond the Culture Wars: How Teaching the Conflicts Can Revitalize American Education* (New York: W. W. Norton & Company, 1993); William Cain, *Teaching the Conflicts: Gerald Graff, Curricular Reform, and the Culture Wars* (New York: Garland Press, 1994).

10. Gerald Graff, *Beyond the Culture Wars*.

11. Paul Barnett, "If What Gets Measured Gets Managed, Measuring the Wrong Thing Matters," *Corporate Finance Review*, January/February 2015, 5–10, https://static.store.tax.thomsonreuters.com/static/relatedresource/CMJ--15-01%20sample-article.pdf.

12. Wanda Teays and Alison Dundes Renteln, eds., *The Ethical University: Transforming Higher Education* (Lanham, MD: Rowman & Littlefield, 2022).

13. Philip Mousavizadeh, "A 'Proliferation of Administrators': Faculty Reflect on Two Decades of Rapid Expansion," *Yale Daily News*, November 10, 2021, https://yaledailynews.com/blog/2021/11/10/reluctance-on-the-part-of-its -leadership-to-lead-yales-administration-increases-by-nearly-50-percent/.

14. David Weil, *The Fissured Workplace: Why Work Became So Bad for So Many and What Can Be Done to Improve It* (Cambridge, MA: Harvard University Press, 2017).

15. David Weil, *Fissured Workplace*.

16. Phillip W. Magness, "The Myth of the 76% Adjunct Majority," https:// philmagness.com/2015/08/the-myth-of-the-adjunct-majority/, blog, argues that adjuncts make up less than a third of the faculty at what most people consider to be "typical" universities and that most non-tenure-track faculty at nonprofit colleges and universities are employed full-time with benefits. Magness also argues that most adjuncts do not have a PhD or other terminal degree; see Magness, "Adjunct Activists and the Terminal Degree Problem," https:// philmagness.com/2016/05/adjunct-activists-and-the-terminal-degree-problem/. Also see, Magness, "The Myth of the Adjunct Majority, Continued," https:// philmagness.com/2015/08/the-myth-of-the-adjunct-majority-continued/; "How Many Adjuncts Are There in Not-for-Profit Higher Ed?," https://philmagness .com/2016/06/how-many-adjuncts-are-there-in-not-for-profit-higher-ed/; "Empirical Evidence of Adjunct Hours and Expectations," https://philmagness .com/2015/05/empirical-evidence-of-adjunct-hours-and-expectations/; and "Do Adjuncts and Full Time Faculty Have Similar Work Loads?," https://philmagness .com/2016/03/do-adjuncts-and-full-time-faculty-have-similar-work-loads/.

17. Randi Weingarten, "When We Fail to Teach Our Kids the Basics about Civics, We Risk Losing Our Democracy," *Newsweek*, October 4, 2022, https://www .newsweek.com/when-we-fail-teach-our-kids-basics-about-civics-we-risk -losing-our-democracy-opinion-1748475.

18. Frederick Hess, "Is Civic Education about Civics? New RAND Survey Suggests Teachers Think Not," *Forbes*, October 5, 2022, https://www.forbes.com /sites/frederickhess/2022/10/05/is-civic-education-about-civics-new-rand -survey-suggests-teachers-think-not.

19. *Educating for American Democracy*, Educating for American Democracy Initiative, March 2021, https://www.educatingforamericandemocracy.org/wp -content/uploads/2021/02/Educating-for-American-Democracy-Report -Excellence-in-History-and-Civics-for-All-Learners.pdf. This effort is led by Edmond J. Safra Center for Ethics at Harvard University, the School of Civic & Economic Thought and Leadership at Arizona State University, Tufts University's Center for Information & Research on Civic Learning and Engagement and Jonathan M. Tisch College of Civic Life, and iCivics.

20. Peter H. Schuck, "James Q. Wilson and American Exceptionalism," unpublished paper, Yale Law School, Public Law Research Paper No. 310 and Yale

Law & Economics Research Paper No. 479 (2013), https://papers.ssrn.com/sol3/papers.cfm?abstract_id=2330375.

### Chapter 14. The Future of the Humanities

1. Jon K. Lauk, "The Ongoing History Crisis," *Middle West Review* 9, no. 1 (2022), https://muse.jhu.edu/pub/17/article/871885.

2. American Academy of Arts & Sciences, "What Becomes of Humanities Majors after College? A New Indicators Report Offers Clues," press release, November 8, 2021, https://www.amacad.org/news/humanities-majors-after-college-survey; Andrew Van Dam, "The Most-Regretted (and Lowest-Paying) College Majors," *Washington Post*, September 2, 2022, https://www.washingtonpost.com/business/2022/09/02/college-major-regrets/.

3. Noah Smith, "The Elite Overproduction Hypothesis," *Noahpinion*, August 25, 2022, https://noahpinion.substack.com/p/the-elite-overproduction-hypothesis.

4. *Authorizing Legislation for FY 1970, before the Joint Comm. on Atomic Energy*, 91st Cong. (1969) (statement of Robert R. Wilson, physicist), https://speakola.com/ideas/robert-wilson-particle-accelerator-congress-1969.

5. Louis Menand, *The Marketplace of Ideas: Reform and Resistance in the American University* (New York: W. W. Norton, 2010).

6. "Daniel Mendelsohn on the Odyssey," *Octavian Report*, August 12, 2021, https://octavian.substack.com/p/daniel-mendelsohn-on-the-odyssey.

7. Shakespeare, *King Lear*, act IV, sc. 1, lines 36–37.

8. Oscar Wilde, *Lady Windermere's Fan*, act 3, http://www.literaturepage.com/read/lady-windermeres-fan-49.html; Quote Investigator, "Quote Origin: Being Irish, He Had an Abiding Sense of Tragedy Which Sustained Him Through Temporary Periods of Joy," https://quoteinvestigator.com/2023/03/21/irish-joy/; Jillian Goodman, "F. Scott Fitzgerald's Hollywood 'Crack-Up,'" *Salon*, June 9, 2013, https://www.salon.com/2013/06/09/f_scott_fitzgeralds_hollywood_crack_up_partner/.

9. Wilfred M. McClay, "Still the Redeemer Nation," *Wilson Quarterly* (Spring 2013), http://archive.wilsonquarterly.com/essays/still-redeemer-nation; Henry James quoted in Steven Mintz, "Art in Early America," *Digital History*, https://www.digitalhistory.uh.edu/topic_display.cfm?tcid=36.

10. Hal Brands and Charles Edel, "The End of History Is the Birth of Tragedy," *Foreign Policy*, May 29, 2017, https://foreignpolicy.com/2017/05/29/the-end-of-history-is-the-birth-of-tragedy/.

11. David Brion Davis, "American Jeremiah," *New York Review of Books*, February 13, 1986, https://www.nybooks.com/articles/1986/02/13/american-jeremiah/.

12. Hal Brands and Charles Edel, *The Lessons of Tragedy: Statecraft and World Order* (New Haven: Yale University Press, 2019).

13. Randall Rothenberg, "Advertising; Is It a Film? Is It an Ad? Harder to Tell," *New York Times*, March 13, 1990, https://www.nytimes.com/1990/03/13/business/the-media-business-advertising-is-it-a-film-is-it-an-ad-harder-to-tell.html.

14. Susan Sontag, "The Pornographic Imagination," *Styles of Radical Will* (New York: Picator, 2002), 35–73, https://www.remittancegirl.org/wp-content/uploads/2015/07/124506505-The-Pornographic-Imagination-by-Susan-Sontag.pdf.

15. Leonard Sweet quoted in "Wikibooks: Future/Quotes," https://en.wikibooks.org/wiki/Future/Quotes.

### Chapter 15. How Innovation Happens

1. The term "wicked problem" was introduced in C. West Churchman, "Wicked Problems," *Management Science* 14, no. 4, Application Series (December 1967): B141–B142.

2. The literature on academic transformation is vast. Good starting points include Jeffrey L. Buller, *Change Leadership in Higher Education: A Practical Guide to Academic Transformation* (San Francisco: Jossey-Bass, 2015); Buller, *Positive Academic Leadership: How to Stop Putting Out Fires and Start Making a Difference* (San Francisco: Jossey-Bass, 2013); Lee G. Bolman and Joan V. Gallos, *Reframing Academic Leadership* (San Francisco: Jossey-Bass, 2011); Donald W. Harward, *Transforming Undergraduate Education: Theory That Compels and Practices That Succeed* (Lanham, MD: Rowman & Littlefield, 2011); Brent D. Ruben, Richard De Lisi, Ralph A. Gigliotti, *A Guide for Leaders in Higher Education: Core Concepts, Competencies, and Tools* (Sterling, VA: Stylus, 2017); Adrianna Kezar, *How Colleges Change* (New York: Routledge, 2013); Elaine P. Maimon, *Leading Academic Change: Vision, Strategy, Transformation* (Sterling, VA: Stylus, 2018).

3. Seymour Papert, "Review: Why School Reform Is Impossible (with Commentary on O'Shea's and Koschmann's Reviews of 'The Children's Machine')," *Journal of the Learning Sciences* 6, no. 4 (1997), 417–27, https://www.jstor.org/stable/1466781.

4. Papert, "Review," 417–27.

5. The classic study of change management, John P. Kotter, *Leading Change* (Cambridge, MA: Harvard Business Review Press, 2012), focuses on institutions that are much more hierarchical than nonprofit colleges and universities, such as corporations and the military. Since top-down approaches to innovation and strategic planning are likely to provoke resistance, the best approach is to encourage creativity and collaboration rather than trying to impose a particular vision.

6. Daniel Seaton, "How MOOC Collaboration Could Aid On-Campus Teaching and Learning," *Chronicle of Higher Education*, December 5, 2018, https://www.insidehighered.com/digital-learning/views/2018/12/05/how-mooc-collaboration-could-aid-campus-teaching-and-learning.

### Epilogue

1. Laura Krantz, "Experimental Colleges Once Were the Future. Now, What Is Their Future?," *Boston Globe*, January 17, 2019, https://www.bostonglobe.com/metro/2019/01/17/experimental-colleges-face-uncertain-fate/tc1uxwTrpcgK2C6EBxNpCI/story.html.

2. Steven Mintz, "The Future Is Now: 15 Innovations to Watch For," *Chronicle of Higher Education*, July 22, 2013, https://www.chronicle.com/article/the-future-is-now-15-innovations-to-watch-for/.

3. George F. Will, "$1.6 Trillion in Student Debt Is a Monument to Destructive Assumptions," *Washington Post*, April 13, 2022, https://www.washingtonpost.com/opinions/2022/04/13/16-trillion-student-debt-is-monument-destructive-assumptions/.

# INDEX

*Academically Adrift* (Arum and Roksa), 6

academic freedom, ix, 8, 84, 217, 221–226, 237, 271

academic misconduct, 229–232

accreditation, 19, 237

active learning, 15, 54, 68, 98, 113, 135–136, 148, 150–151, 167, 299, 304, 312

Adams, Henry, 155

advising and counseling, x, 6, 13–14, 38, 46, 112, 204–205, 277; case management, 16, 31; one-stop, 51; technology-enabled, 54, 205, 291, 307; tiered approach, 108, 317

alternative credentials, 67–68, 79, 304, 307

alternative providers, 18–19, 67, 71–72, 79, 88, 274, 290

applied bachelor's, xiii, 78

Arizona State University, 5

Arrowsmith, William, 157

artificial intelligence, 187–190

assessment, 137; innovative approaches to, 112–113, 172; purpose of, 170–171, 173

Austin Community College, Great Questions project, 254–255

Bard College, 280

Barr, Robert, and John Tagg, 136, 157

Berry, Joe, 235

Big Ten Academic Alliance, 280

*Bildung*, xi, 59

Brandeis, Louis, 198

Brands, Hal, and Charles Edel, 263–264

California State University Long Beach, 41, 191

career preparation, ix, 16, 25–26, 54, 108, 112, 116, 197, 207

Childress, Herb, 235

Cicero, 256, 267

civics education, 240–246

classroom management, 238–240

college: alternatives to, 5; purpose of, 26, 54, 105–106, 120–121; rankings, 227–228

community colleges, 11, 34, 38–39, 42, 64, 69, 73, 81, 93, 124, 192, 199, 284

competency-based education, 53, 74–75, 305

constructivist pedagogy, 136, 147, 300

Cooper, Preston, 195

corequisite remediation, 14, 197, 305–306, 318

corporate universities, 72–73

courseware, 7, 27, 58, 62, 159, 163, 168, 281, 291, 293, 306

Csikszentmihalyi, Mihaly, 185

Cuban, Larry, 110

*cura personalis*, xi, 13

curriculum, 25, 105–106, 113–115, 119–120, 200–201; general education, 113–116, 117–118; humanities in, 131–132; mathematics in, 123–128; new models, 73–79; purpose of, 120–121; science in, 120–123; social science in, 128–131

data analytics, 6, 22–23, 103–104, 206

degree pathways, xi, 14–15, 22, 306, 309, 318

Dewey, John, viii, 91, 151, 153

Drucker, Peter, 228

dual-credit or early-college programs, 67, 73–74

EAB (education consulting firm), 211–212

earn-learn models, 75–76, 310

educational technology, xi, 7, 22–23, 205; history of, 159–161; successful uses of, 162–168

equity, 11, 32, 41–43, 203; barriers to, 191–196, 284; strategies to advance, 196–202

experiential learning, xi, 60, 119, 306, 311

faculty, 20, 54, 76–77; adjuncts, 20, 63–65, 235–238; future of, categorically, 232–238; mindset and, 127, 137, 139, 143, 147, 149, 210, 256, 271, 279, 301, 302, 308; new staffing models, 71, 113; and student success, 211–216

Feldstein, Michael, 11

Fitzgerald, F. Scott, 262

for-profit universities, 58, 59–60

Freud, Sigmund, 225

Geiger, Roger L. 88

general education, 15, 113–118

Georgetown Center on Education and the Workforce, 196, 227

G.I. Bill of Rights (1944), 83

Gibson, William, 109

Goldin, Claudia, and Lawrence F. Katz, 189

graduation rates, collegiate, xiii, 11–12, 21, 24, 28–29, 36–38; improving, 16–17

Graff, Gerald, 181, 225

Great Recession, 4, 5, 30, 49, 56–57, 87

Harvard University, 4, 87, 89, 113, 255

higher education: affordability of, 32–35; challenges facing, 30–50; cost of, 22; disruptors and, 3, 12; enrollment, 30; distinctiveness of American, 91–92; "grammar" of, 23, 110–111; history of, 83–85, 87–88, 89–90, 92–96, 100–101; return on investment and, 45–46; shifting landscape of, viii; stratification of institutions, 2, 65–67

high-impact educational practices, 102–103, 105, 307

Howells, William Dean, 262

Hoxby, Caroline M., and Christopher Avery, 194

humanities, 62–63; applied, 265–266; declining number of majors and

tenured faculty in, 247, 251; defenses of, 250, 255, 256; innovation and, 253; internalizing learning in, 254–254; and job market for majors, 266; strategies for promoting, 252–255, 257–261, 265, 268

Humboldt, Wilhelm von, 221

*in loco parentis*, 218–221, 230

innovation, in higher education: barriers to, xi, 23, 269–272, 275–276; drivers of, 274–275, 276–279; strategies for, 269–282; sustaining and transformational, 273; unintended consequences of, 275

Interstate Passport, 39, 75, 292

James, Henry, 262

Johnson, Matthew, 88

Kezar, Adrianna, 235

King, Reverend Martin Luther, Jr., 198

Kissick, William, 102

Kohn, Alfie, 133

Kotter, John F., 276

Labaree, David, 88

Laude, David, 277

learning, 138–139, 140; durable, 144; psychosocial dimensions of, 144–147; vs. teaching, 133

Levine, Arthur, 117

Mehaffy, George, 11, 22

Menand, Louis, 255

Mendelsohn, Daniel, 256

Microsoft, xii, 71, 274

mindset, 127, 256; of faculty, 137, 271, 279; and student learning, 139, 143, 147–149, 301, 302; in student retention, 210, 308

MIT (Massachusetts Institute of Technology), 4

MOOCs (massive open online classes), 4–5, 57–59, 60–61, 88, 163, 281, 308

Morrill Acts (1862 and 1890), 89

Moses, Robert Parris, 123, 124

Neill, A. S. 156

Newman, John Henry, 147

Niebuhr, Reinhold, 263

Obama, Barack, 36
Ohio State University, 41, 191
online program managers, 7, 81
online universities, 5, 10, 58–59, 71
Open Learning Initiative (Carnegie
    Mellon), 281
OpenStax, 163, 281

pandemic (COVID-19), 30, 36, 59, 85, 99,
    122, 153, 263, 275, 292; impact of, on
    higher education, 1, 2, 8–9, 209
pedagogy, 15, 18, 53–54, 106–107, 310–313;
    effective, 134–135, 149–155, 157–158;
    history of, 155–157
Pinker, Steven, 181
Purdue University, Cornerstones
    certificate, 254–255

rigor, of academics, 175; strategies for
    enhancing, 176–178
Rosofsky, Henry, 119
Rutherford, Ernest, 131

Schrecker, Ellen, 89
Schuck, Peter H., 243
science of learning, 15, 134–135, 139–144,
    147–149
Sheng, Bright, 222, 223, 224
Shirky, Clay, 87
Skinner, B. F., 100
Snow, C. P., 120
Sokal, Alan, 120
Sontag, Susan, 265
Southern New Hampshire University, 5,
    71, 77, 273
Stanford University, 4, 78
Steiper, Michael, 277
Strunk, William, and E. B. White, 180
students: 13–14; debt, 21; gender divide,
    63; learning, 44–44; loans, 35–36, 87;
    pipeline issues, 73, 93, 98; shift away
    from humanities majors, 62; shifting
    demographics of, 21–22, 24, 30–31
student success: cohort programs and,
    208; corequisite remediation and, 14,
    197, 305–306, 318; course design and,
    211; courses on, 206–207; faculty and,
    211–216; mindset and, 127, 137, 139, 143,
    147, 149, 210, 256, 271, 279, 301, 302, 308;

onboarding and, 206; strategies for
    promoting, 106–109, 206–210
student support services, 16, 22, 51, 107–108,
    204–205; technology and, 205–206
Sweet, Leonard I., 268

teaching: as art, craft, and science,
    137–138; effective, 148–155; history of,
    155–157; improving, 157–158; ineffective
    methods of, 147–148; vs. learning, 133,
    135–136; styles, 133–134; training in, 135
tenure, ix, 12, 47, 58, 63–64, 85, 87, 89, 93,
    135, 193, 208; evolution and erosion of,
    231, 233–234, 236–238, 247, 251
text generators (artificial intelligence),
    187–190
Thelin, John, 88
Tolley, Kim, 235
transfer, of enrollment between
    institutions, 38–41; articulation
    agreements and, 304
Treisman, Uri, 124
Trimble, John R., 180
Turchin, Peter, 248
Twain, Mark, 187, 191

University of California, Santa Cruz, 113–114
University of Texas System schools, 26,
    78, 89; Institute for Transformational
    Learning, 26–27

Vedder, Richard, 86
Vygotsky, Lev, 148

Warner, John, 184
Weil, David, 236
Western Governors University, 5, 71, 77, 273
Will, George E., 296
Williams, Joseph M., 180
Wilson, Robert R., 249
writing instruction, 118–119; artificial
    intelligence and, 187–189; classic advice
    for, 180–181; strategies for improving,
    181–183, 184–187

Yale University, 41, 191, 194, 232

Zimmerman, Jonathan, 88
Zinsser, William, 180